Translation and Interpreting as Social Interaction

BLOOMSBURY ADVANCES IN TRANSLATION SERIES

Series Editor:
Jeremy Munday, Centre for Translation Studies, University of Leeds, UK

Bloomsbury Advances in Translation publishes cutting-edge research in the field of translation studies. This field has grown in importance in the modern, globalized world, with international translation between languages a daily occurrence. Research into the practices, processes, and theory of translation is essential and this series aims to showcase the best in international academic and professional output.

A full list of titles in the series can be found at:
www.bloomsbury.com/series/bloomsbury-advances-in-translation

Titles in the series include:

Celebrity Translation in British Theatre, Robert Stock
Collaborative Translation, edited by Anthony Cordingley and Céline Frigau Manning
Community Translation, Mustapha Taibi and Uldis Ozolins
Corpus-Based Translation Studies, edited by Alet Kruger, Kim Wallmach, and Jeremy Munday
Extending the Scope of Corpus-Based Translation Studies, edited by Sylviane Granger and Marie-Aude Lefer
Genetic Translation Studies, edited by Ariadne Nunes, Joana Moura, and Marta Pacheco Pinto
Global Trends in Translator and Interpreter Training, edited by Séverine Hubscher-Davidson and Michał Borodo
Institutional Translation for International Governance, Fernando Prieto Ramos
Intercultural Crisis Communication, edited by Federico M. Federici and Christophe Declercq
Islamic State in Translation, Balsam Mustafa
Music, Text and Translation, edited by Helen Julia Minors
The Pragmatic Translator, Massimiliano Morini
Quality in Professional Translation, Joanna Drugan
Retranslation, Sharon Deane-Cox
Sociologies of Poetry Translation, Jacob Blakesley
Systemic Functional Linguistics and Translation Studies, edited by Mira Kim, Jeremy Munday, and Zhenhua Wang
Theatre Translation, Massimiliano Morini
Translating for Singing, Ronnie Apter and Mark Herman

Translating Holocaust Lives, edited by Jean Boase-Beier, Peter Davies, Andrea Hammel, and Marion Winters
Translating the Poetry of the Holocaust, Jean Boase-Beier
Translating in Town, edited by Lieven D'hulst and Kaisa Koskinen
Translation Solutions for Many Languages, Anthony Pym
Telling the Story of Translation, Judith Woodsworth
Vladimir Nabokov as an Author-Translator, Julie Loison-Charles
What Is Cultural Translation?, Sarah Maitland

Translation and Interpreting as Social Interaction

Affect, Behavior, and Cognition

Edited by
Claire Y. Shih and Caiwen Wang

BLOOMSBURY ACADEMIC
LONDON • NEW YORK • OXFORD • NEW DELHI • SYDNEY

BLOOMSBURY ACADEMIC

Bloomsbury Publishing Plc, 50 Bedford Square, London, WC1B 3DP, UK
Bloomsbury Publishing Inc, 1385 Broadway, New York, NY 10018, USA
Bloomsbury Publishing Ireland, 29 Earlsfort Terrace, Dublin 2, D02 AY28, Ireland

BLOOMSBURY, BLOOMSBURY ACADEMIC and the Diana logo are trademarks of
Bloomsbury Publishing Plc

First published in Great Britain 2024
Paperback edition published 2025

Copyright © Claire Y. Shih and Caiwen Wang and Contributors, 2024, 2025

Claire Y. Shih and Caiwen Wang and Contributors have asserted their right under the
Copyright, Designs and Patents Act, 1988, to be identified as Authors of this work.

For legal purposes the Acknowledgments on p. xiii constitute an extension
of this copyright page.

Cover design: Elena Durey

All rights reserved. No part of this publication may be: i) reproduced or transmitted in
any form, electronic or mechanical, including photocopying, recording or by means of
any information storage or retrieval system without prior permission in writing from the
publishers; or ii) used or reproduced in any way for the training, development or operation
of artificial intelligence (AI) technologies, including generative AI technologies. The rights
holders expressly reserve this publication from the text and data mining exception as per
Article 4(3) of the Digital Single Market Directive (EU) 2019/790.

Bloomsbury Publishing Plc does not have any control over, or responsibility for, any thirdparty
websites referred to or in this book. All internet addresses given in this book were
correct at the time of going to press. The author and publisher regret any inconvenience
caused if addresses have changed or sites have ceased to exist, but can accept no
responsibility for any such changes.

A catalogue record for this book is available from the British Library.

A catalog record for this book is available from the Library of Congress.

ISBN: HB: 978-1-3502-7931-5
PB: 978-1-3502-7935-3
ePDF: 978-1-3502-7932-2
eBook: 978-1-3502-7933-9

Series: Bloomsbury Advances in Translation

Typeset by Deanta Global Publishing Services, Chennai, India

For product safety related questions contact productsafety@bloomsbury.com.

To find out more about our authors and books visit www.bloomsbury.com and
sign up for our newsletters.

Contents

List of Figures		viii
List of Tables		ix
Preface		x
Acknowledgments		xiii
1	Affect and Emotion in Translation Process Research *Claire Shih*	1
2	Translation and Affect and the Notion of a "Center of Attention" *Kirsten Malmkjær*	19
3	Covert Self-talk as a Tool for Dialogue Interpreters *Anu Viljanmaa*	35
4	The Self-Reported Emotional Struggles by Interpreters in the British Judicial System *Zhiai Liu*	55
5	Seeing Omissions from Inside the Interpreter's Mind *Caiwen Wang*	83
6	Interpreting as Communicative and Sociocultural Interaction *Binhua Wang*	107
7	Investigating Sight Translation via Eye Tracking *Monika Płużyczka*	125
8	Conceptual Variations in Legal Translation between "Right" and "權利" *Junfeng Zhao and Jie Xue*	157
9	Cognitive, Linguistic, and Discursive Elements in Metaphor Translation *Sui He*	175
10	Human-Machine Symbiosis to Enhance Overall Understanding *Ming Qian*	197
List of Contributors		219
Index		221

Figures

4.1	Respondent's native languages	63
4.2	Cumulative years of interpreting experience of questionnaire respondents	64
4.3	Questionnaire respondents' average interpreting hours per year	64
4.4	Duties requested by service providers	66
4.5	Duties requested by service users	66
4.6	Reasons respondents feel reluctant to intervene	68
6.1	Major variables shaping the interpreting performance and product	114
6.2	A framework for analyzing mediation in interpreting	115
7.1	Pupil dilation data on paragraphs	139
7.2	Fixation count data on paragraphs	139
7.3	Scan paths of reading for comprehension and sight translation	142
7.4	Selected scan paths illustrating spatial saccadic movements during sight translation from L1 to L2	143
7.5	Selected scan paths illustrating spatial saccadic movements during sight translation	144
7.6	Selected scan paths illustrating spatial saccadic movements during sight translation and pretranslational reading	144
8.1	Conceptual integration between right and 權利	165
9.1	Movement of CMT provenance categories in translation	183
9.2	Movement of CBT provenance categories in translation	184
10.1	Enhanced understanding through human-machine symbiosis	198
10.2	Understanding as a cognitive achievement	198
10.3	Simplified illustrations of sequence-to-sequence model and Transformer architecture	202
10.4	Self-supervised language models: BERT and GPT-3	203

Tables

3.1	Occurrence of linguistic and functional self-talk statements	46
3.2	Examples of reflective first-person self-talk statements	47
3.3	Examples of instructional second-person self-talk statements	48
3.4	Examples of instructional self-talk statements addressing internal listening filters	49
5.1	Speeches generating omissions in SI	93
5.2	Total omissions made by all subjects across all categories	94
5.3	Total and types of omission per subject	94
7.1	Descriptive Statistics for Total Reading Time	135
7.2	Descriptive Statistics for Dwell Time	136
7.3	Descriptive Statistics for Fixation Count	136
7.4	Descriptive Statistics for Revisits	137
7.5	Descriptive statistics for average fixation	138
7.6	Descriptive statistics for pupil dilation	138
9.1	Information about the ST and the TTs	180
9.2	Translation Solutions Overview	182
10.1	Different types of explanations	200
10.2	Localization and culturalization examples	204
10.3	Generating Training Samples for KLSI repair, replace, and SAI Techniques	208
10.4	Few-shot learning using GPT-3	212
10.5	GPT-3 tool extrapolating to unknown conditions	214

Preface

This edited book represents one of the latest contributions to the field of translation studies. Broadly drawing inspirations from the cognitive and sociological approach to translation (see Muñoz Martín 2010; Olohan 2019), it advocates that the triad of social interaction, affect, behavior, and cognition, underpins translators and interpreters' daily activities. In particular, it aims to tap into an increasingly recognized and yet underexplored aspect of the translation and interpreting phenomenon, that is, affect and its interaction with behavior and cognition. This central theme of affect, behavior, and cognition will be examined theoretically, empirically, and methodologically throughout the book with contributions from around the world, featuring literary translation, legal translation, translator training, human and machine translation, and interpreters' practice, and so on.

The chapters included consist of both theoretical and empirical studies, the former represented by Chapters 1, 2, 6, and 8 and the latter by the rest of the chapters. In terms of research methods used, there are eye trackers (Chapter 7), interviews (Chapters 3 and 4), questionnaires/surveys (Chapter 4), retrospective reflections (Chapter 5), case studies (Chapters 5, 9, and 10), and critical reviews of literature (Chapter 1), reflecting a spectrum of both the state-of-the-art and tried-and-tested research instruments in translation studies.

The first four chapters consist of contributions closely linked to affect, focusing on studies tapping into emotion and what role emotion plays in translators' and interpreters' work. It starts with (Chapter 1) an overview of translation affect and emotion within the context of translation process research (TPR) and its parallel development as a mature subdiscipline in translation and interpreting studies. It argues that the investigation of translation affect is closely aligned with the methodological advancement in TPR and psychology. This chapter calls for future researchers to go beyond studying affect as an independent aspect of translation and interpreting so that affect can be understood in the context of translators' and interpreters' mental process (cognition) and physical process (behavior). Chapter 2 focuses on a discussion of affect and its relationship to texts. A literary case study is used to illustrate how a translator's deliberate choices of maintaining eccentricities of the text contribute significantly to the translation's affective potential. Chapter 3 explores how covert self-talk is employed as a self-regulatory tool by dialogues interpreters in handling the so-called listening filters, referring to listener-related, situation-related, or speaker-related factors that negatively impact the listener's ability to hear, process, and understand speaker utterance. It presents an interesting perspective where the role and form of covert self-talk is potentially linked to interpreting performance. In contrast to Chapter 3, Chapter 4 specifically focuses on dialogue interpreters in the legal sector and reveals the extent to which legal interpreters may struggle to cope with strong emotions. The research calls for professional bodies for interpreters, such as the NRPSI in the UK, to provide more support and guidance for the sake of interpreters' well-being.

Chapters 5–10 collectively represent a wide range of empirical and descriptive studies depicting translators' or interpreters' behavior and cognition. Perceiving omissions from simultaneous interpreters' mind and countering historical views, Chapter 5 presents empirical evidence to show that omissions are not always errors, and some types of omissions are actively and effectively utilized as strategies to improve communication. By analyzing interpreters' retrospective reports, the study also identifies triggers for omissions and more crucially how interpreters' own voices can be an external factor that leads to receptive omissions. These findings will have acute implications for interpreter trainers with regard to how omission can be employed or avoided for more optimal communication. Chapter 6 begins with an overview of cognitive approaches in interpreting. It proposes that in exploring the entirety and complexity of interpreting, in addition to cognitive approach, a contextual and sociocultural consideration must not be overlooked. Real-life examples are drawn from a selection of high-profiled interpreting scenarios in press conferences to illustrate this proposal. Chapter 7 presents the results of selected eye-tracking experiments and has provided empirical evidence to support the hypothesis that sight translation cannot be deemed as a "reading" or "reading for comprehension" activity but rather a "reading for translation" activity with unique cognitive characteristics. In addition, as opposed to pupil dilation as an indicator of cognitive load, this study identifies an alternative parameter for cognitive load and its relevant indication for long-term memory in eye-tracking research. This is spatial saccadic movements, or saccades, that occur beyond a text as they appear to be linked to the reduction of cognitive load and information retrieval from the long-term memory. Chapter 8 examines, from a cognitive-sociological angle, the transplantation of the Western concept *right* (*quánlì* 權利) in China and shows how the meaning of a transplanted concept is cognitively and socially constructed and molded by linguistic agents and different groups of recipients, which thus rejects the presupposition of the existence of conceptual equivalents in translation studies. By observing the social interactions among concepts, institutions, and values of law across languages and cultures, it provides a credible explanation for conceptual variations in legal translation. Chapter 9 taps into the field of metaphor analysis in translation. It proposes a dual model of utilizing two cognitive metaphor theories, that is, conceptual metaphor theory and conceptual blending theory, to depict and analyze metaphors and their translation. Data corpus comes from the Chinese translation (both in Simplified and Traditional Chinese) of *Scientific American* produced in 2017. Interviews of the respective translators also shed some lights on the intention and workflow of translating metaphors in popular science texts. Chapter 10 depicts the details of how a symbiosis can be achieved between human and machine. On the one hand, AI tools can be used to assist human comprehension for localization and culturization purposes. On the other hand, human can inform AI tools, via few-shot learning, a type of machine learning algorithm, to generate augmented training data, for the purpose of machine-generated simultaneous interpreting output. A future of a continuous loop of symbiosis is foreseen where human experts can team up with AI tools to further enhance performance of language and translation tasks more seamlessly.

We believe, as the anonymous reviewers do, too, that this book has identified some salient gaps in the existing literature and attempted to examine the role of affect and cognition in translation and interpreting from a wide range of perspectives. It is a timely book tapping into the entirety and complexity of translation and interpreting as social interaction, with a focus on how affect is interwoven into the fabric of translators' behavior and cognition. We hope our readers will appreciate these perspectives.

Claire Shih and Caiwen Wang
June 2023

References

Olohan, M. (2019), Sociological Approaches to Translation Technology, in M. O'Hagan (ed.), *The Routledge Handbook of Translation and Technology*, 384–397, New York and London: Routledge.

Muñoz Martín, R. (2010a), 'On Paradigms and Cognitive Translatology', in G. M. Shreve and E. Angelone (eds), *Translation and Cognition*, 169–187, Amsterdam: John Benjamins.

Acknowledgments

We first of all would like to thank the three anonymous reviewers who were commissioned by Bloomsbury Publishing Plc to assess our book proposal. Their encouraging and constructive feedback is extremely helpful and beneficial as we put together this project, which, as one of the reviewers states, "addresses a relatively new research area (i.e., the role of affect and cognition in translation and interpreting) from various angles." We also would like to thank the anonymous reviewers who reviewed our book before it was published, and we warmly appreciate their commendations.

We are very grateful to Andrew Wardell (who later left Bloomsbury), Becky Holland, Morwenna Scott, Katrina Calsado, Peter Warren, and Laura Gallon at Bloomsbury Academic, an imprint of Bloomsbury Publishing Plc, who offered their much-appreciated professional assistance from the start of this book and throughout.

We thank all the contributors for their enthusiasm to contribute and for their prompt responses during the process of revising and editing. We are indebted to the colleagues who reviewed the manuscripts. Our contributors have asked us to particularly thank the reviewers on their behalf for their feedback.

Last but not the least, we thank our families for their love and support.

1

Affect and Emotion in Translation Process Research

Claire Shih

1 Introduction

A few years ago, I was lucky enough to meet and compare notes with a colleague in psychology. As I was trying to explain my work in translation process research (TPR), I stumbled across a question that startled me, that is, "do you actually study behavior or cognition?" Few scholars in translation studies today would argue against the fact that TPR is deeply rooted in psychology (see O'Brien 2013; Jakobsen 2017; Zhu 2020; Hubscher-Davidson and Lehr 2021). But this question I stumbled across back then has made me reexamine the relationship between TPR and psychology, and it is within this wider context that I contemplate about the evolvement of affect and emotion in TPR to date and beyond.

To be more precise, this chapter aims to unpack the evolvement of translation affect and emotion as a subject of investigation in TPR and argues that such evolvement coincides with the continuous formation of TPR as a subdiscipline within translation studies, particularly in relation to its methodological advancement, which also aligns with conceptualization deeply rooted in psychology.

2 Attitudinal and Affective Factors in Think-Aloud Protocol Studies

There is no doubt that cognitive psychology plays a very important role in TPR. The translation process is often referred to as a cognitive process, cognitive activity, strategic behavior, or cognitive behavior (see Jakobsen 2017). In the early 1990s, TPR was at its infancy. Its customized data collection method was centered around the use of think-aloud protocols (TAPs) (see Kussmaul 1997; Krings 2001). Also known as concurrent verbal reports, TAP was a data collection method directly borrowed from cognitive psychology where subjects verbalized their thoughts. In the methodological history in cognitive psychology itself, TAP was in fact once considered to be an innovative form of the verbal report, which differentiated from retrospective and introspective ones. This was because the retrospective report was conducted after a task was completed and the introspective report was conducted in short intervals during a task, but TAP was the only verbal report method conducted simultaneously during a task, having the advantage of timeliness, minimal data loss, and minimal subjects' self-analysis (see Ericsson and Simon 1984).

A qualitative data collection method by nature, TAP was regularly employed in small-scale case studies, which featured translators' individual differences and idiosyncrasy. It was perhaps no surprise that "affect" presented itself in a handful of early TAP studies. Early TAP adopters, such as Laukkanen, Jääskeläinen, and Tirkkonen-Condit, found many evaluative comments in their TAP data. They were referred to as "attitudinal and affective factors" in the translation process (Laukkanen 1996). It was reported that these evaluative comments were largely related to translators' self-image, their own translation performance, or even the quality of dictionaries they chose to use, and so on (Laukkanen 1996). Tirkkonen-Condit (1997: 69) later named these evaluative comments "expressives" and hypothesized a positive correlation between the proportion and specificity of "expressives" and translation proficiency. In other words, the more and specific a translator is able to articulate or express him/herself through evaluative comments (in TAP), the better s/he is likely to be able to translate. Analyzing her TAP data, Jääskeläinen (1999: 241) also reported very similar results, although she described them as translators' personal involvement either being implicit or explicit. Both Tirkkonen-Condit and Jääskeläinen's studies appeared to lean toward the concept of "metacognition" and its value to translators' performance. Nevertheless, TAP as a research method was not without its controversy (see Jakobsen 2003). For instance, while reflecting on the validity of TAP as a research method, Hansen (2005) alluded that it was absurd to claim that TAP was a concurrent verbal report of thoughts. Given the "firing" speed of neural operations, it was simply not possible to concurrently verbalize one's thoughts. Instead, "What is verbalised is a conglomerate of memories, reflections, justifications, explanations, emotions and experiences, and it seems likely that these cannot be separated from each other" (Hansen 2005: 519).

Interestingly, Hansen's comments probably represented one of the earliest indications and direct acknowledgment that emotion cannot be separated from cognition.

But even though these early TAP studies offered some interesting observation about translators' affect, by and large, "affect" or "affective factors" represented an "offshoot" of translators' idiosyncratic characteristics and occupied a peripheral position in the field (see Bednarova-Gibova and Majherova 2023: 102), which was in stark contrast to the majority of TAP studies that primarily focused on translators' cognition, particularly in relation to their problem-solving and decision-making strategies.

At this point, I would like to share an anecdote when I was a relatively young academic in early 2000. Out of blue, I was contacted by a postgraduate translation student with a request to fill in a questionnaire. This was of course nothing unusual. What stuck in my mind was the fact that this postgraduate student wanted to know why I thought TAP had fallen out of fashion as a research method in TPR. This anecdote highlighted TPR's gradual transition at the time from the nondigital research methods to the subsequent explosion of digital research instruments widely used in TPR. This brings out the discussion of the next section.

3 The Peripheral Position of Affect at the Eve of Digital Instrument Adoption

Ironically, affect appeared to fall out of favor among TPR scholars when digital research instruments, such as keylogging and eye-tracking software, were initially introduced to the field. A plausible reason might be that the notion of "attitudinal and affective factors" is firmly attached to TAP data and that TAP was considered out of date at the time. Yet, a curious question arises: why the introduction of these early digital research instruments did not seem to spark any interests about affect and emotion in TPR? To answer this question, one may have to look into what these early digital research instruments were and what they represented.

Keylogging software, such as Translog, Inputlog, and Scriptlog, represented the earliest digital research instruments adopted in TPR. As the name literally suggests, keylogging software was designed to log keyboard activities. Among these keylogging software, Translog (see Jakobsen 2014) was probably the first and the only digital research instrument not directly borrowed from other adjacent disciplines but specifically created in TPR to capture the translation process. In Jakobsen's (2017: 28) own words, "Translog was developed partly in response to concerns about think aloud data," as controversy exists about how reliable (or scientifically accurate) TAP data could be (see Bernardini 2001; Sun 2011). Translog was therefore developed by Jakobsen to triangulate the cognitive data produced by TAP. While keylogging software represented an exciting advancement into the digital era for TPR, it was not without its shortcoming. This was because as a stand-alone data collection method, the main source of cognitive data in keylogging software peculiarly relied on the passive or "nonbehaviour" of translating, that is, pauses, rather than the active or more visible typing behavior (see Immonen 2006). As Leijten and Van Waes (2013: 1), the developers of Inputlog, admitted, "while [keylogging] allows for ecological data collection, it is often difficult to connect the fine grain of logging data to the underlying cognitive process." On the surface at least, the translation process being observed or the data being captured by keylogging software was predominately behavioral rather than cognitive. This probably planted a seed that even though TPR had been known to be the cognitive process of translation or cognitive translation studies, it was challenging to "tease out" cognition from behavior in most TPR studies. The truth was that by default cognition was "twinned" closely with behavior in TPR studies. This was why I was startled when the psychologist asked me whether TPR was about behavior or cognition, given that behaviorism and cognitive psychology belonged to two distinct subdisciplines in psychology and each following very different theoretical traditions. To be fair and as mentioned before, keylogging software was rarely used alone in TPR. This was probably why Translog-II (see Carl 2012), an updated version of the original Translog, was later developed to be used specifically in conjunction with other data collection methods, primarily eye trackers (see Hvelplund 2017). The combination of Translog-II and eye tracking has been a match made in heaven, as Translog-II logs the behavior or rather "nonbehavior" of keyboard activities, that is, the production process in translation, while eye trackers capture their eye movement (or cognition) on the computer screen, that is, the comprehension process in translation. This was known as the CRITT methodology developed by Copenhagen Business School (see Carl, Schaeffer, and Bangalore 2016), which has been widely adopted in many TPR studies to date. It is worth noting here that unlike keylogging software, eye tracking as a research instrument has a stronger theoretical basis between the data captured (i.e., eye movement) and cognition, due to the renowned "eye-mind hypothesis" (Just and Carpenter 1980), which is widely accepted in cognitive psychology in that eyes are believed to focus on what the mind is processing.

Perhaps it was due to the excitement (or some may argue "complication") of adopting these new digital research instruments from another discipline, and the overwhelming prospect of studying many new aspects of the translation process, affect and emotion did not seem to draw much attention among TPR scholars at least initially. From the perspective of a wider context in the field of translation studies, this was an exciting period when TPR, whose characteristic was interdisciplinarity, had begun to blossom into a subdiscipline of translation studies. Being an inherently interdisciplinary subdiscipline, TPR scholars were acutely aware that they were in constant battles of grappling with new (digital) research instruments particularly at this time when they were first introduced into translation studies. Jääskeläinen (1999: 3) described it as "trying to sit on several chairs at the same time." While this was what drove many TPR scholars to explore the new frontier in translation studies, it became a necessary preoccupation for most TPR scholars to contemplate and critically examine how these new digital research instruments could be better adopted in TPR and what they meant in the field as a whole (see Jääskeläinen 2011).

Another possible reason was that this was also a time when notions of the first-generation cognitive psychology (in contrast to notions in the second-generation cognitive psychology) were prevalent in the field of psychology itself. At the time, cognitive psychologists were largely "deal[ing] with the mental processes between the occurrence of a stimulus and a behavioural response" (Reber 2019: 25). They assumed that the human brain resembled a computer and postulated that human cognition consisted of three components: input (i.e., stimulus), central processor (i.e., memory system), and output (i.e., behavior). Incidentally, this was exactly how most eye-tracking experiments were modelled upon, that is, stimuli, eye movement, behavior. The research focus was on understanding the less observable mental process or cognition that occurred within the central processor. This was also why in TPR, the research efforts largely centered around exploring the "black box" (Holmes 1988: 72), that is, cognition, and its corresponding and consequential behavior.

To sum up, there are several possible reasons why the study of affect and emotion still lies in the periphery when digital research instruments were first introduced to TPR. It was partly due to the fact that TPR scholars were preoccupied with the initial adoption of digital research methods and how such methods could be better utilized for the investigation of translation cognition (to a lesser extent) and translation behavior (to a larger extent). In a wider context outside translation studies, this was also a period when the predominant concept of cognitive psychology, from which TPR regularly borrowed concepts and research methods, largely subscribed to the triad of stimuli, cognition, and behavior.

4 Translation Emotion at the Turn of the Century and Beyond

As mentioned before, behavior and cognition were two pivotal themes constantly investigated by TPR scholars. This was why the translation process was often referred to as a cognitive activity, strategic behavior, or cognitive behavior (see Jakobsen 2017). For many years, such terminologies revealed a taken-for-granted and underlying assumption in TPR, which was that behavior represented a direct result of cognition. However, at the turn of the century, some TPR scholars began to seriously question this assumption: was this really as straightforward as it was assumed to be? Could a behavior be the result of physical discomfort, reflex, or even mere reflection of one's emotional state? Did translators' decisions always make logical sense? Did we assume that because the (more observable) behavioral data were collected at the same time as the cognitive ones, they must explain and complement each other? All these assumptions were probably right, to a large extent. But what they did not account for was other underlying factors, that is, affective ones that may be at play during the translation process. In other words, some TPR scholars began to consider translation affect and emotion in addition to behavior and cognition.

On the one hand, this was also a time when cognitive psychologists gradually moved away from the "classic" analogy of viewing human brain as a computer, known as the first-generation cognitive psychology, and shifted toward motivation and emotion, arguably the driving force behind human cognition and behavior (Reber 2019: 40–58). Parallel to this, in TPR, Muñoz Martín proposed a model or, as he preferred to call it, "a paradigm of cognitive translatology" or 4EA, which stood for embodied, embedded, extended, enactive, and affective approaches (see Muñoz Martín 2010a, 2010b, 2016: 1–20). What Muñoz Martín has done was to advocate an encompassing and paradigmatic archetype for TPR that incorporated concepts from the second-generation cognitive psychology, for example, embodied cognition, situated cognition, distributed cognition, and so on (see Clark 1997; Wheeler 2005), as opposed to those of the first-generation cognitive psychology. For example, the concept of embodied cognition was essentially linking the study of mind (i.e., cognition) and the study of a physical body (i.e., physical brain). This was in fact the most important theoretical foundation for a new subdiscipline in psychology, cognitive neuroscience. This will be referred to later due to its methodological significance to the study of emotion. In the same vein, the concept of situated cognition indicated that cognition should be considered in situ or in its situated environments, which was connected to the ethnographic approach in TPR (see Risku 2017). Similarly, the extended and enactive cognition emphasized the sociological aspect of translation activities, which included the use of external tools and resources, such as the ergonomical approach in TPR (see Enrensberger-Dow 2017). Even though Muñoz Martín did not explicate at length about the A (i.e., affect) in his 4EA paradigm, the fact that it was included in a marked position at the end of the 4EA revealed a tell-tale sign of growing interests in affect and emotion in TPR. These growing interests have been manifested by a swathe of more recent studies that tapped into translators' personality traits (Hubscher-Davidson 2013), emotional intelligence and regulation (Hubscher-Davidson 2016, 2018; Hubscher-Davidson and Lehr 2021), positive/negative effects of emotions on translation (Lehr 2014a, 2014b; Rojo and Ramos 2016), effects of emotional texts on the allocation of cognitive efforts (Lehr and Hvelplund 2020), and resilience and coping strategies of subtitlers (Perdikaki and Georgiou 2023), to name a few. All these studies (the most important of which will be reviewed in detail later in this section) have rooted strongly in the concepts of motivation and emotion in psychology.

On the other hand, in terms of the digital research instruments used, more recent TPR scholars have begun to venture into many newer varieties of digital research instruments used in psychology and its adjacent disciplines, from neurological, for example, fMRI, fNIR, EEG (see Tymoczko 2012; Ren et al. 2019; Zheng et al. 2020), to physiological ones, for example, ECG, EDA/GSR (see Gieshoff, Lehr, and Heeb 2021), and even facial expression analysis software. While these digital research instruments can be used to further examine translators' cognition and behavior or indeed the intertwining relationship between the two, they also open up an excellent platform to step into the study of emotion, as many of these instruments, particularly the physiological ones, are known to be typical measurement for emotions in psychology. For instance, emotional arousal (high vs. low) can be readily measured through bodily reactions (Zachar and Ellis 2012). The basic assumption behind this type of measurement is that the cognitive and behavioral process, particularly the one with salient emotion, manifests itself through physiology (Cacioppo, Tassinary, and Berntson 2007: 14). For example, pupil dilation (elicited from eye trackers) is believed to be linked to one's emotional response. Similarly, skin conductance (e.g., electrodermal activity, i.e., EDA, or sometimes known as galvanic skin response, i.e., GSR) and cardiovascular biomarkers (e.g., heart rate, blood pressure) can all be used to measure the level of emotional arousal. Given the varieties of digital research instruments available, there has never been a better time for TPR scholars to tap into the study of emotion. Interestingly, a recent survey is done on existing research in translation and interpreting studies associated with stress, emotion, or ergonomical demands using physiological instruments (Gieshoff, Lehr, and Heeb 2021). While many of the studies can be considered interdisciplinary rather than translation and interpreting studies per se, the result from this survey suggests that a majority of these studies focus on "cognitive demands," and the most common physiological measurement adopted is pupil dilation (via eye trackers). This shows that while there are gradually more and more interests in studying translation affect and emotion using more varieties of digital research instruments, the use of eye trackers and their relevant metrics (i.e., pupil dilation) still dominates the research landscape in TPR so far.

In contrast to the physiological instruments, the use of neurological instruments, such as EEG, fMRI, and fNIR, is based on an entirely different theoretical assumption. This assumption is rooted in cognitive neuroscience, a relatively new subdiscipline, a cross between cognitive psychology and neuroscience. As Dolan (2002: 1191) puts it,

> Emotion is central to the quality and range of everyday human experience. The neurobiological substrates of human emotion are now attracting increasing interest within neurosciences motivated, to a considerable extent, by advances in functional neuroimaging techniques. An emerging theme is the question of how emotion interacts with and influences other domains of cognition.

Dolan's earlier statement explains the emergence of "cognitive neuroscience" and its increasing interests in emotion. Cognitive neuroscientists believe that the human brain is a biological and physiological representation of the human mind and cognition. In fact, some scholars call the brain "wet mind" (Kosslyn and Koenig 1995). In other words, the brain and the mind are two sides of the same coin. One cannot understand human cognition fully without understanding its physiological and neurobiological construct and functions. TPR's recent adaptation of neurological instruments very much reflects this latest development in psychology, particularly in relation to the way interaction between emotion and cognition may be detected in human brain (see Seth and

Barrett 2007; Storbeck and Clore 2007), although to the best of my knowledge, it is still very early days, given research is scarcely done on translation affect and emotion per se using neurological instruments so far.

While the use of more varieties of digital research instruments offers promising avenues to study translation affect and emotion, it is not the only route to study emotion in TPR. In fact, one of the first monographs on emotion in TPR focused on the use of psychometric tests to study translators' emotional intelligence. In her monograph, *Translation and Emotion: A Psychological Perspective*, Hubscher-Davidson (2018) employed TEIQue test, which identified translators' personality traits in relation to their emotion perception, emotion regulation, and emotion expression. She then attempted to link these traits to professional translators' job profiles, job satisfaction, and career success. One of her key findings was that the length of literary translators' experiences, their emotion intelligence, and their job satisfaction were somehow correlated.

Methodologically speaking, the use of IQ-styled psychometric tests as a research instrument may initially raise an eyebrow in TPR, probably due to potential mispreconception about psychometric tests represented in the popular culture. Yet, it proves to be a unique methodological vantage point in connecting emotion, behavior, and cognition. There is also evidence to suggest that this methodology has inspired new generations of researchers to adapt psychometric tests in their own research design in translation studies (e.g., Coban 2019).

In relation to the personality traits, Hubscher-Davidson (2018) utilized the concept of "emotional intelligence" as a trait (or psychological competence) that could be trained and harnessed by professional translators to enhance their well-being and to deal with potential difficulties faced in their professional and personal lives. With the global pandemic we all faced in recent years, the positive value and implications of emotional intelligence have never been more timely for translators' professional development and training. The introduction of "emotional intelligence" represented the most significant contribution about emotion to date in TPR. This term was first coined by psychologists Salovey and Mayer (1990). It was then popularized by Goleman (1995) in his best-selling book bearing this term in its title. The central notion of emotional intelligence is that (deliberate) awareness, intelligent appraisal (i.e., cognition), and subsequent control of one's emotion could regulate and lead to better behavior. This was a very empowering notion, given its implication that a translator could be potentially trained to grasp such skills or competence, as demonstrated by Hubscher-Davidson and Lehr in their new book, *Improving Emotional Intelligence of Translators* (2021). They cited the method of "cognitive behavioral coaching" (CBC) and its associated ABCDE model, originally developed by Albert Ellis (Carvalho, Matos, and Anjos 2018: 123; cf. Hubscher-Davidson and Lehr 2021: 56). This model was essentially a way "to enhance awareness of one's unproductive emotions and beliefs and remove these barriers so as to help achieve one's goal" (Hubscher-Davidson and Lehr 2021: 55). The A refers to Activate an event or situation, B Belief, C Consequences, D Dispute, and E Exchange. This model was later extended to include an F, which refers to Future. In the same book, Hubscher-Davidson and Lehr also reported a single-subject case study demonstrating how CBC might work in practice for an in-house professional translator as a coachee.

Incidentally, a more well-known psychotherapeutic method than CBC is called "cognitive behavioral therapy (CBT)" (Beck 2011: 12). Widely researched and practiced in clinical psychology, just like CBC, the way CBT works is that it breaks the vicious cycle of negative thoughts so that emotion and behavior can follow suit for the better as a result. Both CBC and CBT subscribe to a fundamental notion in psychology, namely emotion, cognition, and behavior interact closely and constantly in a tripartite model. I believe that this tripartite model can be used to conceptualize what TPR scholars should strive for in the future. In other words, TPR should aim to demystify translators' affect (A), behavior (B), and cognition (C) as a whole. As TPR continues its journey to maturity, it should not just aim to shed more light on "affect" as a seemingly isolated subject of investigation, which is still relatively underresearched so far, but perhaps more importantly it should focus on how and to what extent each of the three components contributes to translators' work and how they interact with or even potentially compete with each other. Without doubts, there are so many questions yet to be answered in this regard. For instance, how does cognition affect translators' emotion and behavior, particularly in the context of emotional intelligence? How does emotion affect translators' cognition and behavior, not just when translators are translating emotional texts? Do interactions among affect, behavior, and cognition differ in different contexts and situations? To what extent does emotion impair translators' cognition and behavior? Ultimately, only by asking and answering these questions, are we able to sketch a fuller and richer picture of how and why translators think, feel, and behave the way they do.

Finally, it is useful to point out that in psychology, newer neurological research instruments can be used to reexamine previous theories about cognition. For instance, in a neurological experiment that is designed to prove that emotion is constructed in a two-way process, that is, bottom-up and top-down processes, as assumed in the first-generation cognitive psychology (Ochsner et al. 2009), participants are asked to conduct two tasks. One is a stimulus-triggered, that is, bottom-up process, with photographs showing adversative events. The other is an appraisal process, that is, a top-down process, with photographs showing neutral events but asking participants to think about adversative events. The brain imaging results show that these two processes activate different parts of the brain, proving that these two processes exist independently. While there are many appraisal theories in psychology, it is generally agreed that the top-down process or a conscious and deliberate appraisal process is an important factor in determining one's emotional state and outcome (Eysenck and Keane 2015: 637–48). This is also an example of how neurological research can be used to inform our understanding about emotional construct and to reinforce the wide application of therapeutic methods, such as CBT, CBC, and the concept of emotional intelligence/regulation, as adopted by Hubscher-Davidson and Lehr (2021) from psychology to translators' continuous professional development.

5 Affect and Emotion

So far, researchers have used both the terms, affect and emotion, in TPR. As shown in the previous sections, the term "affect" or "affective factors" was first used in the 1990s but more recently the use of the term "emotion" appeared to be more in favor. Hubscher-Davidson (2018: 11–12) claims that she does not wish to distinguish the terms "affect," "emotion," or "feeling," even though she seems to use the term "emotion" more than the other two terms in her publications. While categorically outside the subdiscipline of TPR, Koskinen (2020) in her monograph, *Translation and Affect*, put forward an extensive argument with regard to why she prefers to use the term "affect" over "emotion." She contends that "affect" is a broader term that "can function as . . . [a] bridge concept, crossing over the various orientations in translation studies and also cutting through different contexts and modes of translatorial action" (2020: 3). When contrasting these two major monographs, respectively, by Koskinen (2020) and by Hubscher-Davidson (2018) in translation studies, I have found that the former positions itself in the context of cultural studies and social science and the latter in TPR, psychology, and natural science. The disciplinary division probably explains the reasons and preference for the choice of the terms in each monograph. Interestingly, in psychology, just like what Koskinen has argued, affect is considered to be a more holistic concept that encompasses both emotion and mood (Eysenck and Keane 2015: 636). To be more precise, emotion is a more intense and immediate reaction to a given situation whereas mood or feeling is considered to be a potentially more mellow and prolong state of mind. As a result, it can be more difficult to measure or gauge into (the reasons behind) mood than emotion. This is why it is generally easier to measure and detect emotion in psychological experiments. Generally, emotional construct is understood to consist of two dimensions: valence and arousal. Valence refers to a spectrum of emotional state from being very positive to being very negative, and arousal refers to the intensity of emotional response. As mentioned before, many physiological research instruments, such as EDA, GSR, or ECG, and so on, can only measure the arousal, that is, the intensity of emotional response rather than the valence of emotion. A triangulation of other research instruments (such as facial expression or retrospective interview) is therefore often required to determine the type of emotion or the valence of the emotion. This may be an important consideration for future TPR researchers when designing studies with physiological instruments. To put it in another way, given the magnitude of intensity and temporality in emotion measurement, it is crucial to carefully plan the suitability of relevant stimuli so that enough emotional responses are triggered. Otherwise, an experiment could run into the risk of collecting little data and producing inconclusive results. This in itself exposes some inherent limitations of physiological research instruments (and indeed many other psychological instruments) as research methods. First, it may not be possible to capture every single type of emotion, particularly when the intensity of emotion is less prominent. Second, ecological validity may be compromised, given strict controls of stimuli, variables, and experimental conditions are required in order to generate valid and reliable data (see Shih 2023).

While the reasons behind the use of the terms, affect or emotion, in each of the two monographs as mentioned previously, are entirely understandable, I am more inclined to agree with Koskinen (2020) that affect may serve as a more general concept in translation studies as a whole. Affect can certainly be a concept that goes beyond TPR, while emotion serves as a fitting notion of operational values particularly in empirical studies and experiments in TPR. Interestingly, while drawing attention to Clough and Halley's (2007) affective turn in cultural studies, Koskinen (2020: 7) states that she is not about to declare an "affective turn" following the cultural turn in translation studies. I am, however, more optimistic about an "affective turn" we are beginning to witness in TPR. Just like the early evolvement of TPR as a subdiscipline when process was once upon a time investigated independently from product and later alongside product or performance using multi-method approaches, I envisage that it will become more and more difficult to simply ignore affect and emotion from behavior and cognition in TPR studies, given modern psychology has informed us that affect, behavior, and cognition are not only inseparable but also constantly and dynamically interacting with each other. With the advancement of psychological research instruments, TPR researchers are in a better position than ever before to take stock of the latest research instruments to examine when, how, and why translators and their associated agents, including both human and digital ones (i.e., translation technology), interact with each other. But it has to be noted that when these research instruments become increasingly more sophisticated, it may be more and more difficult for TPR scholars to simply "do it alone" by borrowing research instruments from other disciplines. Instead, TPR scholars will have to learn to work alongside psychologists, neurologists, computer scientists, statisticians, and so on in order to move forward in this subdiscipline.

6 Concluding Remarks

This chapter has set out to unpack the evolvement of affect and emotion in TPR and its alignment with TPR's methodological development as a subdiscipline in translation studies. This evolution was also viewed from a wider context of advancement in cognitive psychology. It started off by tapping into the earliest research method, TAP, borrowed from cognitive psychology, and its relevance to the investigation of affect or "affective factors" when TPR was in its infancy. It then drew attention to the period when early digital research instruments, such as keylogging and eye-tracking software, were first used in TPR where research on behavior and cognition appears to be tangled together. On the outset, this period was also a time when notions in first-generation cognitive psychology, including the trinity of stimuli, cognition, and behavior, were more prevalent. This was likely to be another reason why TPR scholars were largely preoccupied with cognition and its corresponding behavior, rather than affect. But, at the turn of the century, when TPR began to embrace an explosion of many newer forms of digital research instruments, such as neurological and physiological instruments, scholars began to recognize that affect and emotion may be the underlying link between cognition and behavior. This was parallel to the latest development of the second-generation cognitive psychology where human cognition cannot be understood without its environments, social contexts, physical bodies, and perhaps, more importantly, affect.

Among the recent studies on emotion, Hubscher-Davidson's introduction of emotional intelligence and emotional regulation was discussed at length, given its pioneering importance in the study of emotion in TPR and in translation studies. Finally, reasons behind the use of the terminologies, affect and emotion, were explained. It was suggested that affect could be considered to be a more holistic notion whereas emotion a more operational one, particularly in empirical experiments in TPR.

To summarize, studies of translation affect and emotion have evolved from idiosyncratic and evaluative comments in early TAP studies from the periphery to the center of investigation where translation emotion is examined as an independent research theme. Koskinen (2020: 55) explains eloquently why it is more and more important to focus on translation affect in translation studies,

> translation work will gradually shift towards an increased dominance of argumentative, persuasive and creative texts rather than technical and repetitive kinds of documents. This warrants the study of affect, as hitting exactly the right tone and affective valence cannot be left for the machine to figure out.

I will go one step further to state that while TPR should of course aim to study translation affect and emotion in all its glory, bias, and weakness in the short to medium term, it is even more pertinent to understand translation as a holistic phenomenon incorporating analysis from the affective, behavioral, and cognitive perspectives in the longer term. This resonates with the 4EA concept advocated by Muñoz Martín, which moves away from the information processing model or brain-as-computer analogy and moves toward a holistic view of seeing translation in its embodied, embedded, enacted, extended, and affective contexts. Wherever possible, it may merit a revisit to some of the previous TPR studies with the lens of affect and emotion in mind.

Psychology as a discipline is sometimes seen as a cross between social science and natural science. Similarly, TPR is also in a unique position in translation studies where it can push the boundary and bridge the divide among humanity and natural science. This is particularly true with the latest adoption of neurological and physiological research instruments in TPR research. There is no doubt that TPR scholars will continue to face challenges in selecting, adapting, and customizing suitable research instruments and research designs from adjacent disciplines for the purpose of investigating the translation process. I share the same sentiment with Hubscher-Davidson (2018: 221) that it is high time for TPR scholars to have a direct dialogue with psychologists rather than simply having a monologue among ourselves. Going back to the conversation I had with the psychologist who partly inspires me to write this chapter, I know that this would not be the last conversation I had with colleagues in psychology.

References

Beck, J. S. (2011), *Cognitive Behavior Therapy: Basics and Beyond*, 2nd ed., New York: Guilford Press.

Bednárová-Gibová, K. and M. Majherová (2023), "Emotions and Literary Translation Performance: A Study Using the Geneva Emotional Competence Test," in S. Hubscher-Davidson and C. Lehr (eds.), *The Psychology of Translation: An Interdisciplinary Approach*, 99–129, Oxon and New York: Routledge.

Bernardini, S. (2001), "Think-aloud Protocols in Translation Research: Achievements, Limits, Future Prospects," *Target: International Journal of Translation Studies*, 13(2): 241–63.

Cacioppo, J. T., L. G. Tassinary, and G. G. Berntson (2007), "Psychophysiological Science: Interdisciplinary Approaches to Classic Questions about the Mind," in J. T. Cacioppo, L. G. Tassinary, and G. G. Berntson (eds.), *The Handbook of Psychophysiology*, 1–16, Cambridge: Cambridge University Press.

Carl, M. (2012), "Translog-II: A Program for Recording User Activity Data for Empirical Reading and Writing Research," in *Proceedings of the 8th International Conference on Language Resources and Evaluation (LREC)*, 4109–12, Istanbul, Turkey.

Carl, M., M. Schaeffer, and S. Bangalore (2016), "The CRITT Translation Process Research Database," in M. Carl, S. Bangalore, and M. Schaeffer (eds.), *New Directions in Empirical Translation Process Research: Exploring the CRITT TPR-DB*, 13–54, Cham: Springer International.

Carvalho, M., M. G. Matos, and M. H. Anjos (2018), "Cognitive-behavioural Coaching: Applications to Health and Personal Development Contexts," *EC Psychology and Psychiatry*, 7(3): 119–29.

Clark, A. (1997), *Being There: Putting Brain, Body and World Together Again*, Cambridge, MA: MIT Press.

Clough, P. and J. O. Halley, eds. (2007), *The Affective Turn: Theorizing the Social*, Durham and London: Duke University Press.

Çoban, F. (2019), "The Relationship between Professional Translators' Emotional Intelligence and their Translator Satisfaction," *International Journal of Comparative Literature & Translation Studies*, 7(3): 50–64.

Dolan, R. J. (2002), "Emotion, Cognition and Behavior," *Science*, 298(5596): 1191–4.

Ehrensberger-Dow, M. (2017), "An Ergonomic Perspective of Translation," in J. W. Schwieter and A. Ferreira (eds.), *The Handbook of Translation and Cognition*, 332–49, Hoboken: Wiley-Blackwell.

Ericsson, K. A. and H. A. Simon (1984), *Protocol Analysis*, Cambridge, MA: MIT Press.

Eysenck, M. W. and M. T. Keane (2015), *Cognitive Psychology: A Student's Handbook*, 7th ed., London and New York: Psychology Press.

Gieshoff, A. C., C. Lehr, and A. H. Heeb (2021), "Stress, Cognitive, Emotional and Ergonomic Demands in Interpreting and Translation: A Review of Physiological Studies," *Cognitive Linguistic Studies*, 8(2): 404–39.

Goleman, D. (1995), *Emotional Intelligence*, New York: Bantom.

Hansen, G. (2005), "Experience and Emotion in Empirical Translation Research with Think-aloud and Retrospection," *Meta: Translators' Journal*, 50(2): 511–21.

Holmes, J. S. (1988/2004), "The Name and Nature of Translation Studies," in L. Venuti (ed.), *The Translation Studies Reader*, 2nd ed., 180–92, London and New York: Routledge.

Hubscher-Davidson, S. (2013), "Emotional Intelligence and Translation Studies: A New Bridge," *Meta: Translators' Journal*, 58(2): 324–46.

Hubscher-Davidson, S. (2016), "Trait Emotional Intelligence and Translation: A Study of Professional Translators," *Target: International Journal of Translation Studies*, 28(1): 132–57.

Hubscher-Davidson, S. (2018), *Translation and Emotion: A Psychological Perspective*, Georgetown: Routledge.

Hubscher-Davidson, S. and C. Lehr (2021), *Improving the Emotional Intelligence of Translators: A Roadmap for an Experimental Training Intervention*, Cham: Springer Nature.

Hvelplund, K. T. (2017), "Eye Tracking in Translation Process Research," in J. Wchwieter and A. Ferreira (eds.), *The Handbook of Translation and Cognition*, 248–64, Hoboken: Wiley Blackwell.

Immonen, S. (2006), "Translation as A Writing Process: Pauses in Translation versus Monolingual Text Production," *Target: International Journal of Translation Studies*, 18(2): 313–36.

Jääskeläinen, R. (1999), *Tapping the Process: An Explorative Study of the Cognitive and Affective Factors Involved in Translating*, Joensuu: University of Joensuu, Publications in the Humanities no. 22.

Jääskeläinen, R. (2011), "Back to Basic: Designing a Study to Determine the Validity and Reliability of Verbal Report Data on Translation Processes," in S. O'Brien (ed.), *Cognitive Explorations of Translation*, 15–29, London: Continuum.

Jakobsen, A. L. (2003), "Effects of Think Aloud on Translation Speed, Revision, and Segmentation," in F. Alves (ed.), *Triangulating Translation*, 69–95, Amsterdam: John Benjamins Publishing.

Jakobsen, A. L. (2014), "The Development and Current State of Translation Process Research," in E. Brems, R. Meylaerts, and L. van Doorslaer (eds.), *The Known Unknowns of Translation*, 65–88, Amsterdam: John Benjamins Publishing.

Jakobsen, A. L. (2017), "Translation Process Research," in J. W. Schwieter and A. Ferreira (eds.), *The Handbook of Translation and Cognition*, 21–49, Hoboken: Wiley-Blackwell.

Just, M. A. and P. A. Carpenter (1980), "A Theory of Reading: From Eye Fixations to Comprehension," *Psychological Review*, 87(4): 329–54.

Koskinen, K. (2020), *Translation and Affect*, Amsterdam: John Benjamins Publishing.

Kosslyn, S. M. and O. Koenig (1995), *Wet Mind: The New Cognitive Neuroscience*, New York: Free Press.

Krings, H. P. (2001), Repairing Texts: *Empirical Investigations of Machine Translation Post-Editing Processes*, ed. G. S. Koby, Kent and London: Kent State University Press.

Kussmaul, P. (1997), "Comprehension Processes and Translation," in Mary Snell-Hornby, Zuzana Jettmarová, and Klaus Kaindl (eds.), *Translation as Intercultural Communication: Selected Papers from the EST Congress, Prague 1995*, 20: 239, Amsterdam: John Benjamins Publishing.

Laukkanen, J. (1996), "Affective and Attitudinal Factors in Translation Processes," *Target: International Journal of Translation Studies*, 8(2): 257–74.

Lehr, C. (2014a), "The Relevance of Emotion for Professional Translation and Translation Studies," in B. Wolfram, B. Eichner, S. Kalina, N. Keßler, F. Mayer, and J. Ørsted (eds.), *Proceedings of the XXth FIT World Congress*, 601–6, Berlin: BDÜ Fachverlag.

Lehr, C. (2014b), "The Influence of Emotion on Language Performance: Study of a Neglected Determinant of Decision-Making in Professional Translators," PhD thesis, University of Geneva, Switzerland.

Lehr, C. and K. T. Hvelplund (2020), "Emotional Experts: Influences of Emotion on the Allocation of Cognitive Resources during Translation," in R. Muñoz Martín and S. L. Halverson (eds.), *Multilingual Mediated Communication and Cognition*, 44–68, London: Routledge.

Leijten, M. and L. Van Waes (2013), "Keystroke Logging in Writing Research: Using Inputlog to Analyze and Visualize Writing Processes," *Written Communication*, 30(3): 358–92.

Muñoz Martín, R. (2010a), "On Paradigms and Cognitive Translatology," in G. M. Shreve and E. Angelone (eds.), *Translation and Cognition*, 169–87, Amsterdam: John Benjamins Publishing.

Muñoz Martín, R. (2010b), "Leave No Stone Unturned: On the Development of Cognitive Translatology," *Translation and Interpreting Studies*, 5(2): 145–62.

Muñoz Martín, R. (2016), "Of Minds and Men – Computers and Translators," *Poznań Studies in Contemporary Linguistics*, 52(2): 351–81.

O'Brien, S. (2013), "The Borrowers: Researching the Cognitive Aspects of Translation," in M. Ehrensberger-Dow, S. Göpferich, and S. O'Brien (eds.), *Interdisciplinarity in Translation and Interpreting Process Research*, 5–17, Amsterdam: John Benjamins Publishing.

Ochsner, K. N., R. R. Ray, B. Hughes, K. McRae, J. C. Cooper, J. Weber, J. D. Gabrieli, and J. J. Gross (2009), "Bottom-up and Top-down Processes in Emotion Generation: Common and Distinct Neural Mechanisms," *Psychological Science*, 20: 1322–31.

Perdikaki, K. and N. Georgiou (2023), "Permission to Emote: Developing Coping Techniques for Emotional Resilience in Subtitling," in S. Hubscher-Davidson and C. Lehr (eds.), *The Psychology of Translation: An Interdisciplinary Approach*, 58–80, Oxon and New York: Routledge.

Reber, R. (2019), *Psychology: The Basics*, London: Routledge.

Ren, H., M. Wang, Y. He, Yan, Z. Du, Z. Jiang, Z. Jing, D. Li, and Z. Yuan (2019), "A Novel Phase Analysis Method for Examining fNIRS Neuroimaging Data Associated with Chinese/English Sight Translation," *Behavioural Brain Research*, 361: 151–8.

Risku, H. (2017), "Ethnographies of Translation and Situated Cognition," in J. W. Schwieter and A. Ferreira (eds.), *The Handbook of Translation and Cognition*, 290–310, Hoboken: Wiley Blackwell.

Rojo, A. and M. C. Ramos (2016), "Can Emotion Stir Translation Skill? Defining the Impact of Positive and Negative Emotions on Translation Performance," in R. Muñoz Martín (ed.), *Reembedding Translation Process Research*, 107–30, Amsterdam: John Benjamins Publishing.

Salovey, P. and J. D. Mayer (1990), "Emotional Intelligence," *Imagination, Cognition and Personality*, 9(3): 185–211.

Seth, D. and L. F. Barrett (2007), "Affect is a Form of Cognition: A Neurobiological Analysis," *Cognition and Emotion*, 21(6): 1184–211.

Shih, C. Y. (2023), *Navigating the Web: A Qualitative Eye Tracking-based Study of Translators' Web Search Behaviour*, Cambridge: Cambridge University Press.

Storbeck, J. and G. L. Clore (2007), "On the Interdependence of Cognition and Emotion," *Cognition and Emotion*, 21(6): 1212–37.

Sun, S. (2011), "Think-aloud-based Translation Process Research: Some Methodological Considerations," *Meta: Translators' Journal*, 56(4): 928–51.

Tirkkonen-Condit, S. (1997), "Who Verbalises What: A Linguistic Analysis of TAP Texts," *Target: International Journal of Translation Studies*, 9(1): 69–84.

Tymoczko, M. (2012), "The Neuroscience of Translation," *Target: International Journal of Translation Studies*, 24(1): 83–102.

Wheeler, M. (2005), *Reconstructing the Cognitive World: The Next Step*, Cambridge, MA: MIT Press.

Zachar, P. and R. D. Ellis, eds. (2012), *Categorical versus Dimensional Models of Affect: A Seminar on the Theories of Panksepp and Russell*, vol. 7, Amsterdam: John Benjamins Publishing.

Zheng, B., S. Báez, L. Su, X. Xiang, S. Weis, A. Ibáñez, and A. M. García (2020), "Semantic and Attentional Networks in Bilingual Processing: fMRI Connectivity Signatures of Translation Directionality," *Brain and Cognition*, 143: 105584.

Zhu, L. (2020), "A Critical Review of the Research on Translation Psychology: Theoretical and Methodological Approaches," *Linguistica Antverpiensia, New Series-Themes in Translation Studies*, 19: 53–79.

2

Translation and Affect and the Notion of a "Center of Attention"

Kirsten Malmkjær

1 Attention and Translation

It is obvious to anyone who has made any serious attempt to translate that the translating activity requires that a considerable amount of attention be paid by the translator to the texts involved and to the circumstances surrounding them; indeed, scholars have been at pains to outline ways in which such attention may be practiced, harnessed, and focused (see, e.g., Nord [1988] 2005; Baker 1992; Vienne 1994; papers collected in Malmkjær 2004 and 2020). But what, exactly, is attention?

According to Hvelplund, "Attention involves focusing on specific environmental stimuli while ignoring other stimuli"; it is "a type of cognitive process by which the mind engages cognitive resources on a specific object" (2021: 279). Such "exclusion-oriented" definitions (my term) derive from James (1890: 403–4), who explains,

> Every one knows what attention is. It is the taking possession by the mind, in clear and vivid form, of one out of what seem several simultaneously possible objects or trains of thought. Focalization, concentration, of consciousness are of its essence. It implies withdrawal from some things in order to deal effectively with others, and is a condition which has a real opposite in the confused, dazed, scatterbrained state which in French is called *distraction*, and *Zerstreutheit* in German.

By "exclusion-oriented," I mean a definition that, like James's and Hvelplund's, includes as an important part of the definition of attention the fact that something is excluded. It implies—at least to me—that a person who is attending to X is deliberately, willfully ignoring something else. Such a definition expresses the paradox that by *willfully* ignoring something, one is very much attending to it.

In empirical translation studies, attention has been measured by way of eye tracking, keystroke logging, or think-aloud protocols, or combinations of these, and, using these methods, considerable progress has been made within translation studies in our understanding of translators' engagement with texts. These investigative methods were preceded by those of Buswell (1935) who made photographic records of the eye movements of art students and of a control group who had not studied art. It is from Buswell's publication that the notion of a center of attention derives (see Buswell 1935: 18).

However, the research methods mentioned tend to force a focus on rather small stretches of text (albeit these can be parts of much longer texts), because small stretches of text are what a working translator looks at, types, or reads out at any one time during the translating process. This focus on small text segments complements exclusion-oriented definition of attention well, but it has what I consider an unfortunate tendency to leave out of consideration the kind of analysis of whole-source texts that translation teachers, and also some theorists (see, e.g., Nord [1988] 2005; Vienne 1994), tend to recommend; and it is possible that current methods of measuring attention in translation studies, in tandem with the exclusiveness definition of attention, regularly force a misrepresentation of translators' activities as these in fact take place outside of a testing situation. In addition, eye tracking, in particular, is wholly focused on visual attention distribution (Kruger 2021: 440), whereas the translators whose descriptions of their activities are cited in Malmkjær (2020), for example, refer to the influence on their individual translation decisions of complex systems of phenomena like alliteration, rhyme, rhythm, and accentual patterns, which they generally bear in mind throughout the process of translating the stretches of text that form the individual foci of their visual attention as they make their way through the text to be translated, looking back and forth between it and the developing translation (on translators' eye movements, see especially Göpferich, Jakobsen, and Mees 2008). Indeed, translators may carry aspects of their wider attention foci over between translating tasks, especially, perhaps, if these involve the same author. If translators did not adopt this more holistic approach to texts, they might run the risk of obscuring the style of an original text and of misrepresenting in the translation the source text's affective aspects. Bearing these issues in mind, and also bearing in mind that translators do not always want to stay as close (in their view) to the source text as possible (though the translator I focus on did want to do so in the case of the translation I discuss), it is my intention here, nonetheless, to illustrate the effect on individual translation choices of a translator's broad attention focus or attention foci. I discuss one translator's translation of one literary text; and it is my contention that the individual translation choices he makes in that text indicate that he adopts a translatorial focus that is significantly broader than each of these individual choices and which affects each of them.

2 The Focal Text[1]

The translation I focus on is a translation into Danish of *The Young Visiters or Mr Salteena's Plan*, written by Daisy (Margaret Mary Julia) Ashford (1881–1972) in 1890, when she was nine years old. The source text was published in 1919 in London by Chatto and Windus/The Hogarth Press, and according to Wikipedia (https://en.wikipedia.org/wiki/The_Young_Visiters), it was reprinted eighteen times in the first year of its publication. *The Young Visiters or Mr Salteena's Plan* is an unusual work insofar as the narrating voice is that of a nine-year-old female child who is its actual author, whereas the child's voice in a number of well-known children's books written as if authored by a child is in fact the adult author's representation of that voice. This is true, for example, of numerous books by Dame Jacqueline Wilson (1991, 1995a, 1995b, 1998a and 1998b, 1999, 2000a and 2000b, 2001), and it is true of the Adrian Mole books by Sue Townsend (e.g., 1982). Other examples that spring to mind are *Goggle-Eyes* by Anne Fine and *Under the Black Flag* by Erik Christian Haugaard. This practice of adults authoring books presented as if written by a child is by no means confined to recent decades. For example, *Treasure Island* by Robert Louis Stevenson, first published in 1883, is presented as if written by a fourteen-year-old boy; and Mary Norton's *The Borrowers* of 1952 begins as if told by "me" before quickly moving into a standard third-person narration. But as mentioned, in contrast to these feats of child impersonation, *The Young Visiters* is written by a real child. The narration is mainly third-person narrative (e.g., it begins "Mr. Saltena was an elderly man of 42 and was fond of asking peaple [sic] to stay with him"); but the narrator self-refers occasionally when addressing her readers, as in chapter one, where she suggests that "Perhaps my readers will be wondering why Bernard Clark had asked My Salteena to stay with him." Occasional direct address to readers is a fairly common literary device in third-person narratives, known perhaps especially famously from Charlotte Brontë's Jane Eyre's exclamation, "Reader, I married him" (1847), and Daisy Ashford uses it with panache. Particularly good examples of her skill in using this literary device are the endings of chapter two, "Here we will leave our friends to unpack and end this chapter" and chapter six, "And now we will leave our hero enjoying his glimpse of high life and return to Ethel Montacue." Also chapter eleven, which tells of Ethel's and Bernard's honeymoon (which Daisy Ashford spells "Honymoon") in Egypt and which ends, "and here we shall leave them for a merry six weeks of bliss while we return to England," and the final chapter, which ends, "So now my readers we will say farewell to the characters in the book."

Of course, despite Daisy Ashford's familiarity with literary convention, she is a child and adopts a child's perspective on many parts of the story that she tells. For example, in chapter one, where she introduces and describes her main characters, she explains that Ethel Monticue, who is seventeen years old, wears "a blue velvit [*sic*] frock which had grown rather short in the sleeves," and at the beginning of chapter two, which takes place on the morning of Ethel's and Mr. Salteena's journey, by train, to visit Bernard, she explains that "When the great morning came Mr Salteena did not have an egg for his breakfast in case he should be sick on the jorney [*sic*]." On the travelers' arrival at Bernard's estate, they are offered "a glorious tea . . . on a gold tray two kinds of bread and butter a lovly [*sic*] jam role and lots of sugar cakes" (p. 26). As these passages illustrate, and as the translator into Danish notes (7–8; my translation), "Daisy Ashford was very good at spelling, but she was only nine years old, and it is quite understandable that her text exhibits a selection of errors." Unusually for published texts (compare with the texts published on sites like, e.g., https://www.tckpublishing.com/child-authors/, which seem improbably error free), the errors in *The Young Visiters or Mr Salteena's Plan* have been retained in the published book, and for many adult readers, they may contribute considerably to the affect experienced when reading the book. For example, the translator sees them as

> curiosities which must certainly not detract from the book's genuine qualities. Let them, rather, enter into a higher, magical unity in Daisy Ashford's world, created in a nursery in a house in the English countryside in the 1890s; and what a world! (Translator's notes, p. 10; my translation)

The translator has populated his translation with the kinds of error that a Danish child of the same age as Daisy Ashford was when she wrote *The Young Visiters or Mr Salteena's Plan* might make in the Danish language. Given the lexical differences between the languages, this strategy means that instead of making an error in the item in the translation that corresponds to an item that Daisy Ashford has spelled incorrectly, the translator has often had to select a different item in the translation to render erroneously, namely one that a Danish child might stumble over. I explore these choices in Section 4. In Section 3 I discuss the notion of affect and the relationship between it and translation.

3 Affect and Translation

Affect is defined by the *American Psychological Association (APA) Dictionary of Psychology* (online) as "any experience of feeling or emotion, ranging from suffering to elation, from the simplest to the most complex sensations of feeling, and from the most normal to the most pathological emotional reactions" (https://dictionary.apa.org/affect, accessed March 15, 2020), and as Hogan (2016; online; accessed March 25, 2022) explains, "Literature is animated by emotion, both at the level of what it concerns and at the level of how readers respond." Of course, texts where affect may be important include not only literary texts but also, for example, journalism, promotional texts, political writing, and historical accounts, but I shall not discuss examples of these genres here.

According to Hubscher-Davidson (2018: 2) there are three forms of emotion that may influence translators. First, material in source texts may engender emotional reactions in a translator. For example, Boase-Beier, Davies, Hammel, and Winters (2017: 7) point out that a translator confronted with a text about the Holocaust may feel especially keenly "the possibilities and limitations of language."

Secondly, and not unrelated to the first form of emotion that may influence translators, a translator's own emotions more generally may affect that translator's decision-making. For example, where a term or a stretch of a source text may have several possible translations, a translator's feelings about the phenomenon referred to may influence which translation option he or she selects. A translator with a strong emotional engagement with the treatment of Jewish people during the second war in Europe, for example, may prefer to render the Hebrew term שואה as "shoah" because this transliteration of the Hebrew term refers exclusively to the killing of Jews by the Nazi regime in Germany, whereas the term "holocaust," which derives from a Greek term that means "sacrifice by fire," has been used for both this and other genocidal atrocities; further, it has been argued that "holocaust" obscenely connotes a religious sacrifice by way of its original Greek meaning (see Evans 1989: 142).

The third kind of emotion that may influence translators, according to Hubscher-Davidson (2018: 2), is the emotions of the source and target text readers. The translator may have a certain readership in mind and make certain assumptions about their reactions to certain aspects of the translation (2018: 175); perhaps the translator wants these to match the reactions he or she experienced him or herself and imagines that the original audience experienced; or perhaps he or she intends for the new readership to have different experiences than those. Either way, the translator will pay attention to what he or she believes are the emotions that his or her text will engender in its prospective readership.

This raises intriguing and somewhat vexed questions concerning the relationship between language and emotion and translation, prominently the following three. First, how is it possible for written text to represent emotion, which may or may not have been felt by its writer and which its readers, including its translator, may then also feel (or not) and, in the case of the translator, "forward" to the readers of the translation? It may seem odd to attribute the ability to generate affect to written text on a page, but according to Oatley (1992: 126), what happens is that "a play or novel allows us to compare an explicitly simulated set of actions and their results with emotions that are our own and that may move us considerably." We read or watch and empathize with the characters on the basis of what our own reactions would be, were we personally to be exposed to the events represented in the play or written text.

The second question, then, concerns the role that language plays in this emulation of reality. In the case of a play, the audience observes a set of events, and although culture is by no means irrelevant to how such a set of events may be understood and reacted to by an audience, a play does at least "imitate reality" more directly, we might say, than a novel or other written text. In written text, language has to do all the representative work for its readers so that, arguably, there is more scope for variation in audience reception with variation in language and culture than in the case of a play, where the language is accompanied by the actions and physical expressions exhibited by members of the cast. The existence of multiple translations of some source texts strongly suggests that not every translator makes the same assumption as every other translator about what would create the same effect (if that is even what a translator is trying to do); or, the existence of multiple translations of the same source text suggests that the translators were affected differently by the source text, which may be why their translations differ; it is also possible, of course, that the translators were in fact affected in similar ways but use different language choices to express this affect; we cannot know precisely, or even approximately, according to some theorists (see, e.g., Quine 1960). But in any case, as Boase-Beier and de Vooght (2019: 17) put it,

> Translation . . . is never about getting it right, about approximating the form or content of the original, about making a copy for those who do not speak Yiddish, or Latvian or French. It is about recognising someone else's story, understanding the way the teller has chosen to tell it, and passing it on to others.

The third question, which is perhaps fundamental, concerns the very nature of emotion. According to Rikhardsdottir (2017: 6), "there is . . . no clear consensus of what 'emotions' really are" or, indeed, of their definition, despite considerable research effort within diverse disciplines, including "psychology, anthropology, philosophy and history" in recent decades, and despite the fact that, according to the Stanford Encyclopedia of Philosophy (https://plato.stanford.edu/entries/emotion/, accessed March 17, 2022), "no aspect of our mental life is more important to the quality and meaning of our existence than the emotions." Rather than discuss approaches to emotions at length, therefore, I will accept this state of affairs as regrettable but adopt the pragmatic attitude that we use what we (think we) know. In other words, most people will have felt emotions that they would name sadness, joy, anger, and so on, and there are certain facial (e.g., smiling, frowning) and bodily (e.g., crying, jumping for joy) characteristics associated with these, which are probably not wholly learnt but which contain elements of more or less spontaneous, "natural" reactions to events. An inability to react to or experience emotion is known in psychology as *alexithymia*, and the fact of the condition being recognized by way of and having been given this Greek reference term reinforces the notion that the ability to empathize and feel affect is normal for humans. Oatley and Jenkins (1996: 49) emphasize that emotions can be recognized cross-culturally and that "although there are substantial differences in emotional life in different cultures . . . emotional commonalities among peoples are larger than the differences." However, as Oatley (1992: 10) points out

> life changes in its emotional patterns from infancy to adulthood. Emotions in childhood seem more salient, more intense, more frequent than in adulthood. There are clear continuities, but there is also the question of whether adult emotions concern different matters than those of childhood.

As mentioned in Section 2, Daisy Ashford perforce adopts a child's perspective on emotions and is unfamiliar, from personal experience, with the emotions that she is aware that her characters are likely to experience given the situations they find themselves in. She knows them by description rather than by acquaintance, as we might say (see Russell 1910–11). The translator does not mention this as a difficulty and, indeed, as an adult, he finds himself in the fortunate position, rather unusual in translation, of knowing more about what is being narrated than the narrator, as far as this issue is concerned. His task, therefore, is to avoid allowing this more advanced knowledge and experience to filter through to the translation because this would risk superimposing an ironic tone on the work, which might diminish its affective potential. He does not mention this as a difficulty, however. In fact, he mentions in his Translator's Notes the zeitgeist as the greatest difficulty afflicting his translation work, followed by the spelling errors, as briefly mentioned in Section 2:

> I have refrained from attempting to represent the way in which a nine-year old girl would misunderstand the Danish of the 1890s. I have used concrete expressions from the period when describing clothes and objects . . . but in descriptive passages as well as in the dialogues, I have brought the language up to our own time as gently as I could.
>
> Another problem was the spelling errors. Daisy Ashford was very good at spelling, but she was only nine years old, and it is understandable that her text exhibits a selection of errors, odd in the case of quite simple words, less surprising when she tackles difficult, adult words. She consistently misspells the word "idea." However, it is unlikely that a Danish child would misspell the Danish word "ide." It is an easy word. In such cases, I have sought to identify a different word in the sentence, which a nine-year old Dane might stumble over. (7–8, my translation)

In the next section, I look at how the translator has accomplished this task.

4 The Translation

Daisy Ashford's book was translated into Danish by Poul Malmkjær under the title, *De unge elskene eller Mr Salteenas plan* (*The Young Lovers or Mr Salteena's Plan*; the word "elskene" is a misspelling of "elskende" ("lovers")). The translation was published in 1986 by Nyt Nordisk Forlag Arnold Busk A/S.

The translator's emotional engagement with the work is made clear in his Translator's Notes:

> One of life's plentiful pleasures is the completion of a piece of enjoyable work. In the case of the translation of Daisy Ashford's novel, however, my joy was admixed with grief that the book wasn't longer, that it ended, that my work was not to continue. (p. 7; my translation)

His engagement with the spelling errors was mentioned at the end of the previous section, where it was also noted that this is not a mere matter of misspelling whenever the author misspells. Rather, to create affect through the misspellings, these must be believable, logical, and consistent in the context of the language of the translation, which means, interestingly, that the representation of spelling errors works best when close equivalence with individual items in the source text in this aspect is *avoided* rather than aimed for. For example, in the first sentence of the story, Mr. Salteena is said to be "fond of asking peaple to stay with him" (Ashford 1919/1984 edition: 19), and this "peaple" is the first misspelling in the book. The translator places an error in the chapter heading, where he spells the term "temmelig," which would correspond to the original's "Quite" in "Quite a young Girl" as "temlig," which is how the term is pronounced; this error then recurs in the second sentence (Ashford and Malmkjær 1986: 19). Such consistency in misspelling is important to ensure credibility across the translation, and the translator ensures credibility further by exploiting other aspects of the Danish spelling system where pronunciation is either an imprecise or a misleading guide to spelling. In particular, within words, the same consonantal sounds can be represented by either gg/g or kk/k [g], or by either dd/d or tt/t [d], or by either pp/p or bb/b [b]. Some vowel sounds can be represented by different letters, for example, [œ] can be represented by either æ or e; in addition, some letters are redundant for pronunciation purposes, as in so many languages (including English), especially, in the case of Danish, at the ends of syllables.

In the first two chapters, the spelling errors listed later occur in the original and in the translation. I have not provided the correct spelling for the English words, though I have for the Danish to illustrate the strategies the translator has used. In the examples, bold typeface indicates that the meanings of the English and Danish word coincide. Numbers after the example indicate the book pages where the example occurs. Where a term is only represented under one of the language headings (ENGLISH TEXT or DANISH TEXT), there is no misspelling in the corresponding term in the other language.

ENGLISH TEXT	DANISH TEXT	CORRECT DANISH
peaple (19; 21)		
	temlig (19; 21)	temmelig (rather)
wiskers (19)	**Baggenbarder (19)**	**Bakkenbarter**
thorght (19)		
velvit (19; 22)	**fløjels (22)**	**fløjls**
quear (19 x 2)		
	udseene (19)	udseende (looking)
tishu (20)		
	indsvøpt (20)	indsvøbt (wrapped)
rarther (20)		
	vinddruer (20)	vindruer (grapes)

compleat (20; 28)		
certinly (20)	**selføllelig (20)**	**selvfølgelig (of course)**
parshial (20)		
	ligger (21)	lægger (places)
valud (21)	**værsatte (21)**	**værdsatte**
partys (21)		
	afsidsliggene (21)	afsidesliggende (remote)
presumshious (21)		
	temlig (21)	temmelig (rather)
jorney (22)		
	oprant (22)	oprandt (came)
ruuge (22)	**ruuche (22)**	**rouge**
superier (22)		
	spis (22)	spids (sharp)
rithum (22)	**rytteme (22)**	**rytme**
idiotick (22)		
survayed (22)	**tog et overblig (22)**	**overblik**
colors (22)		
	hångklæde (23)	håndklæde (towel)
dont (22 × 2; 26)		
	chenert (23)	genert (shy)
bronkitis (22)	**bronkitis (23)**	**bronchitis**
	oprømpt (24 × 2)	oprømt (excited)
	unniform (24)	uniform
	impornerene (24)	imponerende (impressive)
conveyance (24)		
	baggachen (24 × 2)	bagagen (the luggage)
thankyou (24; 25)	**mangetak (24)**	**mange tak**
	parongen (24)	perronen (the platform)
cariage (24)	**Karret (24)**	**karet**
	baggache (24; 25)	baggage (luggage)
perlitely (24)	**høflit (24)**	**høfligt**
gracefuly (24)		
	karreten (24)	kareten (the carriage)
	tøjletbord (25)	toiletbord (dressing table)
beleeve (25)		
	i værtifald (25)	i hvert fald (in any case)
cant (25)		
the sceenery (25)	**seneriet (25)**	**sceneriet**
	skintæppe (25)	skindtæppe (fur rug)
the cariage (25)	**karreten (25)**	**kareten**
beautifull (25)		
pillers (25)		
majic (25)	**tryldeslag (25)**	**trylleslag**
	skinnene (25)	skinnende (shiny)
viacle (25)		
	Bleg (ansigt) (25)	blegt (pale)
	venlit (25)	venligt (friendly)
	udseene (25)	udseende (air/look)

	koridor (25)	corridor
	indtændst (26)	intenst
partys (26)	selvskaber (26)	selskaber
Socierty (26)	selvskabslivet (26)	selskabslivet
crid (26)		
	fornøjgelse (26)	fornøjelse (pleasure)
lovly (26 × 2)		
	dypt (26)	dybt (deep)
role (26)	rulade (26)	roulade
Ethels (26 × 2)		
	adskelige (26)	adskillige (several)
rarther an idear (26)		
	gallandt (26)	galant (gallant)
	hyggelit (26)	hyggeligt (cozy)
	mundert (27)	muntert (cheerfully)
	lukale (27)	locale (room)
	nyanse (27)	nuance
(the) toilit (set) (26)	tøjlet(bordet) (27)	toilet(bordet) (the dressing table)
	lila (27)	lilla (purple)
cosly varse (27)	kosbar vase (27)	kostbar vase (costly/precious vase)
supprise (27)		
	skildedøren (27)	skilledøren (the dividing door)
decerated (27)		
	Blejgult (27)	bleggult (pale yellow)
somber (27)	mellenkolsk (27)	melancholy
tip up baison (27)	vibbebadekar (27)	vippebadekar
jellus (27)	chalu (27)	jaloux (jealous)

In the first two chapters of the book, there are marginally more spelling errors in the translation than in the source text, because the spelling convention-related strategy for error representation in the translation is applied consistently, as it has to be, to be credible. There is also the typical child phrase "i værtifald" instead of "i hvert fald," which means more or less "in any case" in the sense of "at least." In some cases, the translator has inserted an element that might amuse in the translation. For example he translates "a huge pale face" (p. 25) as "et stort bleg ansigt" (p. 25), which, because of the lack of a "t" after "bleg" suggests "a large pale-face" in the sense that this term might occur in Cowboy/Indian stories.

5 Conclusions

By using a largely pronunciation-guided strategy, the translator ensures credibility of the errors in the target text and sustains the aspect of the story's affective potential provided by the spelling. Any story is sustained by not only the events that are narrated in it but also the manner in which they are narrated (Genette 1972); similarly, character depiction depends not only on what is expressed but also on how it is expressed. In the case in focus here, spelling and its role in creating potential for affect are important aspects of the narrative. The translator's consistent and logical representation of this feature ensures that it enriches the translation as much as it enriches the original story.

Of course, erroneous spelling is not the only feature of Daisy Ashford's work that marks it out as the work of a child or that adds to its charm. For example, the idea with which the story opens that a person of forty-two is elderly is enchanting, and so is the entire course of events, which I will not dwell on, because it offers no resistance to translation between the two languages involved. Ambiguity also plays its part; for example, Mr. Salteena sits down at the breakfast table to "eat the egg which Ethel had so kindly laid for him" (p. 20). Again, since chickens also "lay" eggs in Danish, and eggs might be "laid" on a table too, translation poses no difficulty.

The original also contains what would undoubtedly be considered instances of double entendre in a work authored by an adult; as it is, it is uncertain and probably unlikely that the second meaning was intended (and yet . . .). One of these instances occurs just before Ethel and Mr. Salteena are to leave to go and stay with Bernard. Mr. Salteena goes upstairs "to say goodbye to Rosalind the housemaid" (p. 22):

> Mr S. skipped upstairs to Rosalinds [sic] room. Good-bye Rosalind he said I shall be back soon and I hope I shall enjoy myself.
> I make no doubt of that sir said Rosalind with a blush as Mr Salteena silently put 2/6 on the dirty toilet cover.

Be that as it may. I believe that the case I have discussed illustrates that a translator may (probably most often does) focus on the work he or she has to translate as a whole in his or her effort to convey to readers the affect that the work has had on the translator him or herself. I hope I have made it clear that I am aware that not all translators of all texts desire to do this; but I have selected a text and translation pair in the case of which it is attested by the translator that the work affected him and that he tried to convey it into its new language in such a way that its affective potential would be retained.

For further discussion of the relationship between translation and emotion, see, for example, Lehr (2021).

Since affect belongs within the realm of what Austin (1962) refers to as perlocution (the effect of a speech act on a listener: what it makes him or her understand, feel, or do), it is not in the translator's power (any more than it actually is in the power of the author of the original) to guarantee what it will be. But the translator may, if they wish to convey to the readers of the translation the affect that the original had on them themselves, seek to select the translations for individual items that will in their unison, in the translator's opinion, convey that affect to the readers of the translation.

Note

1   I have previously written on this topic in an article entitled "Centres of Attention in (Literary) Translation" published in *Journal of Languages and Translation (JLT)*, Vol. 7, Issue 1, pp. 1–15 | October 2020 Print ISSN: 2735-4520 | E-ISSN: 2735-4539. I am grateful to the editors of *JLT* for permission to take up the topic again here and to reproduce the data from the previous article.

References

American Psychological Association (APA) Dictionary of Psychology. https://dictionary.apa.org/affect (accessed March 15, 2020).

Ashford, D. (1919/1984), *The Young Visiters or Mr Salteena's Plan*, London: Chatto and Windus/The Hogarth Press.

Ashford, D. (1919/1986), *De unge elskene eller Mr Salteenas Plan*. Translated by Poul Malmkjær from *The Young Visiters or Mr Salteena's Plan*, Copenhagen: Nyt Nordisk Forlag Arnold Busck A/S.

Austin, J. L. (1962), *How to do Things with Words*, Oxford: Oxford University Press.

Baker, M. (1992), *In Other Words: A Coursebook on Translation*, London: Routledge.

Boase-Beier, J., P. Davies, A. Hammel, and M. Winters, eds. (2017), *Translating Holocaust Lives*, London: Bloomsbury.

Boase-Beier, J. and M. de Vooght, eds. (2019), *Poetry of the Holocaust: An Anthology*, Todmorden: Arc Publications.

Brontë, C. (1847), *Jane Eyre*, London: Smith, Elder & Co. Published under the pen name "Currer Bell".

Buswell, G. T. (1935), *How People Look at Pictures: A Study of the Psychology of Perception in Art*, Chicago: The University of Chicago Press.

Evans, R. (1989), *In Hitler's Shadow*, New York: Pantheon.

Genett, G. (1972), *Discours du recit*, Paris: Editions due Seuil.

Göpferich, S., A. L. Jakobsen, and I. M. Mees (2008), *Looking at Eyes: Eye-Tracking Studies of Reading and Translation Processing*, Copenhagen: Samfundslitteratur.

Hogan, P. C. (2016), "Affect Studies," in *Oxford Research Encyclopedia*. https://oxfordre.com/literature/view/10.1093/acrefore/9780190201098.001.0001/acrefore-9780190201098-e-105.

Hubscher-Davidson, S. (2018), *Translation and Emotion: A Psychological Perspective*, London: Routledge.

Hvelplund, K. (2021), "Translation, Attention and Cognition," in F. Alves and A. L. Jakobsen (eds.), *The Routledge Handbook of Translation and Cognition*, 279–93, London: Routledge.

James, W. (1890), *The Principles of Psychology*, New York: Henry Holt and Company.

Kruger, J.-L. (2021), "Translation, Multimodality and Cognition," in F. Alves and A. L. Jakobsen (eds.), *The Routledge Handbook of Translation and Cognition*, 433–44, London: Routledge.

Lehr, C. (2021), "Translation, Emotion and Cognition," in F. Alves and A. L. Jakobsen (eds.), *The Routledge Handbook of Translation and Cognition*, 294–309, London: Routledge.

Malmkjær, K., ed. (2004), *Translation in Undergraduate Degree Programmes*, Amsterdam: John Benjamins Publishing.

Malmkjær, K. (2020), *Translation and Creativity*, London: Routledge.

Nord, C. (1988/2005), *Textanalyse und Übersetzen: Theoretische Grundlagen, Methode und didaktische Anwendung einer Übersetzungsrelevanten Textanalyse*, Heidelberg: Gross. Published in English as *Text Analysis in Translation: Theory, Methodology, and Didactic Application of a Model for Translation-Oriented Text Analysis*, Amsterdam: Rodopi.

Norton, M. (1952), *The Borrowers*, London: J. M. Dent & Sons.

Oatley, K. (1992), *Best Laid Schemes: The Psychology of Emotions*, Cambridge: Cambridge University Press.

Oatley, K. and J. M. Jenkins (1996), *Understanding Emotions*, Cambridge: Blackwell Publishers Inc.

Quine, W. v. O. (1960), *Word and Object*, Cambridge, MA: MIT Press.

Rikhardsdottir, S. (2017), *Emotion in Old Norse Literature: Translations, Voices, Contexts*, Cambridge: D. S. Brewer.

Russell, B. (1911), "Knowledge by Acquaintance and Knowledge by Description," *Proceedings of the Aristotelian Society (New Series)*, XI(1910–1911): 108–28.

Stevenson, R. L. (1883), *Treasure Island*, London: Cassell & Co.

Townsend, S. (1982), *The Secret Diary of Adrian Mole Aged 13 ¾*, London: William Heinemann.

Vienne, J. (1994), "Towards a Pedagogy of 'Translation in Situation,'" *Perspectives: Studies in Translatology*, 1: 51–9.

Wilson, J. (1991), *The Story of Tracy Beaker*, London: Doubleday.

Wilson, J. (1995a), *Double Act*, London: Doubleday.

Wilson, J. (1995b), *How to Survive Summer Camp*, Oxford: Oxford University Press.
Wilson, J. (1998a), *Buried Alive*, London: Doubleday.
Wilson, J. (1998b), *Girls under Pressure*, London: Doubleday.
Wilson, J. (1999), *The Illustrated Mum*, London: Doubleday.
Wilson, J. (2000a), *Superstars*, London: Corgi Yearling.
Wilson, J. (2000b), *Vicky Angel*, London: Doubleday.
Wilson, J. (2001), *Dustbin Baby*, London: Doubleday.

Covert Self-talk as a Tool for Dialogue Interpreters

Anu Viljanmaa

1 Introduction and Background

This article addresses the phenomenon of covert self-talk as a tool for dialogue interpreters to address and manage internal listening filters (Viljanmaa 2020: 477–9). The study approaches dialogue interpreting from a listening-centered perspective. In listening-centered communication, listening is seen as "the primary process influencing communication outcomes" (Brownell 2010: 143) and is defined as "the process of receiving, constructing meaning from, and responding to spoken and/or nonverbal messages" (ILA 1996: 4). Listening is a dynamic and multidimensional process that takes different shapes and forms depending on the context where it is used. It is a complex everyday phenomenon that contains a cognitive, affective, and behavioral dimension (Halone et al. 1998: 64; Pecchioni and Halone 2000) (see Section 2.1). The dimensions come to play in all listening settings, including interpreting.

The effectiveness of the listening process can be compromised by listener-related, situation-related, or speaker-related factors that negatively affect the listener's ability to hear or process and understand the uttered information. These factors are part of what is called listening filters (see Section 2.1). Various kinds of external and internal listening filters can come to play in interpreting situations and interfere with the interpreter's listening process and affect it negatively. Interpreters address them in different ways.

Self-talk is similar to listening in that it is also a complex everyday phenomenon. It refers to verbalizations or statements people make to themselves, either internally (covert) or aloud (overt) (Theodorakis, Hatzigeorgiadis, and Chroni 2008: 11; Hardy 2006: 84). Talking to oneself is a "ubiquitous human phenomenon" (Kross et al. 2014: 321). However, there is a growing body of evidence that self-talk can be used deliberately to improve individual performance in highly demanding settings, such as in sports (e.g., Hardy 2006; Theodorakis, Hatzigeorgiadis, and Chroni 2008).

So far, there is only a very limited number of studies on the role of self-talk in interpreting (see Section 2.2). This study tries to contribute to this area by investigating the specific functions and linguistic forms of self-reported covert self-talk statements used by dialogue interpreters during interpreting. It revisits qualitative interview data from the author's PhD research that investigated the dialogue interpreter's professional listening competence at different stages of the listening process (Viljanmaa 2020: 481–8). In the research data that consisted of the in-depth interviews of twenty-two dialogue interpreters, interpreters reported two kinds of verbal metacognitive activities during the processing stage of their listening process. These activities were coded as examples of personal thoughts (*eigene Gedanken*) and inner voice (*innere Stimme*) (Viljanmaa 2020: 338–46). Personal thoughts referred to an interpreter's general thoughts in the situation when listening to a speaker. These thoughts were evoked by the interpreting context, the participants, or the content to be interpreted, and they contained the interpreter's personal experience or opinion, among other elements (Viljanmaa 2020: 338–43). Inner voice was defined as metacognitive talk used by the interpreter to talk to themselves, that is, interpreters' directing the words to themselves, which is covert self-talk. Instances of reported self-talk in interpreting situations included moments when the interpreter became aware of personal emotions, wandering thoughts, or other internal distracting factors and reacted to them internally in a verbal manner, that is, with covert self-talk (Viljanmaa 2020: 338–46).

One specific finding from the qualitative analysis in my PhD research was that interpreters used covert self-talk statements to address internal listening filters (Viljanmaa 2020: 477–9). However, due to the scope of the PhD project it was not possible to investigate the overall occurrence, the other functions, and the linguistic form of covert self-talk statements in the data. The aim of the current chapter is to gauge into the aforementioned. In other words, it will use theoretical concepts from self-talk research in other domains (see Section 2.3) to first investigate the functions and linguistic forms of all covert self-talk statements in the qualitative interview data and then follow up specifically on the function and linguistic form of those covert self-talk statements used by interpreters to address internal listening filters.

The article starts by presenting a theoretical framework, that is, the concept of listening filters and the listening-centered approach to dialogue interpreting, and then it looks at previous research on self-talk in interpreting and on self-talk in other domains. On the basis of these, more detailed research questions are formulated (see Section 2.4).

2 Theoretical Framework and Research Questions

2.1 Listening Filters and a Listening-Centered Approach to Dialogue Interpreting

From a listening-centered perspective, dialogue interpreting can be conceptualized as a listening process containing three main stages: perceiving (sensing), processing (constructing meaning), and responding (Viljanmaa 2020: 18; Comer and Drollinger 1999; Drollinger, Comer, and Warrington 2006; ILA 1996). In the sensing stage, the interpreter perceives various verbal and nonverbal information signals (Viljanmaa 2020: 303–6). In the processing stage, the interpreter constructs meaning from the perceived signals by employing various subprocesses. This stage also contains the processing of the interpreter's personal feelings and other reactions to the perceived information; it can also contain metacognitive elements, namely the interpreter's personal thoughts and self-directed covert talk (Viljanmaa 2020: 346–52). In the responding stage, the interpreter reacts to the perceived and processed signals. The interpreter's response stage can be further divided into two substages. These are the initial behavioral, cognitive, and/or affective reaction of the interpreter to the perceived and processed information and the production of the interpretation in the target language (Viljanmaa 2020: 406–14).

The different process stages overlap and are interrelated. The interpreter's listening process is thus an interplay of affect, cognition, and behavior. The affective dimension consists of the interpreter's affective and emotional reaction to the perceived signals. The cognitive dimension covers the processing of various information perceived from external sources, for example, from the participants in the interpreted communication, from the physical location, and from internal sources, that is, the interpreter's personal emotions and other personal reactions. Finally, the behavioral dimension consists of the interpreter's acting responses upon the basis of the perceived and processed external and internal information signals.

The concept of listening filters is an umbrella term that refers to factors and variables that affect the interpreter's listening process (Viljanmaa 2020: 481–8; Brownell 2010: 144). They can influence the aspects of the listening situation either negatively or positively (Thompson et al. 2010: 272). Listening filters can be further divided into internal and external listening filters. Internal listening filters are individual factors related to the listeners themselves that interfere with or complicate the listening process. These factors can be related to the listener's own background, his/her current physical or mental condition or state, or the listener's attitude toward the speaker or the topic, among others (Brownell 2010: 150–1). External listening filters are factors related to the speaker, the location, or the situation, which similarly influence the effectiveness of the listening outcome (Brownell 2010: 151). The speaker might mumble, speak quietly or very fast, the location can be noisy or have bad acoustics, and the situation can be a tense or a threatening one. An effective listener recognizes, analyzes, and addresses the influence of negative listening filters either in advance or as they occur during the listening event (Thompson et al. 2010: 273).

In dialogue interpreting, it is the speaker's poor articulation, overlapping speech, or disturbing background noises that can create an external listening filter in the interpreter's listening process (Viljanmaa 2020: 483). Internal listening filters in dialogue interpreting are, on the other hand, interpreters' physical exhaustion, their positive or negative emotions, their wandering thoughts or reawakening of personal experiences from the past, and so on (Viljanmaa 2020: 485). Personal emotions can form an internal listening filter for the interpreter if the interpreter pays too much attention to them. The same applies to wandering thoughts or the prolonged searching for a certain word in the target language. All these elements or factors negatively affect the interpreter's ability to listen comprehensively and attentively if they remain unaddressed. As such, they need to be managed effectively so that their negative effect on the listening and interpretation processes remains minimal. Interpreters address distracting external and internal listening filters in various ways, both during the interpreting and before and after (Viljanmaa 2020: 481–8).

2.2 Existing Studies on Self-Talk in Interpreting

As a phenomenon of intrapersonal communication, self-talk can be further defined as self-directed or self-referent overt or covert speech that serves a variety of self-regulatory and other functions (Brinthaupt 2019: 2). It is the syntactically recognizable articulation of an internal position where the sender of the message is also the intended receiver (Van Raalte, Vincent, and Brewer 2016: 141). The phenomenon of covert self-talk has been studied under different names such as *inner speech* (e.g., Morin, Duhnych, and Racy 2018; Alderson-Day and Fernyhough 2015; Lee, Wang, and Ren 2020), *private speech* (e.g., Deniz 2009; Winsler, Fernyhough, and Montero 2009), and *self-talk* (e.g., Hatzigeorgiadis, Theodorakis, and Zourbanos 2004; Kross et al. 2014). It has also been investigated by scholars in different fields, such as psychology (e.g., Furman, Kross, and Gearhardt 2020; Morin, Duhnych, and Racy 2018; Alderson-Day and Fernyhough 2015), sports psychology (e.g., Hardy 2006; Hardy, Oliver, and Tod 2009; Hatzigeorgiadis et al. 2011), and educational psychology (e.g., Deniz 2009; Lee, Wang, and Ren 2020), among others. However, to the best of my knowledge, there is only one existing study on self-talk in interpreting. This is a survey conducted by Maddux and Nicodemus (2016). Their study reported on the experiences of 445 American Sign Language (ASL)–English interpreters and their reports of self-talk in terms of its frequency, valence, overtness, self-determination, motivation, and function. The findings in Maddux and Nicodemus's study (2016: 186) verified that self-talk is a ubiquitous phenomenon among interpreters as 94 percent of ASL–English interpreters reported experiencing self-talk. Self-talk was also reported to occur frequently: 41 percent of the respondents who reported self-talk experienced self-talk at least six times or constantly in their work, and 54 percent of them experienced self-talk between one and five times during their assignment (2016: 186). As for valence (i.e., positive self-talk vs. negative self-talk), 62 percent of the respondents stated their self-talk was a mix of both positive and negative messages, 46 percent reported they felt their self-talk served to facilitate interpreting, and 43 percent respondents stated that their self-talk was a mix of facilitative and debilitative messages (2016: 189). As for the conscious or unconscious nature of self-talk, the survey asked the participants if they felt their self-talk was carried out consciously or whether it occurred unconsciously. Almost half of the respondents (48 percent) reported that self-talk was a mix of both conscious and unconscious thoughts, 29 percent stated that their self-talk was always unconscious, and 19 percent said that their self-talk was always conscious (2016: 191). As for self-talk functions, the most reported function in the survey was "improving interpreting," followed by "preparation," "awareness," and "mental focus" (Maddux and Nicodemus 2016: 192). Three of these functions, namely "improving interpreting," "awareness," and "mental focus," can be directly linked to the function of self-talk as a tool for interpreters to manage internal listening filters during interpreting, as they can all be linked to improving concentration levels and to refocusing the interpreter's attention on the speaker. However, the question is, do spoken-language interpreters also employ self-talk in a similar manner? The results from Maddux and Nicodemus (2016) cannot be generalized as such, because there are differences in the interpreting process between sign-language (SL) interpreters and spoken-language interpreters. This is because spoken-language dialogue interpreters interpret mostly consecutively, whereas SL interpreters interpret in the simultaneous mode. The listening processes also involve input channels (audio, visual) differently, which applies to the delivering of the interpretation.

In my PhD research, spoken-language dialogue interpreters did report examples of covert self-talk. Covert self-talk was found to happen prior, during, and after the actual interpreting assignment. It was linked to situations where an interpreter needed to calm down, was afraid of irritating a client, wanted to refocus on the actual task (interpreting), or needed to remind themselves to stay focused, among other instances (Viljanmaa 2020: 343–6). The results of the analysis in my PhD study showed that covert self-talk was also used as a tool for addressing internal listening filters both prior to interpreting and during the interpreting assignment (Viljanmaa 2020: 477–9). During the interpreting assignment self-talk was used to regain focus on the actual task of interpreting or to return to the "here and now" from personal memories evoked by the client's story. Interpreters also reported instances where self-talk was accompanied by a physical touch or where the interpreters talked to themselves using their first name or another reference (e.g., "honey") (Viljanmaa 2020: 477–9). The actual linguistic forms of the reported covert self-talk statements and their different functions were not studied in my PhD research and will form part of the focus of the present study.

2.3 Existing Studies on Self-Talk in Other Domains

The current study draws upon an abundance of previous research on self-talk in sports psychology. Just like sports, interpreting can be seen as a complex performative act that requires highly trained skills and an intense concentration so that maximal performance can be executed. In addition, both interpreters and athletes rely on extensive preparation in advance. As such, the assumption is that interpreters may exhibit certain similarities with athletes, particularly related to their self-talk and its related effects.

In sports psychology, self-talk is divided into motivational self-talk and instructional self-talk. The roles and functions of instructional and motivational self-talk differ (e.g., Hase, Hood, Moore, and Freeman 2019). Motivational self-talk refers to self-talk cues that encourage and motivate (e.g., "let's go," "I can do it"), maximize effort (e.g., "give it all"), or build confidence (e.g., "I can do it") (Hatzigeorgiadis et al. 2011: 349). Instructional self-talk includes self-talk cues that aim at focusing or directing attention and providing instruction regarding technique, strategy, or the kinesthetic attributes of a skill (Hatzigeorgiadis et al. 2011: 349).

Furthermore, self-talk can be categorized into proactive and reactive self-talk (Van Raalte, Vincent, and Brewer 2016: 141). Proactive self-talk is used with a specific intention or outcome in mind, and its use requires mental effort from the performer. In contrast to proactive self-talk, reactive self-talk occurs as a response to an emotionally charged and bias-driven situation (Van Raalte, Vincent, and Brewer 2016: 141). Finally, self-talk can be conceptualized as goal-directed and undirected self-talk (Latinjak et al. 2014).

Results from various sports psychology studies suggest that self-talk can improve athletes' performance. This improvement is linked to the various functions that self-talk seems to serve (Tod, Hardy, and Oliver 2011: 680; see also Hatzigeorgiadis et al. 2011: 348). For example, the results of two experiments conducted by Hatzigeorgiades, Theodorakis, and Zourbanos (2004) indicate that the use of self-talk has an important impact on the reduction of unwanted interfering thoughts irrespective of self-talk content. Later, Theodorakis, Hatzigeorgiadis, and Chroni (2008: 25–7) have identified five functions for self-talk in sports: attentional focus, regulating effort, increasing confidence, controlling cognitive and emotional reactions, and triggering automatic execution. The results of their study further indicated that athletes' self-talk mostly served to regulate effort, control attention, and build confidence (2008: 25–7). More recent research by Morin, Duhnych, and Racy (2018) on university students' self-talk indicated that the most frequently self-reported self-talk activities were self-regulation, self-reflection, and critical thinking (see also Lee, Wang, and Ren 2020: 545). From the listening perspective, many of the functions listed earlier would also appear to be relevant to measures or functions for addressing distracting internal listening filters (e.g., control effort and emotional reactions, control attention, reducing number of unwanted interfering thoughts) during interpreting.

One particularly interesting element is the linguistic manifestation of self-talk. Self-talk can occur as immersed first-person self-talk (e.g., "I have to go now," "I have to do this") or as a distanced, non-first-person self-talk using one's name and the second-person singular (e.g., "Emily, you have to speak up now") or the third-person singular including a name (e.g., "Emily needs to speak up"). Research has shown that using non-first-person self-talk can have many positive effects. These include promoting self-distancing (Kross et al. 2014), strengthening intentions and task performance (Dolcos and Albarracin 2014), reducing emotional reactivity (Moser et al. 2017; Nook, Schleider, and Somerville 2017; Orvell et al. 2021), and so on. Furthermore, Zell, Warriner, and Albarracin (2012: 553) found that the use of second-person self-talk and the use of the imperative co-occurred in situations where self-control was required. The use of these kinds of self-talk forms was more frequent during activity and action than during behavior planning and evaluation (2012: 553). Distancing self-talk (non-first-person ST) thus seems closely linked to self-talk during action.

Research on self-talk in sports psychology indicates that self-talk improves performance mostly by helping athletes to control attention, to regulate emotions, and to reduce the occurrence of interfering or distracting thoughts. Using distanced self-talk, that is, non-first-person self-talk, can further enhance the positive effects of self-talk on athletes' performance. It is thus interesting to find out whether non-first-person self-talk could also be an effective tool when addressing distracting internal listening filters in dialogue interpreting.

2.4 Research Questions

Based on existing studies on the functions and the use of self-talk, this study sets out to explore the overall functions and the linguistic forms of covert self-talk statements originally collected for my PhD research. Furthermore, the study also sets out to investigate potential relationships between the function and linguistic form of covert self-talk statements specifically used to address strong distracting emotions and other interfering internal listening filters during interpreting. Three research questions (RQs) are formulated below:

> RQ 1. In terms of the functions of covert self-talk: What are the main functions of covert self-talk? How much of covert self-talk is instruction related and how much is motivation related?
> RQ 2. In terms of the linguistic forms of self-talk: What are the main linguistic forms of covert self-talk? How much of the covert self-talk is first-person self-talk and how much is non-first-person self-talk?
> RQ 3. What are the potential relationships between the functions and the linguistic forms of covert self-talk and their implications?

3 Research Methods and Data Source

The data for this study was derived from a 233,600-word corpus containing the transcriptions of twenty-two individual in-depth interviews with practicing dialogue interpreters in Finland. I compiled the corpus originally for my PhD research (Viljanmaa 2020). The qualitative semi-structured interviews were conducted between May 2016 and May 2018. The interviews were conducted in Finnish, which was one of the working languages of all the interviewees. Their other languages included: Albanian, Arabic, Chinese, Dutch, English, French, German, Italian, Japanese, Kurdi, Persian, Portuguese, Russian, Somali, Spanish, Swahili, Thai, Turkmen, and Turkish. Some interpreters had more than two working languages. The interpreters ranged in age from twenty-nine to sixty-one years (mean age forty-five) and their educational backgrounds varied. All informants had several years of working experience as dialogue interpreters in various community and/or court interpreting settings. Some of them also had additional experience in conference interpreting. (For further granular demographic data, see Viljanmaa 2020: 250–4.)

The interview corpus contains a large number of narratives and anecdotes about the dialogue interpreters' work as perceived and recounted by the interpreters themselves. The semi-structured interviews focused on the interviewees' personal experience of carrying out their work in different communicative settings. There were four main themes in the interviews: manifestation and goals of the interpreter's professional listening behavior throughout the interpreting process (pre-process, in-process, post-process), listening filters, interpersonal relationships and interaction management in interpreting, and listening competence in relation to professional identity and self-efficacy. For all four main themes there were several questions. The interpreters were invited to express themselves freely but to maintain professional secrecy. They were instructed to describe how they usually work and what they do and also to elaborate on individual assignments of their choice, that is, recount in their own words particular cases they remembered well. These could be cases from the day of the interview or the day before or cases dating several years back. (For further data on the interviews, see Viljanmaa 2020: 237–50.)

It must be noted that neither metacognitive talk, inner voice nor covert self-talk was specifically asked about in the interviews, and yet the category "Metacognition—inner voice" emerged from the content-based analysis of the data in Viljanmaa (2020). The current study focuses on this particular category.

To be more precise, it contains interview excerpts referring to one or more of the following elements: interpreters' inner voice, interpreters reminding themselves of something that needs to be done, interpreters' talking to themselves using their inner voice either before, during, or after the interpreting assignment. The category consists of a total of 114 direct quotations from the interview data. For the current study, I revisited these 114 quotations. As the first step, I selected all quotations directly referring to situations during interpreting for further analysis. Those quotations containing only implicit references to the interpreter's personal thoughts without an explicit self-talk statement were deselected. Only those quotations that contained at least one explicit verbal self-talk statement (e.g., "keskity nyt mitä sanot," "now focus on what you say") were kept. These self-talk statements were explicit statements that were immediately preceded or followed by a reference about oneself or commanding oneself to do something (e.g., "mä koko ajan *mietin* että älä ärsytä tota," "I kept *thinking* all the time that don't irritate that guy") or explicit statements that clearly indicated that the interpreter reported to a self-talk statement that had occurred in the situation (e.g., "*hei*. mä oon tulkki. mä oon täällä," "*hello*. I'm the interpreter. I'm here"). This resulted in seventy-eight quotations stemming from twenty individual interviews. The quotations contained the interpreter's description of a specific moment during interpreting. The quotations were of different length. Some of the quotations contained several self-talk statements related to the situation and others contained only one self-talk statement. These seventy-eight quotations constitute the research data source for the current study.

In the first round of analysis, the seventy-eight quotations were categorized as either immersed "first-person self-talk" or distanced "non-first-person self-talk" according to the linguistic form of the self-talk statements reported in them. The quotations in the category "non-first-person self-talk" were then further divided into the subcategories "second-person self-talk" and "third-person self-talk" according to their actual linguistic forms. Most quotations contained only one kind of self-talk statements, but in some quotations interpreters reported two different kinds of self-talk statements (e.g., first-person self-talk statements and second-person self-talk statements, first-person self-talk statements and third-person self-talk statements, or second-person self-talk statements and third-person self-talk statements). In these cases, the quotations were thus coded into both categories, respectively. The result is eighty-two cases of reported self-talk statements for the current study stemming from seventy-eight interpreting situations.

These cases were then further categorized into situations where covert *instructional* self-talk statements were reported and those where covert *motivational* self-talk statements were reported. The categories were named "instructional self-talk" and "motivational self-talk," respectively. During this analysis round a third category emerged. This category includes instances of self-talk where an interpreter was talking to themselves without a clear instructional or motivational focus. For example: "What should I do?" These self-talk statements were all reflective in nature, and the category was thus named "reflective self-talk." In all stages specific attention was paid to covert self-talk statements that were used to address internal listening filters.

4 Data Analysis and Results

The results of the data analysis are presented in Table 3.1. It shows the number of cases for each type and subtype of self-talk statements under investigation as well as their functions.

There was more first-person self-talk in the data (forty-six cases) than non-first-person self-talk (thirty-six cases), but both categories are well represented. As for the function of self-talk in the data, the category reflective self-talk was the biggest category (fifty-one cases), followed by instructional self-talk (thirty cases). Detailed analysis can be found in Section 4.1.

4.1 Functions of Covert Self-Talk

RQ 1 addressed the function of reported covert self-talk. It is found that there are three main categories: instructional self-talk, motivational self-talk, and reflective self-talk. The third category, reflective self-talk, referred to covert self-talk statements where the interpreter pondered and/or wondered about situational or setting-specific elements. This category turned out to be the biggest category among the three (see Table 3.1). In fact, more than half of the quotations contained reflective self-talk statements. The reflective self-talk statements were often reactive as a response from the interpreter to the situation. However, the situation did not need to be emotionally charged and bias-driven in order for the reflective self-talk of the interpreter to occur (cf. Van Raalte, Vincent, and Brewer 2016: 141; see also Section 2.3). Out of the fifty-one reflective self-talk statements, twenty-six are found to be related to clients' behavior or reactions,

Table 3.1 Occurrence of linguistic and functional self-talk statements

	Occurrence of Linguistic and Functional Self-Talk Statements			
	First-Person Self-Talk	Non-First-Person Self-Talk	Subcategory: Second-Person Self-Talk	Subcategory: Third-Person Self-Talk
Instructional Self-Talk	8	22	14	8
Motivational Self-Talk	1	0	0	0
Reflective Self-Talk	37	14	1	13
Total	**46**	**36**	**15**	**21**

whereas twenty-five are related to the interpreters' personal performance or other personal thoughts.

Instructional self-talk was found in twenty-eight out of the seventy-eight quotations (two quotations contained two linguistic types of instructional self-talk, so there is a total number of thirty cases of instructional self-talk). This instructional self-talk was mostly reactive in nature. The majority of instructional covert self-talk found in the data was self-talk that served to address internal listening filters (see Section 4.3). However, there were also two occasions where the interpreter used instructional self-talk to instruct herself to behave or act in a certain way, that is, not to irritate the client and to take shorter and more logical notes, respectively.

Surprisingly, there was only one quotation portraying motivational self-talk. The interesting feature of motivational self-talk was that it did not appear during the interpreting assignment but it did appear before and after the assignment.

4.2 Linguistic Forms of Covert Self-Talk

RQ 2 addressed the linguistic forms of covert self-talk in dialogue interpreting. It asked what the main linguistic forms were and how much were first-person self-talk and how many were non-first-person self-talk. First-person self-talk has been described as immersive self-talk, whereas non-first-person self-talk is distanced. The results of the analysis showed that first-person self-talk statements were found in forty-six out of the seventy-eight quotations and non-first-person self-talk statements in thirty-six out of the seventy-eight quotations. It is worth mentioning here that the total number of reported self-talk statement cases (i.e., 46 + 36= 82) is bigger than the total number of quotations analyzed (78), because some of the quotations contained two different kinds of self-talk statements and they were coded into both categories, respectively. Interestingly, the result also reveals that the use of the linguistic forms might be linked to the function of self-talk, as first-person self-talk statements are mostly reflective, whereas non-first-person self-talk statements are often instructional.

Of the forty-six immersed first-person self-talk statements, the majority (thirty-seven quotations) is reflective self-talk. This self-talk was all reactive self-talk, that is, self-talk that resulted as a response to the situations from the interpreter. It was either related to specific factors in the situation (see Examples 1 and 2 in Table 3.2) or related to the interpreters' meta-observations or reflections on their personal reactions and performance (see Examples 3 and 4) or even extending to what they should do next as a result of such reflections (see Examples 5–7).

The non-first-person self-talk category, on the other hand, contained more instructional rather than reflective or motivational self-talk. The analysis showed that twenty-two out of the thirty-six non-first-person self-talk quotations were instructional self-talk. When non-first-person self-talk is further divided into the subcategories of second-person self-talk and third-person self-talk, the results became even clearer: fourteen out of a total of fifteen second-person self-talk quotations are instructional in nature, whereas in the third-person self-talk subcategory, only eight out of twenty-one, for example, approximately one-third, are instructional. These results indicate that there may be a link between instructional self-talk and distanced, for example, non-first-person self-talk in general, but especially between instructional self-talk and second-person self-talk.

Table 3.3 illustrates some examples of second-person instructional self-talk statements made by interpreters. Most of the instructional second-

Table 3.2 Examples of reflective first-person self-talk statements

Example No.	Original Finnish Self-Talk Statements	English Translation
Example 1	ei helkkari mihin mä olen päätynyt	damn what have I got myself into
Example 2	mitä tuokin tuossa häiritsee tätä mun työtä	why does that person there disturb me when I'm doing my work
Example 3	aha. nyt mulla jäi toi sana.	a-ha. now I missed that word
Example 4	ei hitto, mä en tiedä, että osaanko mä enää tätä	oh man, I don't know if I'll manage this any longer
Example 5	mä en halua sanoa	I don't want to say it
Example 6	uskallanko mä kysyä että suuttuuko se nyt mulle	do I dare to ask or will he be angry with me
Example 7	mitä mä teen että olenko vaan hiljaa annanko mennä vaan	what should I do or should I just remain silent should I simply let go

Table 3.3 Examples of instructional second-person self-talk statements

Example No.	Original Finnish Self-Talk Statements	English Translation
Example 8	muista roolisi hoida työsi, tulkkaa asiallisesti älä anna tämän vaikuttaa	remember your role, do your job, interpret appropriately, do not let this have an effect
Example 9	suppress, paina se heti pois	suppress, put it away immediately
Example 10	fokusoi fokusoi fokusoi	focus focus focus
Example 11	sulle ei makseta siitä mitä sä tunnet. vaan sulle maksetaan siitä että sä autat näitten kommunikointia. sano nyt mitä hän sanoi.	you're not paid for what you feel. you're paid for helping them communicate. now say what he said
Example 12	älä ärsytä tota	don't annoy that guy

person self-talk statements were used to address internal listening filters (see Section 4.3), but in the data there were also two instances where instructional second-person self-talk is used for other purposes. They were linked to the interpreter's instruction of oneself in how (not) to behave or (not) to act (see Example 12).

4.3 The Relationships between the Functions and Linguistic Forms of Self-Talk and Their Implications

RQ 3 focused on the potential relationship between the functions and linguistic forms of the reported covert ST statements. The results show that a total of twenty-eight out of the thirty instructional covert self-talk instances are actually self-talk that served to address internal listening filters. Based on these empirical data, one could argue that addressing internal listening filters is a core function of instructional self-talk in dialogue interpreting.

The interpreters' instructional self-talk statements used to address internal listening filters referred to various situations in which the interpreter's attention was drawn to phenomena other than listening to the current speaker. These included, for example, a situation where a participant or specific content made the interpreter feel uneasy (see Examples 13 and 14 in Table 3.4). Another example was that the interpreter failed to recall a specific word in the target language (Example 15). A further example was that the interpreter needed to refocus his/her attention on the task at hand after being distracted by personal memories that were acute and emotional (Examples 16–19). A further reason for the interpreter to engage in instructional self-talk was fatigue (Examples 20 and 21).

Table 3.4 Examples of instructional self-talk statements addressing internal listening filters

Example No.	Finnish Original Self-Talk Statement	English Translation
Example 13	keskity nyt ja tulkkaa mitä se sanoo	concentrate now and interpret what he says
Example 14	mun tehtävä on tulkata	my task is to interpret
Example 15	hani jo unohda se	honey, forget it already
Example 16	hei. mä oon tulkki. mä oon täällä.	hello. I'm the interpreter. I'm here.
Example 17	ei, kun nyt tulkataan.	no, now we interpret.
Example 18	ei nyt. ei nyt itke.	not now. no crying now.
Example 19	ole läsnä. ole läsnä. it's not about me.	be present. be present, it's not about me.
Example 20	nyt täysin mukana. kuuntele.	now fully attentive. listen.
Example 21	tässä on käänne. tarkkana.	that's a turning point. pay attention.

Examples for the self-talk statements as mentioned earlier can be found in Table 3.4.

As for the linguistic form of covert self-talk statements used to address internal listening filters, the question was whether self-talk statements were expressed in first-person or in non-first-person form. The results show that the instructional self-talk statements used to address internal listening filters were most often in the linguistic form of non-first-person self-talk, more specifically in second-person self-talk. There was, however, also evidence that this kind of instructional self-talk could occur as first-person self-talk (e.g., Example 16 in Table 3.4). In the data, the most frequent function of instructional self-talk was to manage internal listening filters by refocusing the interpreter's attention on their task at hand and/or controlling and addressing distracting thoughts and other distracting elements, such as the interpreter's personal emotions (see examples in Table 3.4). This finding largely tallies with those from previous studies in psychology (e.g., Kross et al. 2014; Hatzigeorgiadis and Galanis 2017).

5 Conclusion

This study set out to investigate the use of covert self-talk during dialogue interpreting in general as well as to study specifically the linguistic forms and functions of covert self-talk. The analysis showed that twenty-eight of all eighty-two self-talk occurrences, for example, approximately a third, are concerned with instructional self-talk used for addressing internal listening filters. Although instructional self-talk does not appear to be the most used type of covert self-talk during interpreting, it is found to play a crucial role for the quality of the interpreter's listening process due to its function and mitigating effect on internal listening filters.

As for the actual linguistic manifestation of covert self-talk in interpreting, the results show that although some instructional self-talk statements took the form of immersed first-person self-talk, most instructional self-talk occurs as distanced non-first-person self-talk and more specifically as second-person self-talk. The types of self-talk statements reported in the data of this study are very much in line with the samples of self-talk reported by ASL–English interpreters in Maddux and Nicodemus (2016: 187), where covert self-talk during assignments concerned both non-first person instructional self-talk ("Stay calm. Focus. Breathe, breathe") and more reflective or reactive first-person self-talk ("I am really bored with this discussion," "I can see this person is getting upset. Get ready") (2016: 187). One could argue that from the two self-talk types, non-first-person instructional self-talk is likely to be an effective way to address listening filters as it creates self-distancing that benefits emotion regulation and attention and helps reduce the occurrence of interfering thoughts.

In addition, the results of this study showed that a large part of the reported covert self-talk during interpreting is concerned with reflective self-talk. Reflective self-talk points to instances where dialogue interpreters engaged in reactive self-talk with themselves by reflecting on and thinking about various topics related to the situation or the speaker. The large amount of reflective self-talk in the data would point to the experienced interpreters' ability to perceive and process various other details of the communicative situation in addition to the actual verbal and nonverbal content of the speaker. These include the reactions and behavior of the other clients as well as the interpreters' personal reactions, among many other factors.

While successfully demonstrating the importance of self-talk in dialogue interpreting, the present study also has its limitations. First, the data is derived from a small sample, with seventy-eight self-talk quotations stemming from twenty individual interviews with dialogue interpreters. In addition, the data was collected with a specific focus on elements of the dialogue interpreters' professional listening competence, which undoubtedly has influenced the topics that interpreters report on. Furthermore, for the validity of the reported self-talk statements, it must also be noted that research on self-talk always carries an amount of vagueness. As Oleś et al. (2020: 8) stated, not all intrapersonal communication is conscious, and self-talk statements are also highly context-dependent. Therefore, self-talk data is often limited to situations and experiences that respondents are able to recall or infer based on their consciousness and awareness. Despite this, we can learn from the covert self-talk reports and experiences that interpreters do recall and remember.

The role of covert self-talk in interpreting deserves more attention from interpreting researchers. After all, self-talk can serve a variety of functions in interpreting as indicated by Maddox and Nicodemus (2016). Also, the role of covert instructional self-talk in the management of internal listening filters (Viljanmaa 2020) points to the direction of pedagogical implications. In other words, future interpreting students may benefit from learning more about different self-talk functions and their benefits and possible effects on interpreting performance. Equally, interpreting practitioners could also benefit from more information on the role of instructional self-talk and its effect on their performance.

Meanwhile, a question arises as to whether the use of covert instructional or motivational self-talk is something that needs to be learned deliberately or it is a natural human phenomenon that will occur anyway (cf. Orvell et al. 2019: 570). The interpreters interviewed for this study clearly already used instructional self-talk frequently in their practice. At the same time, evidence from self-talk research in the field of sports psychology would suggest that focusing on specific self-talk cues and paying attention to the linguistic forms of self-talk can actually improve performance. It would be interesting to find out whether or to what extent this also applies to interpreting. More research is needed to determine and confirm the various functions of instructional and motivational self-talk in interpreting as well as its effects. In addition, self-talk that occurs before and after an interpreting assignment would need to be investigated. A more holistic picture of spoken-language interpreters' self-talk uses is also needed. Future research could address this with the help of self-reports elicited through a questionnaire with prompts that have been successfully used in previous self-talk research in other domains (e.g., Morin, Duhnych, and Racy 2018: 379).

References

Alderson-Day, B. and C. Fernyhough (2015), "Inner Speech: Development, Cognitive Functions, Phenomenology, and Neurobiology," *Psychological Bulletin*, 141(5): 931–65.

Brinthaupt, T. M. (2019), "Individual Differences in Self-talk Frequency: Social Isolation and Cognitive Disruption," *Frontiers in Psychology*, 10. https://doi.org/10.3389/fpsyg.2019.01088

Brownell, J. (2010), "The Skills of Listening-Centered Communication," in A. D. Wolvin (ed.), *Listening and Human Communication in the 21st Century*, 141–57, Chichester: Wiley-Blackwell.

Comer, L. B. and T. Drollinger (1999), "Active Empathetic Listening and Selling Success: A Conceptual Framework," *The Journal of Personal Selling and Sales Management*, 19(1): 15–29.

Deniz, C. B. (2009), "Early Childhood Teacher's Awareness, Beliefs, and Practices toward Children's Private Speech," in A. Winsler, C. Fernyhough, and I. Montero (eds.), *Private Speech, Executive Functioning, and the Development of Verbal Self-Regulation*, 236–46, Cambridge: Cambridge University Press.

Dolcos, S. and D. Albarracin (2014), "The Inner Speech of Behavioral Regulation: Intentions and Task Performance Strengthen When You Talk to Yourself as a You," *European Journal of Social Psychology*, 44: 636–42.

Drollinger, T., L. B. Comer, and P. T. Warrington (2006), "Development and Validation of the Active Empathetic Listening Scale," *Psychology and Marketing*, 23(2): 161–80.

Furman, C. R., E. Kross, and A. N. Gearhardt (2020), "Distanced Self-talk Enhances Goal Pursuit to Eat Healthier," *Clinical Psychological Science*, 8(2): 366–73.

Halone, K. K., T. M. Cunconan, C. G. Coakley, and A. D. Wolvin (1998), "Toward the Establishment of General Dimensions Underlying the Listening Process," *International Journal of Listening*, 12(1): 12–28.

Hardy, J. (2006), "Speaking Clearly: A Critical Review of the Self-talk Literature," *Psychology of Sport and Exercise*, 7: 81–97.

Hardy, J., E. Oliver, and D. Tod (2009), "A Framework for the Study and Application of Self-talk within Sport," in S. D. Mellalieu and S. Hanton (eds.), *Advances in Applied Sport Psychology: A Review*, 37–74, London: Routledge.

Hase, A., J. Hood, L. J. Moore, and P. Freeman (2019), "The Influence of Self-talk on Challenge and Threat States and Performance," *Psychology of Sport & Exercise*, 45: 101550.

Hatzigeorgiadis, A. and E. Galanis (2017), "Self-talk Effectiveness and Attention," *Current Opinion in Psychology*, 16: 138–42.

Hatzigeorgiadis, A., Y. Theodorakis, and N. Zourbanos (2004), "Self-talk in the Swimming Pool: The Effects of Self-talk on Thought Content and Performance on Water-Polo Tasks," *Journal of Applied Sport Psychology*, 16: 138–50.

Hatzigeorgiadis, A., N. Zourbanos, E. Galanis, and Y. Theodorakis (2011), "Self-talk and Sports Performance: A Meta-Analysis," *Perspectives on Psychological Science*, 6(4): 348–56.

ILA (1996), "The All New, State-of-the-Art ILA Definition of Listening: Now that We Have It, What Do We Do With It?," *The Listening Post*, 53: 1–5.

Kross, E., E. Bruehlman-Senecal, J. Park, A. Burson, A. Dougherty, H. Shablack, R. Bremner, J. Moser, and O. Ayduk (2014), "Self-Talk as a Regulatory Mechanism: How You Do It Matters," *Journal of Personality and Social Psychology*, 106(2): 304–24.

Latinjak, A. T., N. Zourbanos, V. Lopez-Ros, and A. Hatzigeorgiadis (2014), "Goal-Directed and Undirected Self-talk: Exploring a New Perspective for the Study of Athletes' Self-talk," *Psychology of Sport and Exercise*, 15: 548–58.

Lee, S., T. Wang, and X. Ren (2020), "Inner Speech in the Learning Context and the Prediction of Students' Learning Strategy and Academic Performance," *Educational Psychology*, 40(5): 535–49.

Maddux, L. and B. Nicodemus (2016), "'The Committee in My Head.' Examining Self-talk of American Sign Language – English Interpreters," *Translation and Interpreting Studies*, 11(2): 177–201.

Morin, A., C. Duhnych, and F. Racy (2018), "Self-reported Inner Speech Use in University Students," *Applied Cognitive Psychology*, 32(3): 376–82.

Moser, J. S., A. Dougherty, W. I. Mattson, B. Katz, T. P. Moran, D. Guevarra, H. Shablack, O. Ayduk, J. Jonides, M. G. Berman, and E. Kross (2017), "Third-Person Self-talk Facilitates Emotion Regulation without Engaging Cognitive Control: Converging Evidence from ERP and fMRI," *Scientific Reports*, 7(4519). www.nature.com/scientificreports/, https://doi.org/10.1038/s41598-017-04047-3

Nook, E. C., J. L. Schleicher, and L. H. Somerville (2017), "A Linguistic Signature of Psychological Distancing in Emotion Regulation," *Journal of Experimental Psychology*, 146(3): 337–46.

Oleś, P. K., T. M. Brinthaupt, R. Dier, and D. Polak (2020), "Types of Inner Dialogues and Functions of Self-talk: Comparisons and Implications," *Frontiers in Psychology*, 11. https://doi.org/10.3389/fpsyg.2020.00227

Orvell, A., Ö. Ayduk, J. S. Moser, S. A. Gelman, and Ethan Kross (2019), "Linguistic Shifts: A Relatively Effortless Route to Emotion Regulation?," *Current Directions in Psychological Science*, 28(6): 567–73.

Orvell, A., B. D. Vickers, B. Drake, P. Verduyn, O. Ayduk, J. Moser, J. Jonides, and E. Kross (2021), "Does Distanced Self-talk Facilitate Emotion Regulation Across a Range of Emotionally Intense Experiences?," *Clinical Psychological Science*, 9(1): 68–78.

Pecchioni, L. L. and K. K. Halone (2000), "Relational Listening II: Form & Variation across Social and Personal Relationships," *International Journal of Listening*, 14(1): 69–93.

Theodorakis, Y., A. Hatzigeorgiadis, and S. Chroni (2008), "Self-talk: It Works, but How? Development and Preliminary Validation of the Functions of the Self-talk Questionnaire," *Measurement in Physical Education and Exercise Science*, 12(1): 10–30.

Thompson, K., P. Leintz, B. Nevers, and S. Witkowski (2010), "The Integrative Listening Model: An Approach to Teaching and Learning Listening," in A. D. Wolvin (ed.), *Listening and Human Communication in the 21st Century*, 266–86, Chichester: Wiley-Blackwell.

Tod, D., J. Hardy, and E. Oliver (2011), "Effects of Self-talk: A Systematic Review," *Journal of Sport and Exercise Psychology*, 33(5): 666–87.

Van Raalte, J. L., A. Vincent, and B. W. Brewer (2016), "Self-talk: Review and Sport-specific Model," *Psychology of Sport and Exercise*, 22: 139–48.

Viljanmaa, A. (2020), *Professionelle Zuhörkompetenz und Zuhörfilter beim Dialogdolmetschen*, Berlin: Frank & Timme.

Winsler, A., C. Fernyhough, and I. Montero (2009), *Private Speech, Executive Functioning, and the Development of Verbal Self-regulation*, Cambridge: Cambridge University Press.

Zell, E., A. B. Warriner, and D. Albarracin (2012), "Splitting of the Mind: When the *You* I Talk to is Me and Needs Commands," *Social Psychological and Personality Science*, 3(5): 549–55.

4

The Self-Reported Emotional Struggles by Interpreters in the British Judicial System

Zhiai Liu

1 Introduction

A lot has been made of the roles of legal interpreters, for example, impartiality, confidentiality, and faithfulness. However, legal interpreters' emotional issues have seldom been explored, particularly from the practitioners' perspective, though scholarly work (Schweda-Nicholson 1989; Mikkelson 1998; Berk-Seligson 2002; Valero-Garcés 2003; Hale 2004; Napier and Spencer 2008; Russell, Hale, and Morris 2008; Lee 2009) has extensively addressed the stressful nature of legal interpreting and the complexity of interpreter-mediated legal proceedings. The challenges legal interpreters face are often far beyond understanding, and interpreting seems to have complicated legal glossaries or legal discourse. Interpreters are expected to adopt multiple roles (e.g., to interpret, to deal with cultural discrepancies, and to facilitate communication), to command different abilities (e.g., cognitive, linguistic, and ethical) and to integrate these abilities into the special features of particular settings (e.g., social, cultural, gender, and asymmetrical knowledge or power) (Valero-Garcés 2003). Such complex and onerous expectations are highly likely to create multitudinous ethical dilemmas for interpreters and consequently challenge the interpreters' emotional stability.

The cognitive and emotional demands of interpreters' work may overburden their mental and psychological capacities and thus lead to work-based fatigue and distress (Hubscher-Davidson 2020). However, in legal proceedings, all parties expect a calm and impartial interpreter. A dearth of research has provided evidence that expecting interpreters to be completely invisible or to perform a machine-like role is a false notion (Berk-Seligson 2002; Nakane 2009; Kaczmarek 2012; Inghilleri 2013), and it is impractical to believe that the presence of an interpreter does not bring any changes to the courtroom (Eades 2010). Moreover, interpreters are positioned between service providers and service users, so they could be emotionally influenced by other parties' emotions or by the content of a case. Consequently, an ethical dilemma emerges when interpreters desire, and are expected to abide by, the professional principle of being impartial while they also need to manage their own emotional struggles.

Hence, exploring legal interpreters' emotional struggles for interpreter-mediated interactions is a vital aspect of research into legal interpreters' roles.

Public service interpreting (PSI) and community interpreting are the terms used synonymously in the UK to refer to interpreting activities within a range of public services, including "legal, health, education, employment, housing and other social services" (Rabadán-Gómez 2016: 2).

Legal interpreting, the focus of the current study, is a specialized branch of PSI. It is a broad field that encompasses interpreting in criminal, civil proceedings, or administrative proceedings (Kadrić 2021, "such as lawyer-client interviews, immigration-related interviews, police-related matters, tribunal hearings and court hearings and trials" (Hale and Gonzalez 2017: 200).

2 Sources of Negative Emotional Impact

Since the 1990s, scholars have recognized the influential role emotions play in the process of translation and interpreting. Evidence from psychological studies has proved that emotions and the cognitive system work in a complementary manner (Rojo 2017). Emotion is the product of a person's interpretation of objects, events, or circumstances (Jiménez and Voss 2014). The action components of emotions direct people's reactions to emotional situations (Rojo 2017) and thus play a key role in directing people's decision-making and behaviors (Damasio 1994). From this perspective, emotions can be considered to have a crucial impact on the work of translation and interpreting.

2.1 Ethical Stress

Ethical stress, also known as occupational stress, is defined by Hubscher-Davidson (2020: 415) as the stress that "results from disparities between one's ethical values and expected behaviours." Making ethical decisions can be particularly challenging for legal interpreters, especially as they may find themselves constantly entangled in ethical dilemmas and pushing professional boundaries. Long-term exposure to ethical stress may cause a series of psychological symptoms, such as anxiety, depression, secondary traumatic stress, and burnout (Christodoulou-Fella et al. 2017).

Scholars (González, Vásquez, and Mikkelson 1991; Morris 1995; Barsky 1996; Fenton 1997; Fowler 1997; Corsellis 2002; Angelelli 2004; Cambridge 2005; Kaczmarek 2012; Munyangeyo 2016) have found that one of the main sources of ethical dilemmas in legal interpreting is the conflict of expectation, which is the result of a general lack of understanding of the profession from service providers and service users and the unpredictability of situations in which interpreter-mediated triadic exchanges occur.

Interpreters, service providers, and service users seldom share the same ideologies, aims, and emotions (Hubscher-Davidson 2020), but interpreters are required to render these differentiated ideologies, aims, and emotions in the target language and culture. The situation may become more complex when the interests of different parties in the adversarial legal system are in conflict. These additional difficulties can be attributed to service providers' demands beyond interpreters' professional boundaries. Law enforcement officers may, for instance, expect interpreters to take a more active role in criminal investigations. Service users may seek to establish a stronger emotional bond with the interpreter due to a shared cultural and ethnic group status. This emotional demand may conflict with interpreters' professional requirement to remain neutral (Cambridge 2005). Additional conflicting factors also include: interpreters' sharing biographical details or previous experiences with the service user; the service user's psychological and emotional instability; unpleasant content of conversations; and interpreters' failure to help service users. This inherent misalignment requires constant effort from interpreters to suppress any negative emotional reactions while striving to maintain professionalism (Hubscher-Davidson 2020).

A lack of trust has also been recognized as a situation that may lead to interpreters' ethical stress and certain unethical behaviors (Samad et al. 2010). Moreover, legal settings are notoriously rigid, hierarchical systems with strict and formulaic procedures, which may force interpreters to act in a self-protecting manner and choose not to raise ethical concerns. This daunting environment may, therefore, increase interpreters' ethical stress and can profoundly impact their interpreting performance. Interpreters may, for example, compromise their professional role by reducing the complexity of the original utterances, which is done to avoid being blamed for any misunderstandings (Hubscher-Davidson 2020).

There is evidence that contending with moral dilemmas makes the UK interpreters who are engaged in PSI distressed (Munyangeyo 2016). The most prominent difficulties reported by interpreters include fighting to avoid becoming emotionally involved in sensitive issues against their personal principles or values and balancing between the inherent desires to help people and worrying about being viewed as unprofessional, which might cause distrust and anger from the non-native English speaker side (Valero-Garcés 2015; Munyangeyo 2016).

2.2 Vicarious Trauma

In addition to ethical stress, legal interpreters' work involves interpreting for violent or vicious traumatic cases. These cases can be another main source of emotional challenges because of the traumatic nature of the interpreting task, such as "disputes, client anxiety, negotiations, social vulnerability, child abuse, domestic abuse, the presence of corpses and discrimination" (Valero-Garcés 2015: 94).

The content of traumatic narratives can bring back painful memories of service users, which can indirectly result in interpreters becoming engaged in these experiences due to the need to interpret disturbing imagery and descriptive feelings of the speakers' memories. McCann and Pearlman (1990), discussing trauma therapists, point out that therapists' cognitive schemas and imagery systems may be negatively affected if they work with victims' traumatic experiences, with the term "vicarious traumatization" being used to define this type of transformation. "The inability to process the traumatic material is reflected as 'burnout'" (McCann and Pearlman 1990: 134). Moreover, according to McCann and Pearlman (1990: 133), "burnout" can be the "psychological strain of working with difficult populations." Thus, it is fair to say that when interpreting for people who have directly experienced traumatic events and violence, and who retell or relive these experiences, interpreters are prone to secondary traumatization in much the same manner as therapists. Vicarious trauma can be reflected in symptoms of "stress, frustration, grief, anxiety, irritability, fear, mood swings, confusion, feeling disturbed" (Valero-Garcés 2015: 89), "feeling pressure, anguish, difficulty in remaining impartial and increased heart rate" (Valero-Garcés 2015: 92).

The situation may also be aggravated when interpreters strive to conceal their emotions on account of their professional code of conduct, which requires them to remain emotionless and neutral at all times (Hubscher-Davidson 2020).

The incongruence between a person's displayed emotions and his or her true feelings can lead to emotional dissonance, which may lead to problematic ethical behaviors (Grootegoed and Smith 2018). Bakker and Heuven (2006: 426) pointed out that police officers' management of emotions has a conflicting nature, as they need to switch between being "neutral, solid, and controlled" and "compassionate and understanding" when dealing with aggressive criminals or with victims of crime, respectively. Legal interpreters' work also contains this challenge. The professional codes for interpreting require the effective restraint of personal emotions so that the requirements of neutrality and impartiality are fulfilled. It is widely accepted that the accuracy and faithfulness of interpreting in the legal setting should include both linguistic and paralinguistic contents (Berk-Seligson 1987; De Jongh 1991; González, Vásquez, and Mikkelson 1991; Mason 2009; Inghilleri 2013). Moreover, "police officers need to master the art of constantly switching between this human and disciplinary emotional expression" (Bakker and Heuven 2006: 426), which can again apply to legal interpreters' work. Interpreters need to absorb the speakers' feelings and emotions when seeking to achieve accuracy and faithfulness in their interpretation while also displaying an emotionally detached professional attitude. This challenging task may produce distorted emotional reactions.

Studies have established that interpreters working in the public service context may be continually exposed to substantial psychological and emotional stress while performing a highly demanding job (Roberts 2015; Schwenke 2015; Korpal and Jasielska 2019; Hubscher-Davidson 2020). Evidence has shown that it is challenging for interpreters to maintain their professional role when contending with emotional influences (e.g., Bancroft 2017). According to Valero-Garcés (2015: 91), the most prominent emotional challenges faced by interpreters are "maintaining neutrality, discomfort with the topic at hand, being affected by the distress and anxiety of the service users and feeling powerless to be able to help clients directly."

2.3 Lack of Training or Professional Support

The issue of a lack of training or professional support in dealing with emotional management has gained scholars' attention (Knodel 2018; Gutiérrez and Rausch 2020). Gutiérrez and Rausch (2020) point out that few interpreting courses prepare interpreters with the knowledge of the emotional difficulties they may encounter, the potential impacts caused by experiencing negative emotions, and any strategies to avoid or reduce these impacts.

In addition to training, providing professional support to ensure effectiveness for practitioners is recognized by many organizations as an ethical responsibility to ensure practitioners' effectiveness, for example, the International Committee of the Red Cross (ICRC), the Australian Sign Language Interpreters Association (ASLIA), the American Psychological Association (APA) Practice Organisation, and the British Association for Counselling and Psychotherapy (BACP). Catherall (1995) highlights the importance of organizational support and official support in frontline practitioners' education to protect them from the negative impacts of occupational stress. Strategies to cope with traumatic and stressful environments rely on personal resilience, which helps a person to find available support and utilize the support to recover from stressful experiences (Hobfoll et al. 2007). Support for interpreters, as recommended by Hetherington (2012), should be organized to involve psychological consultations and peer discussions. This support, which could enable interpreters to offload difficult emotional experiences, has proven to be effective in a pilot project carried out by Medical Justice (MJ). MJ is a UK NGO that works with immigration centers in the UK. Interpreters who attended the workshops with professional psychologists and more experienced interpreters reported that they gained a better understanding of their ethical dilemmas, a stronger ability to offload themselves from the emotional burden, and the know-how for better performance in the future (Gutiérrez and Rausch 2020).

3 Research Questions

There has been awareness of emotional factors and their potential negative impacts on interpreters' effectiveness (Roberts 2015; Schwenke 2015; Valero-Garcés 2015; Bancroft 2017; Korpal and Jasielska 2019; Hubscher-Davidson 2020), which further influences interpreters' cognitive capacity in processing speakers' utterances and delivering an accurate rendition of information while keeping up with the flow of speech (Gile 2009). Despite this, the National Register of Public Service Interpreters NRPSI appears to have failed to acknowledge the emotional nature of public service interpreters' work. The NRPSI sets out, on its website, that "Ensuring high professional standards is essential if interpreting is to function safely and effectively" and claims that the NRPSI Code of Professional Conduct "provides guidance setting out skills, practices and knowledge for interpreters to use in their professional lives" (October 24, 2022). Nevertheless, a search of the NRPSI's website yielded no mentions of organized support for registrants in respect of addressing or supporting interpreters' emotional struggles. This failure to incorporate emotional considerations reflects a disconnection between the drafting of the NRPSI Code of Professional Conduct and the practical side of public service interpreters' work. Consequently, the fulfilment of the principal standards of impartiality, confidentiality, and accuracy is potentially compromised.

Workers in highly stressful or sensitive settings such as police officers, healthcare personnel, and social care workers receive training in relation to potential occupational stress factors, while also receiving guidance about self-care and awareness of organizational support. Legal interpreting has often been considered a psychologically and emotionally taxing activity (Schweda-Nicholson 1989; Mikkelson 1998; Berk-Seligson 2002; Valero-Garcés 2003; Hale 2004; Napier and Spencer 2008; Russell, Hale, and Morris 2008; Lee 2009), but their professional need to manage high levels of emotional impact seems to be ignored. Most studies that explore the significance of emotions in influencing the process of interpreting either deal with the whole PSI sector or focus largely on healthcare interpreting. How emotional struggles may increase the level of difficulty in legal interpreting has been under-investigated. To explore the complicating factors of emotional influences in connection with legal interpreters' unique professional demands and their common subjective experience of working in the legal setting, the current study will address the following two research questions:

RQ1: What are the contributing factors to emotional challenges in legal interpreting that are perceived by legal interpreters?

RQ2: What types of support are expected by interpreters working in the British judicial system?

4 Methodology

4.1 Instruments

The data presented in this chapter are taken from part of a larger study investigating the roles of legal interpreters that used a combination of questionnaire surveys and semi-structured interviews. A set of self-administered questionnaires was distributed electronically to registrants on the NRPSI.

The NRPSI is "the UK's independent voluntary regulator of professional interpreters specialising in public service" (October 22, 2022). The NRPSI currently represents around 1,800 public service interpreters who offer services in 100 languages. To become a "Full Status" registrant, applicants must hold "a qualification that meets the requirements of the National Occupational Standards for Interpreting" and is "at QCF Level 6 or higher." Also, the NRPSI requires interpreters to have gained 400 proven PSI interpreting hours and meet the minimum of 10 hours of PSI interpreting experience annually to qualify for annual renewal of membership. All registrants are bound by the NRPSI Code of Professional Conduct.

At the time of conducting the survey, there were around 1,500 registrants on the NRPSI. The main questionnaire data in relation to this chapter was elicited from three questions, which explored ethical conflicts in terms of service providers' and service users' expectations toward legal interpreters' role and their misunderstanding of the way interpreters work, respectively. These three questions offered multiple choices that respondents could select and more than one answer could be selected as appropriate. At the end of each question and at the end of the questionnaire, respondents were provided with a section to expand on their responses related to their experiences if they wished. The three questionnaire questions are:

1. Have you ever been asked by the criminal justice staff to perform duties other than interpreting during an assignment and what were you required to do?
2. Have you ever been asked by the non-native English speakers to perform duties other than interpreting during an assignment and what were you required to do?
3. What are the reasons you feel reluctant to intervene?

During the second phase of data collection, ten semi-structured interviews were conducted with legal interpreters who had indicated a willingness to be interviewed in their questionnaire responses. The interviews were conducted either face-to-face or via telephone conversations, and all were audio recorded. Each interview lasted around one hour. The discussions in this chapter are mainly based on the analysis of data in relation to conflict of role expectations; cross-cultural and interactional difficulties they encountered; and their strategies to deal with these situations.

4.2 Participants

All participants are professional interpreters registered on the UK NRPSI. A total of 1,508 emails with a link to the questionnaire were sent out. A total of 155 responses were received, constituting a response rate of 10 percent.

The first part of the questionnaire contained questions about the demographic information of respondents (such as their native languages, duration of interpreting experience, and interpreting hours per year). Responses to these questions indicate that the respondents represented the general perceptions of legal interpreters from a range of linguistic and cultural backgrounds and varying levels of interpreting experience. As shown in Figure 4.1, their native languages cover many European, Middle East, and Asian languages.

Respondents' number of years of experience, presented in Figure 4.2, varies from one year to more than thirty years. Of the 155 responses, 108 respondents' experiences fell into the category of "10 to 19 years" (37 percent) with "5 to 9 years" (32 percent) being the second most populated category.

The pattern of respondents' interpreting hours each year is summarized in Figure 4.3. Nearly half of them, seventy-six interpreters, interpret between 100 and 499 hours every year.

It is fair to conclude that these respondents' responses can represent interpreters' views and opinions from a variety of linguistic and cultural origins with different levels of experiences, and that these respondents are valid and reliable sources to generate data for this study.

Among those who had indicated a willingness to be interviewed (ten in total) their native languages include English, French, Mandarin, Romanian, Polish, and Arabic. They are all practicing PSI interpreters with experience that varies from one year to more than twenty years and their interpreting hours range from 100 to 500 hours.

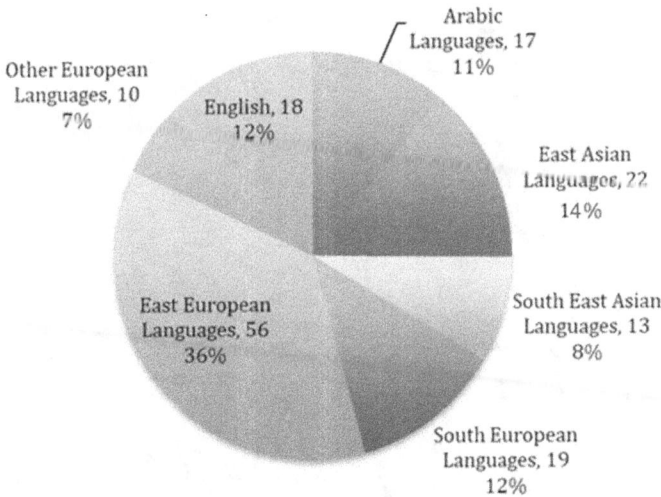

Figure 4.1 Respondent's native languages.

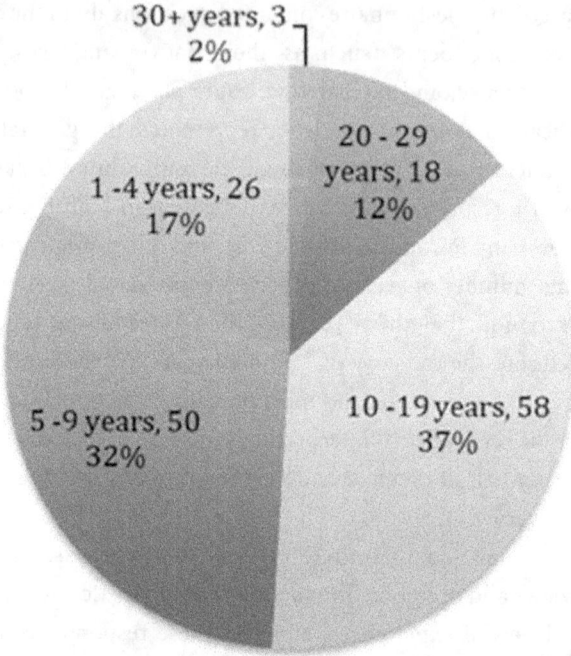

Figure 4.2 Cumulative years of interpreting experience of questionnaire respondents.

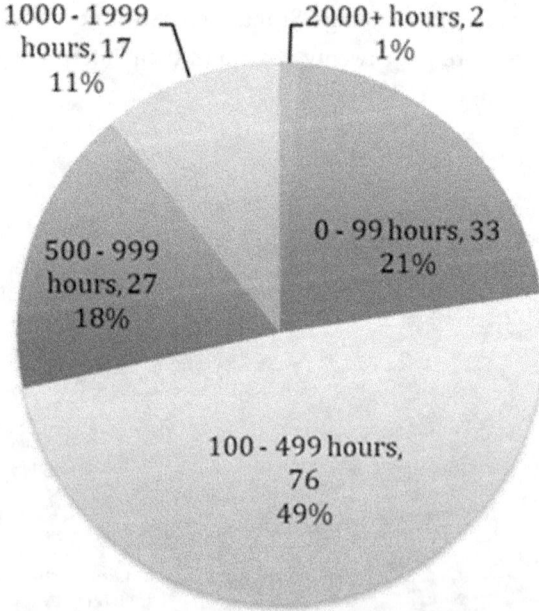

Figure 4.3 Questionnaire respondents' average interpreting hours per year.

4.3 Data Analysis

The analysis and discussion in this chapter focus on the emotional and psychological challenges reported by participants in their questionnaire responses and the interview discussions. Thematic analysis was adopted to analyze the interview data. The data analysis followed the process of organizing, categorizing, and identifying themes, as recommended by Brewer (2000). As this study explores perceptions, how the participants' discussions were similar to or different from each other was examined to ensure meaningful interpretation. Data were analyzed from three perspectives: ethical stress, vicarious trauma, and lack of training or a support system. For confidentiality purposes, interviewees have been anonymized and represented with chronological numbers.

5 Data Analysis Results and Discussion

Two overriding themes are presented in this section, which address the two research questions in this chapter. First, participants in this study identified two main contributing factors that may lead to emotional problems: ethical stress and vicarious trauma. Second, participants raised the issue of a lack of training and called for stronger organizational support.

5.1 Ethical Stress

Just as ethical stress is a recognized source of occupational stress for translators and interpreters when they need to make a judgment that is contradictory to the prescribed professional code of ethics (Hubscher-Davidson 2020), it is also one of the most profound difficulties reported by legal interpreters in this study. The participants' responses indicate that ethically difficult situations may take place due to a conflict in the expectations of the role, a lack of understanding of how interpreters work, the contents of the case, and other parties' attitude.

5.1.1 Conflict in Role Expectations

The majority of the 155 questionnaire respondents reported that it is common for them to face difficult ethical decisions about whether or not to step outside of their professional boundaries. Respectively, 41 percent, 68 percent, 52 percent, and 53 percent of them were asked by service providers to explain

Question 1: Have you ever been asked by the criminal justice staff to perform duties other than interpreting during an assignment and what were you required to do? Please tick as many as apply.

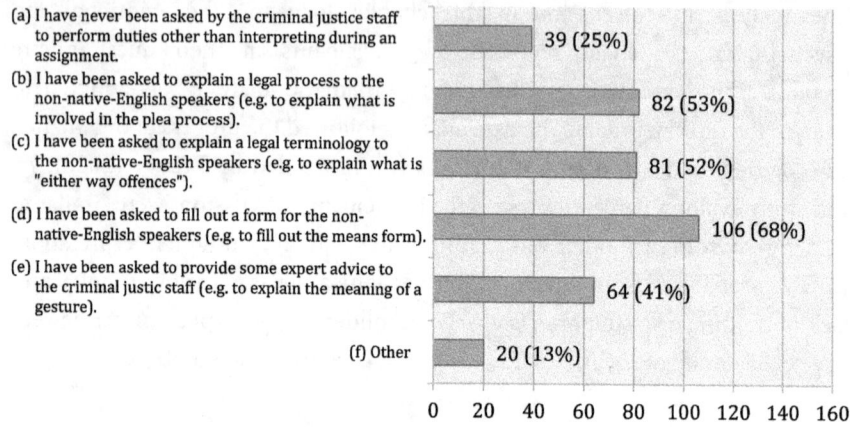

Figure 4.4 Duties requested by service providers.

Question 2: Have you ever been asked by the non-native-English speakers to perform duties other than interpreting during an assignment and what were you required to do? Please tick as many as apply

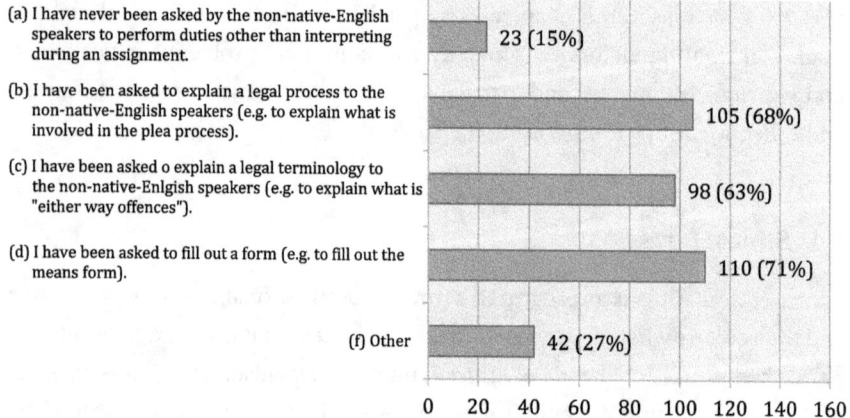

Figure 4.5 Duties requested by service users.

a legal process, to explain legal terminology, to fill out a form for non-native English speakers, and to provide some expert advice to the criminal justice staff. Meanwhile, respectively, 71 percent, 63 percent, and 68 percent of the participants were asked by service users to fill out a form, to explain a legal process, and to explain legal terminology. The results are shown in Figures 4.4 and 4.5, respectively.

During the interviews, the participants also discussed their experiences of being regularly expected, by both the service providers and the service users, to perform multirole tasks. In Excerpt 1, Interviewee 3 commented that some of these roles are beyond their remit as a legal interpreter and thus create stressful situations.

Excerpt 1

Researcher: Have you been asked to perform duties other than interpreting?

Interviewee 3: That could actually happen to me many, many times.

Researcher: How do you feel about these kinds of requests?

Interviewee 3: And interpreters should not be put in that position ... because that's not within our remit. We are not some kind of legal assistant for the solicitor or the barrister ... Interpreters are there to interpret. That's our sole function.

Hubscher-Davidson (2020: 415) notes that interpreters "are part of a complex network of people." When the interpreter is required by other parties to take on a variety of duties, interpreters are likely to ask themselves whether it is morally justified for them to step outside of their professional boundaries to meet the requests of others. If interpreters refuse to perform duties because they feel such duties conflict with their professional code of ethics, it may affect the other parties' attitude and make their work more difficult. Interpreters who constantly face conflict in the expectations of their role from service providers and service users could find the situations mentally draining, and therefore they may suffer from an increased level of stress.

5.1.2 Lack of Understanding of the Way Interpreters Work

The misunderstanding of the legal interpreters' role by other parties in the legal system has emerged as a cause for interpreters to face ethical dilemmas. These misunderstandings could also occur in relation to the way interpreters work. For example, legal interpreters may often need to intervene to ask for clarifications or repetitions, a requirement that ensures they can break down lengthy utterances or allows them to correct an interpreting error to achieve accuracy. However, interpreters may have concerns about interrupting proceedings and thus be hesitant to intervene, even when it is necessary. Question 3 of the questionnaire sought to determine whether interpreters felt they could interrupt proceedings, and if not, why not. The results are presented in Figure 4.6. Of the 155 questionnaire respondents, 30 percent felt

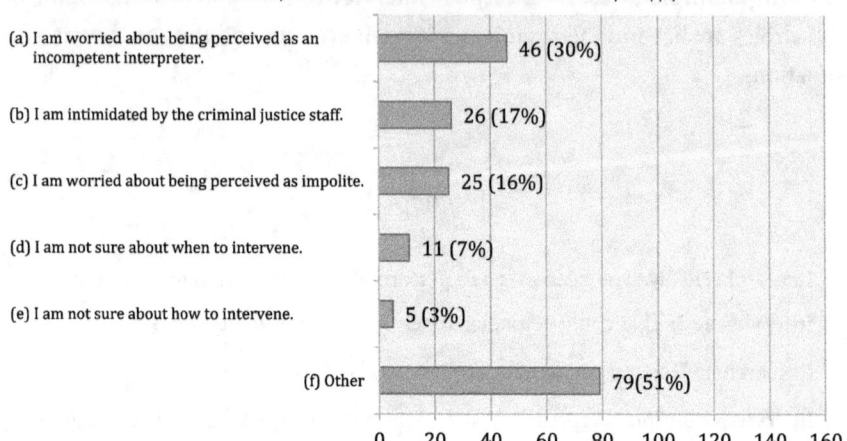

Figure 4.6 Reasons respondents feel reluctant to intervene.

worried about being perceived as an incompetent interpreter, 16 percent were intimidated by the criminal justice staff, and 17 percent were worried about being perceived as impolite.

Questionnaire respondents also commented in the space provided at the end of this question that feeling intimidated by service users' arrogant and ignorant attitude was one of the significant reasons for not interrupting the proceedings. For example, one respondent commented, "arrogant judges: looking down on you as an unwelcome presence/expense. Judges are not always sympathetic to the interpreting process, and do not look kindly on 'interpreter speaking.'" Other respondents related their reluctance to intervene to not wishing to interrupt the trial proceedings. One respondent reported, "I don't think that staff want the process to be halted for any reason." Moreover, interpreters may feel stressed when they need to correct an interpreting error to ensure accuracy, as reported by Interviewee 5 in Excerpt 2. Acknowledging and correcting interpreting errors could be perceived as negatively impacting on the other parties' impression of the interpreter's capability and thus lead them to doubt the whole interpreting performance.

Excerpt 2

Researcher: What areas of legal interpreters' ethical rules do you feel it is difficult to follow and why?

Interviewee 5: I find it [corrections] very troublesome ... if you correct it, which may make all the parties (in) the court doubt your interpretation. Although you think you just make that one mistake, it may still make others doubt all your interpretation.

Lee (2009) argued that interpreters' professional behavior in seeking interventions could be perceived as an undesirable intrusion by judges and lawyers as well as a cause for the questioning of the professional performance of the interpreter. This, therefore, reveals a key dilemma that interpreters face, namely that they must intervene to achieve satisfactory interpreting quality, yet such interventions are not always appreciated, such as the disapproval of the criminal justice staff (Morris 1995). Interventions are possibly the only situation where the interpreter speaks in his or her own right, yet some criminal justice staff may see interpreting as a mere "mechanical process" (Lee 2009: 110). Therefore, interpreters risk suffering ethical stress due to wavering between a desire not to be seen as an undesirable intrusion by the criminal justice staff and not wishing to compromise the professional role of interpreting accurately and faithfully.

5.1.3 Content of the Case

Several interpreters reported, in the interviews, feeling uncomfortable or embarrassed when seeking to replicate certain speech elements, including aggressiveness, harsh body language, shouting, and rude language, because it does not suit their personalities. Interviewee 3, for instance, made efforts to include body language in the interpretation, although this action did not come naturally or comfortably, as evident from the interview, namely Excerpt 3.

Excerpt 3

Researcher: So, what are the difficulties when you are trying to keep the original style of speech?

Interviewee 3: I'm reflecting the tone of voice, the register, or even the body language to some extent of the person I'm interpreting for, even if it's actually quite unpleasant. Sometimes very difficult, sometimes actually very embarrassing.

Regarding rude language, in Excerpt 4, Interviewee 6 expressed shyness, describing how they would turn red in the face and lose eye contact with others or simply look down. However, this speech element was still interpreted as it was deemed essential to ensure a faithful interpretation. Therefore, the interpreters sought to fulfil the professional code of "faithfulness," which surpasses any personal discomfort.

Excerpt 4

Researcher: Do you find it difficult to swear to the judge?

Interviewee 6: [When interpreting rude words] I always go red. And I dare not look up. But you've got to do it. Absolutely, it's not our personality, but we just have to do it for the job. But as long as you say it at the beginning, explain your role, and "I'll interpret," well, you do the affirmation, or you swear, before it, and you say "I will faithfully interpret, explanation made of all such matters that shall be required of me," so that includes everything. But it's embarrassing sometimes.

Interpreting for sex-related topics or genital parts also appears to cause some emotional issues for some interpreters. Interviewee 5's reflection, as presented in Excerpt 5, confirms the difficulty of interpreting "intimate body parts and activities." This finding is also acknowledged in Cambridge (2005: 153). Interviewee 5 has been an interpreter for many years and reported becoming brave and calm over that time. Yet not all interpreters, especially newly qualified interpreters, can maintain such a professional manner when they encounter certain topics, such as a rape or sexual assault case.

Excerpt 5

Researcher: What are the main challenges and difficulties in relation to culture that you have encountered during an assignment? How do you deal with them? Can you give examples?

Interviewee 5: For example, a rape or a sexual assault case . . . But the questioning process was in a lot of detail. There were a lot of questions about genitals. The opposite gender of the suspect might feel uncomfortable. I didn't turn red. Really; I was interpreting calmly.

5.1.4 Other Parties

Interviewee 4 reported, as seen in Excerpt 6, developing emotional challenges when interpreting for an uncooperative non-native English speaker. During a police interview, a detainee, who was suffering from depression, behaved in an angry and aggressive manner and constantly verbally abused the interpreter.

Excerpt 6

> **Researcher:** Are there any misunderstandings or dilemmas that you have experienced during an assignment which affected your ability or quality of interpreting? How do you deal with them? Can you give examples?
>
> **Interviewee 4:** After the police interview finished, my mood collapsed. When it collapsed, I couldn't handle it anymore. It was extremely difficult and challenging . . . I also have my own emotions, I am also a human being, and I am not a robot. I had to do my best not to be influenced by her aggressive attitude and her abuse.

Commenting on the specific situation raised in Excerpt 6, Interviewee 4 felt the interaction and situation went beyond a reasonable tolerance level. This interpreter reflected that it is natural for an interpreter to have emotions and to be affected by other parties' attitudes. This situation is similar to Hochschild's (1979) discussion of airline stewardesses' difficulties in behaving appropriately when dealing with unpleasant customers, where there is a severe discrepancy between the outward presentation and the internal stress.

The ethical guidelines constructed by the NRPSI prescribe the normative professional standards of behaviors but fail to respond to real-life situations. The participants in the current study reported extensive firsthand experiences involving conflicting expectations of their role, lack of trust or understanding from others, and procedural pressure. Hubscher-Davidson (2020: 4) raises this important question: "What if the codes demand behaviour that cannot always be displayed in practice?" Inevitably, these ethical dilemmas can work as environmental and external stimuli that aggravate interpreters' degree of stress and impair their performance.

5.2 Vicarious Trauma

When the researcher asked the interviewees: "What are the main challenges and difficulties in relation to language and interpreting that you have encountered during an assignment? How do you deal with them? Can you give examples," many interpreters discussed their emotional struggles. Interviewee 5 felt, as presented in Excerpt 7, that interpreters' emotions could inevitably be affected by "those vicious cases, such as rape or murder."

Excerpt 7

> **Interviewee 5:** I remember I did a case where two female students were murdered in [city name]. That girl was suffocated to death. Her mouth was stuffed with a face towel. The police used that face towel as an exhibit, and put it in a picture frame, and displayed it in the picture frame. When they presented the exhibit, they asked us to pass it on to each other to see the towel mounted inside the frame. I felt very sick and very horrified . . . When you look at those things, you are still human beings, and you will be affected anyway. This is very difficult.

This example outlines the darker side of interpreting in legal proceedings, such as when interpreters need to deal with the exhibits from murder cases. Interpreters, like other humans, may find it difficult to face such fear-inducing scenarios. This example appears typical of how the traumatic nature of an interpreting task could influence the interpreter. Similar reports of the influence of the nature of the interpreting task were also made by interpreters in the study by Splevins et al. (2010) and those in studies reviewed by Valero-Garcés (2015).

Furthermore, Interviewee 1 reported struggling with becoming too emotionally involved in cases, especially in the early days of the profession, as evident in Excerpt 8 of the interview.

Excerpt 8

> **Researcher:** What are the main challenges and difficulties in relation to language and interpreting that you have encountered during an assignment? How do you deal with them? Can you give examples?
>
> **Interviewee 1:** Emotion, I struggled emotionally when I first started . . . That was initially mostly I struggled when I first started. I was a little bit soft and a little bit inexperienced, so I put myself in the shoes of the witness. I could feel the sarcastic tone and the aggressive tone, then I emotionally absorbed it for the defendant.

The content of domestic violence cases can also affect an interpreter emotionally. This is seen in the response from Interviewee 7 about a female colleague, as discussed in Excerpt 9.

Excerpt 9

Researcher: What are the main challenges and difficulties in relation to language and interpreting that you have encountered during an assignment? How do you deal with them? Can you give examples?

Interviewee 7: [A colleague of mine . . .] She finds the emotional side difficulties. If she sees certain domestic issues, she gets really upset. She gets into it. And that's what she finds difficult, and I find I am the same.

In Excerpt 10, Interviewee 2 reflected upon another element of the emotional struggle, which was caused by "the unwanted sympathy," which could lead to their alterations to the original testimony.

Excerpt 10

Interviewee 2: Misunderstandings or dilemmas are sometimes caused by the unwanted sympathy that court interpreters might have when working in court.

Interpreters are not immune to associations with traumatic cases, which can result in negative emotional reactions. The long-term exposure to these feelings may increase the level of difficulty for the interpreter, as described in Excerpt 11 by Interviewee 10.

Excerpt 11

Researcher: What are the main challenges and difficulties in relation to language and interpreting that you have encountered during an assignment? How do you deal with them? Can you give examples?

Interviewee 10: Once I interpreted for a defendant in a case for several months. She was convicted with solid evidence. But she committed the crime because another dependent took advantage of her. In the series of

> legal consultations to prepare for her case, I got to know her background and her story inside out. By the end, I kind of developed some kind of sympathy for her. I know I shouldn't. I know this is not that professional . . . but when she was sentenced to prison, I felt very sorry for her and this feeling lasted for a long period even after the case was over.

Interpreters commonly consider showing emotions as being unprofessional (Cambridge 2005), as clearly stated by Interviewee 10 in Excerpt 11. The difficulty of fighting against becoming emotionally involved is a common finding of several studies as reviewed by Valero-Garcés (2015). These studies covered all public service interpreting sectors and across several European countries. Their findings support the notion that it is natural for interpreters to be sympathetic to people in more disadvantageous situations. In Brisset, Leanza, and Laforest's view (2013), this type of emotional problem is due to the conflict between an interpreter's need for impartiality and their need for commitment to the case. A higher level of commitment to the service user can be reflected as showing more empathy, and this could lead to the loss of an interpreter's neutrality (Brisset, Leanza, and Laforest 2013). Additionally, the emotional drain of perpetually being empathetic is highly likely to cause psychological strain, namely "burnout" (McCann and Pearlman 1990: 134).

Participants in this study reported that legal interpreters' work can be emotionally intensive, and several forms of extreme emotional confrontation can occur in their work (e.g., instances of death and violence) or victims of crimes. Legal interpreters may, therefore, face the ethical decision between the restraint from displaying their own emotions as a professional etiquette and processing the emotional demands of the interactions. The work and behavior of legal interpreters are officially prescribed in the NRPSI Professional Code of Conduct, which focuses on impartiality, confidentiality, and faithfulness. "Impartiality" asks for emotional detachment from the speakers they interpret for, whereas "faithfulness" demands an entry into the speakers' emotional experience and a deep absorbance of their feelings. These two demands actually contradict with each other. Interpreters' emotions provoked by "vicarious traumatization" must be suppressed to maintain professionalism. This means interpreters face the challenge of constantly switching between their interactive emotions and their organismic emotions, which can at times counter biological instincts. As a consequence, struggling between the required emotion and their own emotions is likely to lead to an impaired performance (Bakker and Heuven 2006).

5.3 Lack of Training or a Support System

Legal interpreters are not emotionless machines, and their emotions could influence the smooth running of legal proceedings. Valero-Garcés (2015) identified the significant consequences of emotional factors on interpreters' work. However, this issue has not been realized across the legal setting, as Interviewee 7 notes in Excerpt 12. Interpreters are expected to maintain a professional manner with an impartial and calm stance, which is not always realistic.

Excerpt 12

> **Interviewee 7:** Other legal professionals think you don't get affected ... When there is a problem, what you do is just you deal with it ... Emotion can be a big problem, but if there is a problem, that could affect in big terms. Absolutely.

The benefits of emotion-related education and organized support from the interpreting profession have started to be appreciated by scholars in the field (Anderson 2011; Hetherington 2012). When discussing their emotional struggles, participants in this study reflected that a lack of training and a mechanism for consoling themselves can result in feelings of isolation and loneliness. For example, Interviewee 1 expressed a strong sense of loneliness and complained about the lack of training and support resources for NRPSI registrants, as in Excerpt 13.

Excerpt 13

> **Researcher:** How do you deal with the emotional problems? As you said, there is not actually any training about emotional or psychological problems.
>
> **Interviewee 1:** I learned through the school of life experience. I'm a bit harder now, a bit more experienced, sort of to switch off the emotions. I have got no training, or counselling, or support, nothing at all. Interpreters are very individualized, isolated. They cannot go to the NRPSI's therapist, or something, or receive training about how to deal with these cases.

Interviewee 1 explained that they could only use a strategy developed from the practice to cope with the emotional involvement. Without emotional education or psychological training, legal interpreters are not as prepared as other frontline practitioners. Interpreters can only rely on their self-developed coping strategies when they feel frightened or emotionally exhausted. This is in line with the finding in Splevins et al.'s study (2010) that interpreters working in therapeutic sessions with trauma survivors develop their own coping strategies after an initial stage of struggling with the emotional shock. Moreover, the NRPSI does not provide a support system for interpreters in the British judicial system as other European countries do, such as Germany, or as other professions in the legal system in the UK do, such as the police force. In Excerpt 14, Interviewee 7 shared some information about the psychiatric services on offer for interpreters in Germany.

Excerpt 14

> **Interviewee 7:** I was told that interpreters in Germany are required to go through a psychiatric assessment every six months to keep up with their registration and there are always psychiatric services like that available.

Professional isolation is one of the major factors contributing to therapists' "burnout" (McCann and Pearlman 1990: 134), and interpreters working in the British judicial setting are likely to suffer from a similar sense of professional isolation. Participants in this study complained that the NRPSI fails to equip interpreters with a sense of belonging. This highlights the need for the NRPSI to reconsider, as the professional association representing public service interpreters in the UK, how to provide practical psychological support and training, how to fulfil their role as pastoral support, and how to build up a sense of belonging and trust for their registrants.

6 Conclusion

The legal interpreters in this study strongly indicate that emotional aspects of their work can negatively impact their professionalism and consequently push the boundaries of their occupations. Ethical dilemmas are identified as significant sources of occupational stress for legal interpreters. Legal interpreters' work extends beyond dealing with highly complicated legal discourses and complex legal procedures in a manner fitting to the professional code of ethics of impartiality, confidentiality, and accuracy that interpreters are required to abide by. They also face the multilayered pressure of being positioned between the conflict of expectations and problematic attitudes of service providers and service users. Legal interpreters also need to combat vicarious trauma caused by the emotionally taxing nature of legal proceedings and the distressing content of certain types of cases.

The findings of this study indicate that policymakers and service users in the British legal system have not currently recognized these difficulties, and there is a lack of professional guidance on dealing with various unexpected emotional situations and a lack of a solid support system. These findings call for the need to address the lack of training interpreters receive regarding emotional issues in their occupation and to train service providers to accommodate interpreters' emotional needs in legal proceedings.

The emotional struggles reported in this study may have significant implications for the development of a more comprehensive education and training system for legal interpreters in the UK. A general public service interpreter training course cannot fulfil the purpose of dealing with the complexities of emotional and psychological issues that are relevant to working in the British judicial setting. Based on Valero-Garcés's (2005: 2) recommendation on interpreters' psychological education, a similar program can be adapted to include the following areas:

- Types and content of vicious cases that may present emotionally difficult aspects (e.g., murder, assault, domestic violence, etc.);
- Basic psychological training regarding core concepts (stress, anxiety, emotional transfer, behavioral alterations, etc.);
- Recognizing potentially stressful factors (e.g., service providers' or service users' arrogant attitude, service providers' refusal to accommodate vital interpreting needs, legal interpreters' efforts in reflecting emotional elements of speech while observing legal interpreters' professional code of ethics in term of impartiality, confidentiality, and accuracy, etc.);
- Recognizing symptoms and developing strategies to deal with the possible psychological impact related to legal interpreting (e.g., fear, embarrassment, anger, etc.).

Both prevention and coping strategies should be taught to guide interpreters, rather than teaching them a set of prescriptive measures. Interpreters may be able to integrate the earlier mentioned psychological knowledge into their understanding of the code of ethics. For example, interpreters can understand that the traumatic content of some assignments in the legal setting is likely to cause feelings of distress, anxiety, or sympathy. These feelings do not indicate a failure of professionalism, and there are self-care strategies available to offload their emotional burdens. Also, interpreters have the ability to weigh up different factors and reach a sound professional judgment when faced with a difficult interpreting scenario that requires strong emotional management. Nevertheless, if educators and professional organizations allow legal interpreters to continue as they are without any emotional training or organized support, interpreters run the risk of being overwhelmed by their emotional involvement. Legal interpreters' inability to control their emotions may impair their performance in meeting their professional standards and thus indirectly damaging the integrity of the legal system.

This study adds to existing literature by recognizing the factors contributing to the emotional challenges legal interpreters face in the British judicial system. More research is needed on the negative emotional and psychological impacts on legal interpreters so that interpreter training and service user training can be developed and be of assistance to interpreters. For example, how emotional dissonance affects legal interpreters' psychological mechanisms and disrupts their performance is yet to be explored thoroughly.

References

Anderson, A. (2011), "Peer Support and Consultation Project for Interpreters: A Model for Supporting the Well-Being of Interpreters Who Practice in Mental Health Settings," *Journal of Interpretation*, 21(1): 2.

Angelelli, Claudia V. (2004), *Revisiting the Interpreter's Role: A Study of Conference, Court, and Medical Interpreters in Canada, Mexico, and the United States*, Amsterdam: John Benjamins Publishing.

Bakker, A. B. and E. Heuven (2006), "Emotional Dissonance, Burnout, and In-Role Performance among Nurses and Police Officers," *International Journal of Stress Management*, 13(4): 423.

Bancroft, M. A. (2017), "The Voice of Compassion: Exploring Trauma-Informed Interpreting," in C. Valero-Garcé and R. Tipton (eds.), *Ideology, Ethics and Policy Development in Public Service Interpreting and Translation*, 195–219, Bristol: Multilingual Matters.

Barsky, R. F. (1996), "The Interpreter as Intercultural Agent in Convention Refugee Hearings," *The Translator*, 2(1): 45–63.

Berk-Seligson, S. (1987), "The Intersection of Testimony Styles in Interpreted Judicial Proceedings: Pragmatic Alterations in Spanish Testimony," 25(6): 1087–1126, http://doi.org/10.1515/ling.1987.25.6.1087.

Berk-Seligson, S. (2002), "The Miranda Warnings and Linguistic Coercion: The Role of Footing in the Interrogation of a Limited-English-Speaking Murder Suspect," in J. Cotterill (ed.), *Language in the Legal Process*, 127–43, London: Palgrave Macmillan.

Brewer, J. (2000), *Ethnography*, Buckingham, England: Open University Press.

Brisset, C., Y. Leanza, and K. Laforest (2013), "Working with Interpreters in Health Care: A Systematic Review and Meta-Ethnography of Qualitative Studies," *Patient Education and Counseling*, 91(2): 131–40.

Cambridge, J. (2005), "The Public Service Interpreter's Face: Rising to the Challenge of Expressing Powerful Emotion for Others," <u>Revista Canaria de Estudios Ingleses</u>, 51: 141-57.

Catherall, D. R. (1995), "Coping with Secondary Traumatic Stress: The Importance of the Therapist's Professional Peer Group," in B. H. Stamm (ed.), *Secondary Traujatic Stress: Self-care Issues for Clinicians, Researchers, and Educators*, 80–92, The Sidran Press.

Christodoulou-Fella, M., N. Middleton, E. D. Papathanassoglou, and M. N. Karanikola (2017), "Exploration of the Association between Nurses' Moral Distress and Secondary Traumatic Stress Syndrome: Implications for Patient Safety in Mental Health Services," *BioMed Research International, 2017*.

Corsellis, A. (2002), "Creating a Professional Context for Public Service Interpreters," *Community Interpreting and Translating: New Needs for New Realities*, January, 29–36.

Costa, B., R. L. Gutiérrez, and T. Rausch (2020), "Self-Care As An Ethical Responsibility: A Pilot Study on Support Provision for Interpreters in Human Crises," *Translation and Interpreting Studies*, 15(1): 36–56.

Damasio, A. (1994), *Descartes' Error: Emotion, Rationality and the Human Brain*, 352, New York: Putnam.

De Jongh, E. M. (1991), "Cultural Proficiency and Nonverbal Communication in Court Interpreting," *Confluencia*, 7(1): 99–106.

Eades, D. (2010), "Sociolinguistics and the Legal Process," in D. Eades (ed.), *Sociolinguistics and the Legal Process*, Bristol: Multilingual Matters.

Fenton, S. (1997), "The Role of the Interpreter in the Adversarial Courtroom," in *The Critical Link: Interpreters in the Community*, 29, Amsterdam: John Benjamins Publishing.

Fowler, Y. (1997), "The Courtroom Interpreter: Paragon and Intruder?," in *The Critical Link: Interpreters in the Community*, 191, Amsterdam: John Benjamins Publishing.

Garcés, C. V. (2003), "Soñé con una melodía y escuché voces dispersas: Barreras en la comunicación interlingüística en los centros de salud," in *Discursos (Dis) Con/Cordantes: Modos y Formas de Comunicación y Convivencia*, 89–108, Madrid: Editorial Universidad de Alcalá.

Garcés, C. V. (2015), "The Impact of Emotional and Psychological Factors on Public Service Interpreters: Preliminary Studies," *Translation & Interpreting*, 7(3): 90–102.

Gile, D. (2009), *Basic Concepts and Models for Interpreter and Translator Training*, Revised Edition, Amsterdam: John Benjamins Publishing.

González, R. D., V. F. Vásquez, and H. Mikkelson (1991), *Fundamentals of Court Interpretation, Theory, Policy, and Practice*, 2nd ed., Carolina Academic Press.

Grootegoed, E. and M. Smith (2018), "The Emotional Labour of Austerity: How Social Workers Reflect and Work on Their Feelings Towards Reducing Support to Needy Children and Families," *The British Journal of Social Work*, 48(7): 1929–47.

Hale, S. and E. Gonzalez (2017), "Teaching Legal Interpreting at University Level: A Research-Based Approach," in C. Letizia and N. Niemants (eds.), *Teaching Dialogue Interpreting*, 200–16, Amsterdam: John Benjamins Publishing.

Hale, S. B. (2004), *The Discourse of Court Interpreting : Discourse Practices of the Law, the Witness, and the Interpreter*, Amsterdam: John Benjamins Publishing.

Hetherington, A. (2012), "Supervision and the Interpreting Profession: Support and Accountability through Reflective Practice," *International Journal of Interpreter Education*, 4(1): 5.

Hobfoll, S. E., P. Watson, C. C. Bell, R. A. Bryant, M. J. Brymer, M. J. Friedman, … and R. J. Ursano (2007), "Five Essential Elements of Immediate and Mid-Term Mass Trauma Intervention: Empirical Evidence," *Psychiatry*, 70(4): 283–315.

Hochschild, A. R. (1979), "Emotion Work, Feeling Rules, and Social Structure," *American Journal of Sociology*, 85(3): 551–75.

Hubscher-Davidson, S. (2020), "Ethical Stress in Translation and Interpreting," in K. Koskinen and N. K. Pokorn (eds.), *Routledge Handbook of Translation and Ethics*, 415–30, London: Routledge.

Inghilleri, M. (2013), *Interpreting Justice: Ethics, Politics and Language*, London: Routledge.

Jiménez, F. R. and K. E. Voss (2014), "An Alternative Approach to the Measurement of Emotional Attachment," *Psychology & Marketing*, 31(5): 360–70.

Kaczmarek, L. (2012), "Addressing the Question of Ethical Dilemmas," *Global Trends in Translator and Interpreter Training: Mediation and Culture*, 6: 217.

Kadrić, M. (2021), "Legal Interpreting and Social Discourse," in M. Ji and S. Laviosa (eds.), *The Oxford Handbook of Translation and Social Practices*, 501–20, Oxford: Oxford University Press.

Knodel, R. K. (2018), "Coping with Vicarious Trauma in Mental Health Interpreting," *Journal of Interpretation*, 26(1): 2.

Korpal, P. and A. Jasielska (2019), "Investigating Interpreters' Empathy: Are Emotions in Simultaneous Interpreting Contagious?" *Target. International Journal of Translation Studies*, 31(1): 2–24.

Lee, J. (2009), "Interpreting Inexplicit Language during Courtroom Examination," *Applied Linguistics*, 30(1): 93–114.

Mason, I. (2009), "Role, Positioning and Discourse in Face-to-Face Interpreting," in R. D. P. Ricoy, I. Perez, and C. Wilson (eds.), *Interpreting and Translating in Public Service Settings. Policy, Practice, Pedagogy*, 52–73, Manchester: St. Jerome Publishing.

McCann, I. L. and L. A. Pearlman (1990), "Vicarious Traumatization: A Framework for Understanding the Psychological Effects of Working with Victims," *Journal of Traumatic Stress*, 3(1): 131–49.

Mikkelson, H. (1998), "Towards a Redefinition of the Role of the Court Interpreter," *Interpreting*, 3(1): 21–45.

Morris, R. (1995), "The Moral Dilemmas of Court Interpreting," *The Translator*, 1(1): 25–46.

Munyangeyo, T. (2016), "Insight into Ethical Dilemmas in Public Service Interpreting and Interpreters' Training Needs," in T. Munyangeyo, G. Webb, and M. Rabadán-Gómez (eds.), *Challenges and Opportunities in Public Service Interpreting*, 161–89, London: Palgrave Macmillan.

Nakane, I. (2009), "The Myth of An 'Invisible Mediator': An Australian Case Study of English-Japanese Police Interpreting," *Portal: Journal of Multidisciplinary International Studies*, 6(1): 1–16.

Napier, J. and D. Spencer (2008), "Guilty or Not Guilty? An Investigation of Deaf Jurors' Access to Court Proceedings via Sign Language Interpreting," in S. Hale and D. Russell (eds.), *Interpreting in Legal Settings*, 72–122, Washington, DC: Gallaudet University Press.

Rabadán-Gómez, M. (2016), "Professionalisation and Standardisation of Public Service Interpreting," in T. Munyangeyo, G. Webb, and M. Rabadán-Gómez (eds.), *Challenges and Opportunities in Public Service Interpreting*, 47–85, Cham: Palgrave Macmillan.

Roberts, G. (2015), "Public Service Interpreters: The Emotional and Psychological Impact of Interpreting Within Public Service Settings," Doctoral diss., Cardiff University.

Rojo, A. (2017), *The Role of Emotions. The Handbook of Translation and Cognition*, 369–85, Hoboken, NJ: John Wiley & Sons.

Russell, D. and S. Hale (2008), *Interpreting in Legal Settings*, Washington, DC: Gallaudet University Press.

Samad, N. I. A., Z. Hashim, S. Moin, and H. Abdullah (2010), "Assessment of Stress and Its Risk Factors Among Primary School Teachers in the Klang Valley, Malaysia," *Global Journal of Health Science*, 2(2): 163.

Schweda-Nicholson, N. (1989), "Ad Hoc Court Interpreters in the United States: Equality, Inequality, Quality?," *Meta: Translators' Journal*, 34(4): 711–23.

Schwenke, T. J. (2015), "Sign Language Interpreters and Burnout: Exploring Perfectionism and Coping," *JADARA*, 49(2): 7.

Splevins, K. A., K. Cohen, S. Joseph, C. Murray, and J. Bowley (2010), "Vicarious Posttraumatic Growth among Interpreters," *Qualitative Health Research*, 20(12): 1705–16.

Valero-Garcés, C. (2005), "Emotional and Psychological Effects on Interpreters in Public Services: A Critical Factor to Bear in Mind," *Translation Journal*, 9(3): 1–13.

Seeing Omissions from Inside the Interpreter's Mind

Caiwen Wang

1 Introduction

Omissions in interpreting were first studied by Barik in 1971 and were defined as "items present in the original version which are left out of the translation by the T" (1971: 200; "T" = interpreter). Barik went on to categorize omissions into four types by comparing the interpreting product with the source speech. The four types are skipping omissions, comprehension omissions, delay omissions, and compounding omissions and are all "departures of the translation from the original which to some degree affect the meaning of what is said" (1971: 202). Along similar lines, Altman (1994: 26) treated omissions as errors on the ground that "the interpreter's prime task is to communicate a message between the original speaker and a listener (or group of listeners) under a given set of circumstances." These earlier empirical studies should be lauded as they have taught us much about omissions in interpreting.

Among the four types of omission, Barik touched upon the causes of comprehension omissions and delay omissions but not the other two. The former, as the term suggests, are due to comprehension problems on the interpreter's part. The latter are the consequence of cognitive overloading:

> This (delay omission; note added) would happen when, as the T was giving his translation of a segment of the text, the S resumed speaking, with the result that some of what S said did not seem to « register » with the T, who would then either wait until the beginning of a new unit of meaning or else would bypass what had been said in order to « catch up » . . . had the T not lagged behind in his translation and had he been able to pay attention to what was being said, he may have been able to translate it. (1971: 201)

Altman (1994: 34) provided the below list of causes for all types of error she found, including omissions:

(i) excessive concentration on a preceding item due to processing problems, resulting in a lack of attention and hence omission;
(ii) attempt to improve TL style, leading to a tendency to overstate the case or to embroider the text unnecessarily;
(iii) difficulty in finding the correct contextual equivalent for a given lexical item;
(iv) drawing erroneously upon one's store of background/general knowledge;
(v) compression of two information items into one, thereby producing a third, incorrect item;
(vi) shortcomings in mastery of the FL, leading to misunderstandings and therefore misinterpretations of the original speech.

It is clear that these analyses of causes are the theorist's assumption, since no relevant data reported by the interpreters themselves are referred to. As Altman stated, while attempting to analyze the causes of errors, "we are compelled to remain at the level of conjecture: . . . we have no access to the psychological mechanisms at work in the interpreter's mind during the listening process" (1994: 33–4). This indicates that Altman believed that access to the interpreters' cognitive processing is crucial for our knowledge about omissions and their triggers. Nevertheless, since Altman, there has been little research in this area, especially when compared to the amount of research into what is going on in translators' mind during the translation process. It was not until 2004 that Napier examined sign language interpreters' omissions and for the first time combined observations of the interpreting product with interpreters' retrospective reflections on their cognitive processing at the time of omissions.

Napier grouped omissions from a cognitive perspective and identified five categories: unconscious, conscious strategic, conscious intentional, conscious receptive, and conscious unintentional. Based on her findings, Napier argued that among these five types, conscious strategic omissions should not be treated as errors and instead should be favored in interpreting as effective communication. This suggests that when omissions occur in interpreting, only some of them can be categorized as errors. This further entails that in interpreter training, there is a need to encourage the use of some types of omission while discouraging the use of other types for the purpose of better interpreting quality. Nonetheless, while Napier's study focused on omissions in signed language interpreting, it remains unclear what the picture is like for spoken-language interpreting.

I therefore hope that the current study will begin to fill this gap. The current study draws upon Napier's framework since according to her,

> the findings can be extrapolated to interpreters working in other languages as well. The interpreters in this study showed high levels of metalinguistic awareness, and there is no reason to doubt that this would be the case for other interpreters in different contexts using different signed or spoken languages. (2004: 137)

Two research questions are asked in the current study:

> RQ1: What is the nature of omissions in spoken-language interpreting in the simultaneous mode?
>
> RQ2: What kind of cognitive factors led to the omissions identified?

2 Background

2.1 The Cognitive Approach

"Translation has been carried out for millennia but understanding the particularities of the complicated process of transforming a piece of information from one language into another increasingly intrigues researchers around the world" (Ferreira and Schwieter 2017: 3). Despite this, process research into Translation appears to focus more on the transforming of information in the written genre than in the oral genre[1] and also to be unclear in its cognitive stance. Perhaps this is what has led to Muñoz Martín's fair statement that "The label *translation process research* ... does not clarify that it refers to cognitive approaches to translation and whether it also includes interpreting" (2017: 567; italics original). In the interpreting literature, Daniel Gile is arguably the only scholar whose cognitive approach is clear right from the beginning, and he is renowned for his several models explaining the cognitive process of interpreting, such as the Effort Model, respectively, for consecutive interpreting and simultaneous interpreting (1995, 2009). For omissions specifically, Gile (2009: 210) has distinguished two scenarios. In one scenario, interpreters are not conscious of the occurrence of omission:

> Interpreters may miss information without even noticing it because they did not have enough processing capacity available for the Listening and Analysis Effort when the speech segment carrying it was being uttered. They may also omit it because it disappears from short-term memory.

In the other scenario, interpreters are conscious of the occurrence of omission:

> an interpreter decides deliberately not to render in his/her target speech information present in the source speech.

Omissions in the second scenario are referred to as a coping tactic or forced option due to "situations of cognitive saturation where the only possibility of keeping interpreting and serving best the interests of the participants" is to omit (Gile 2009: 210), though Gile also mentioned gatekeeping as an additional reason.

Gile's treatment of omissions is reminiscent of Barik's (1971) and Altman's (1994) in that we are left to treat omissions as suboptimal solutions or errors and thus as something that interpreters should endeavor to avoid. In reality, it is not uncommon for interpreters to hear and interpret chunks of a speech that are not well structured or which are even redundant. It is therefore worth pondering whether in such cases interpreters still strive not to omit or whether they strive to "communicate a message between the original speaker and a listener (or group of listeners) under a given set of circumstances" (Altman 1994: 26; see also the introduction section) and omit deliberately in order to convey the message effectively. This requires us to see omissions from the interpreters' point of view at the time of their occurrence.

2.2 Empirical Studies of Omissions in Simultaneous Interpreting

Previous major empirical studies of omissions in simultaneous interpreting include those by Altman (1994) and Barik (1971), as mentioned earlier. According to Altman, omissions are a type of error that constitutes "an obstacle to communication" (1994: 26). But as discussed earlier, one wonders if all cases of omissions are detrimental to communication. Barik's findings, in addition to his categorization of omissions, are that:

> Although the difference in the number of omissions associated with more-qualified and less-qualified Ts does not at first glance seem particularly striking..., the two groups differ in the degree of "seriousness" of the omissions: whereas about 80% of the omissions of the more-qualified Ts are of the minor *skipping* variety... and thus only about 20% are more "serious," for less-qualified Ts roughly half or 50% of their omissions fall in the latter category. Whereas more-qualified Ts have about the same omission measures associated with interpretation in either direction (from their weaker into their dominant language or *vice versa*), less-qualified Ts, interestingly, usually do "better" when translating from the

dominant into their weaker language, making fewer omissions and omitting less material in that situation than when translating from their weaker into their dominant language, which is the more "natural" direction. (1971: 134)

These findings suggest that in interpreting training, interventions may be different depending on the types of omission made by students when compared to those by professionals and that interventions may also depend on the directions of interpreting.

In 1999, four years after having proposed his cognitive Effort Models for the first time (1995), Gile investigated omissions to test his Tightrope Hypothesis for simultaneous interpreting. While his analysis confirmed the Tightrope Hypothesis, two points are especially relevant to the current research. Firstly, in coding omissions, Gile excluded cases where "what may be identified as an error or omission in a transcript may be an acceptable rendition in an oral presentation of the speech," and he only included "instances of what appeared to me as flagrant errors or omissions" (1999: 161). This indicates that Gile was aware of omissions that were acceptable in interpreting, though he decided not to study them. Secondly, Gile used his data to conclude that "at least for these e/o's, no intrinsic difficulty of the affected source-speech segments is involved (that no specialty-specific or language-specific difficulty is involved will appear clearly to readers)" (1999: 168). Given that Gile's research subjects are all seasoned professional interpreters and considering his research purpose, this conclusion is not surprising. However, it is also important to investigate omissions that are potentially related to the intrinsic difficulties of speeches, such as fast pace and lexical density, which are particularly challenging for interpreting students. This would be useful for pedagogic purposes as tutors and students would want to learn how to counter such difficulties.

Analyzing the same datasets as Gile (1999), Pym (2008) compared the omissions made by interpreters in their first and second renditions and concluded that omissions indicate interpreters' effort at risk analysis: interpreters strive not to omit when possible; if they do, the omissions they make are mostly low risk and interpreters omit by weighing contextual factors. These insights suggest that omissions can potentially be used as a conscious pragmatic strategy when interpreters are analyzing the risk of omitting for a current communicative event. Depending on how well an interpreter uses this pragmatic strategy, the omission can be acceptable (data showing this are unfortunately excluded from Gile's datasets) and can be low or high risk for the success of communication (as shown by Pym's analysis of Gile's data). For training purposes, it is therefore useful to examine the omissions that are made by interpreting students. Specifically, it would be useful to investigate whether or not students are aware when they make omissions and what is going on in their minds when they decide to omit.

Korpal (2012) undertook an experimental study of omissions among both professional and trainee interpreters. He hypothesized that interpreters are sensitive to the omissions they make in interpreting and that omissions are made with the intention to eliminate redundancy. To test these hypotheses, he prepared two speeches that "comprised the addition of many digressions, hedges, discourse markers, cultural allusions and message redundancy" and analyzed the omissions made in the interpreting products (2012: 106). He also conducted a survey among his research participants focusing on whether they thought they had omitted or not, and if so, why and whether or not they "accept omission in SI as a deliberate act" (109). Korpal's interpreting product analysis showed that both groups of interpreters made omissions and that there was not much discrepancy between the omissions made by the two groups. Korpal's questionnaire analysis showed that both groups of interpreters knew they omitted, and that

> many participants from both experimental groups claimed that the speeches were so disorderly that they felt they needed to make them more organised. A great many professionals and trainees said that they had the impression that they should have omitted some information to make the speeches more communicative. Some of them reported that, while interpreting the fast speaker, failure to omit redundancies would have made it impossible for them to interpret the more crucial elements. (2012: 110)

Korpal's findings indicate that interpreters, be they experienced or in training, purposefully use omissions as a strategy to deal with redundancy and to make communication more effective. Nonetheless, Korpal's study was designed to draw interpreters' attention to the "many digressions, hedges, discourse markers, cultural allusions and message redundancy" that he deliberately injected into the speeches used for his experiments. I contend that these injections had made these speeches unnatural because the deliberate insertion of redundant segments has inflated the degree of redundancy that usually occurs in a speech naturally given by a speaker, so much so that it would be impossible for one not to become aware of them and subsequently do something. One thus wonders how interpreters deal with redundancy of a lesser degree as in prepared or spontaneous speeches given by speakers in normal circumstances (i.e., where interpreting is needed for communication). Additionally, one wonders if Korpal's participants made omissions when interpreting segments that were not redundant in the way that he designed the speeches for his research.

The above mentioned studies all focus on spoken-language interpreting and have contributed to our understanding of the cognitive aspects of omissions. As is clear, however, no comprehensive study has yet been made of all kinds of omissions and, except for Korpal's understanding, most views of omissions are from the perspective of an external observer, rather than from the perspective of interpreters, whose input would be most useful for us to learn about the particularities of the complicated process that involves omissions in interpreting.

In contrast, Napier (2004) employed retrospective interviews to collate signed language interpreters' input when categorizing all the omissions she observed in her research. This is probably the first interpreting study to invite interpreters to talk about their interpreting process. Since Napier's framework will also be the framework for the current study, it will be presented in detail following my review of relevant research methodologies employed thus far.

2.3 Methodological Considerations

As the performance of interpreting involves speaking itself, typical methods of process research in written translation, such as Think Aloud Protocol (Ericsson and Simon 1984/1993), Screen Recording (Angelone 2012), and Keystroke Logging (Jakobsen 2014), "cannot be implemented in interpreting" (Gile 2011: 202), and retrospective introspective methods provide the major data for investigating interpreters' cognitive processing (Ahrens 2017: 448). This said, according to Ericsson and Simon (1984/1993), when used alone, retrospective introspective methods compromise the reliability of data if there is a delay of more than eight to ten seconds between task performance and retrospection. Studies such as Hansen (2006), Angelone (2015), and Vottonen and Jääskeläinen (cited in Jääskeläinen 2017) on the other hand have shown that the reliability of retrospection can be enhanced if combined with other methods. Since interpreters' omissions were used as cues in her retrospective interviews, Napier's research helped generate data on the cognitive process involving omissions in the way corroborated by Hansen (2006) and mitigated the reliability issue found by Ericsson and Simon (1984/1993). In the studies mentioned earlier, Korpal (2012) and Napier (2004) both employed retrospective methods with Napier being more specific and detailed with regard to the kinds of thought processes behind omissions.

With respect to sampling, the aforementioned empirical studies are modest in size in terms of both the number of participants and the length of speech used to generate the omission data. Altman (1994) recorded five students' French-English interpreting of five 2.5-minute-long speeches. Barik (1971) recorded the French-English and English-French interpreting by two professionals, two students, and two amateurs, and he standardized the length of the speech for investigation to 100 words. Gile (1999), and subsequently Pym (2008), examined the English-French interpreting by ten professionals interpreting a speech text of 245 words and lasting 1 minute and 40 seconds in delivery. Korpal (2012: 107) recruited eleven students and six professionals for his study, and "[t]he participants were asked to imagine they were interpreting for an audience at an international conference." He used two texts with different delivery rates, one lasting 2 minutes and 48 seconds at the speed of 177 wpm and 3 minutes and 48 seconds at the speed of 130 wpm and the other lasting 2 minutes and 51 seconds at the speed of 180 wpm and 3 minutes and 56 seconds at the speed of 130 wpm. The data source was English to Polish interpreting. Napier (2004) recruited ten English-Auslan ("Auslan" refers to the Australian Sign Language) professionals and the speech (extracted from a lecture) she used for interpreting was thirty minutes long.

3 Theoretical Framework

Napier's comprehensive categories of omissions reflect the cognitive focus that is important in a study of omissions. Unlike Gile (1995), Napier carried out her study by strictly following the definition of omissions by Barik (1971), though she did not make this perspective explicit, and thus captured all the cases and contexts where omissions occurred. Using retrospective interviews with interpreters together with their omissions in interpreting, she probed interpreters' accounts of their cognitive processes of omissions thus avoiding overt guesswork or conjecture. As Napier's study is on sign language interpreting and since no similar research into spoken-language interpreting exists, the current study is the first to attempt to give a cognitively focused account of omissions in simultaneous interpreting. This will allow us to see how signed language interpreting compares with spoken-language interpreting in terms of omissions. Napier's five categories of omissions are reproduced here (2004: 125):

1. *Conscious strategic omissions*—omissions made consciously by an interpreter, whereby a decision is made to omit information in order to

enhance the effectiveness of the interpretation. The interpreter applies his or her linguistic and cultural knowledge to decide what information from the source language makes sense in the target language, what information is culturally relevant, and what is redundant.
2. *Conscious intentional omissions*—omissions contributing to a loss of meaningful information. The interpreter is conscious of the omission and has opted for it intentionally due to a lack of understanding of a particular lexical item or concept, or an inability to retrieve an appropriate equivalent in the target language.
3. *Conscious unintentional omissions*—omissions that contribute to a loss of meaningful information. The interpreter is conscious of the omission, but has not chosen it intentionally. Having heard the lexical item, s/he decides to "file it" before interpreting it, waiting for more contextual information or depth of meaning. Due to further source-language input and lag time, however, the particular lexical item is not retrieved, and is ultimately omitted.
4. *Conscious receptive omissions*—omissions contributing to a loss of meaningful information. The interpreter is aware of these, but cannot properly decipher what was said, due to (reported) poor sound quality.
5. *Unconscious omissions*—omissions contributing to a loss of meaningful information. The interpreter is not conscious of the omission and does not recall hearing the particular lexical item(s).

4 Methodology

The current investigation seeks to study omissions in spoken-language interpreting by (1) examining the interpreting product and (2) examining interpreting students' own retrospective or reflective reports of what happened when omissions occurred during the course of interpreting. It comprises two parts: a quantitative part that classifies omissions utilizing Napier's framework for omissions (2004) and a qualitative part that details the reasons for the occurrence of the omissions as explained by the interpreters themselves in their retrospections.

4.1 Data Source

The data source of this research is seven MA dissertations on simultaneous interpreting. The dissertation in question is a practical project designed to introduce students to the major procedures of professional interpreting. The practical project required that a student examine one or two interpreting issues in their own interpreting learning that concerns or interests them particularly. For this purpose, they are free to choose an interpreting mode but are required to source on the internet an authentic speech or excerption of a speech delivered by a speaker within the last four years on a subject area interesting to them. The speech or speech excerption used for the project needs to be around thirty minutes long, and the delivery rate needs to be at 100–120 wpm, which is the optimal speed for interpreters according to Li (2010) and thus would enable students to focus on the interpreting issue(s) for examination. The project contains an element that asks students to prepare a glossary, to research the speaker of the sourced speech, and to gather relevant extralinguistic knowledge before interpreting. Students are required to design an interpreting brief similar to Korpal's (2012) but more detailed regarding speaker and audience information, as it needs to reflect the purpose of the event where the speech in question was delivered in real life. They are required to do their interpreting and then transcribe both the source speech and their interpreting in order to investigate their interpreting performance. Students' examination of their interpreting performance with respect to the chosen interpreting issue(s) amounts to an empirical study where they draw upon existing literature on the issue(s), look into the frequency of occurrences of the phenomenon or phenomena in question, and investigate the triggers leading to each occurrence as they recall them. Regular workshops are given over the academic year to prepare for the dissertation.

I believe data of omissions thus generated are more "naturalistic" than those reported in the existing literature and will therefore better capture the characteristics of omissions as they occur in real-life interpreting. As for the subjects' retrospective reflections of the triggers of their omissions, these were sourced as they were presented in the students' actual project. Since as students, the research subjects were free to choose a relevant theoretical framework to investigate their own performance regarding the specific interpreting issue(s), they were able to examine their performance at a depth that reflects "genuine self-reflection" and "how much knowledge the students have developed on the course" (Lambert 2022). The retrospective reports by the research subjects all drew upon concepts from Gile's Effort Model for simultaneous interpreting (2009).

4.2 Data

The data were collected between 2018 and 2021, covering four academic years, and they were drawn from those projects focused on omissions that achieved a Merit or Distinction score to ensure validity of the students' research. In total,

Table 5.1 Speeches generating omissions in SI

Subject	Interpreting Direction	Speech Source
S01	English-Italian	Theresa May: https://www.youtube.com/watch?v=6H6BCp31THU
S02	English-French	Theresa May: https://www.youtube.com/watch?v=m9OOF29xJmE
S03	English-Spanish	Kimberlé Crenshaw: https://www.youtube.com/watch?v=4_gnxRlRf9c&t=153s
S04	English-Chinese	Mark Zuckerberg: https://www.youtube.com/watch?v=QM8l623AouM&t=933s
S05	English-Chinese	Almeida Theatre and Andrew Scott: https://www.youtube.com/watch?v=H8MhNWVI6gU&list=WL&index=6&t=171s
S06	English-Chinese	Mark Zuckerberg: https://youtu.be/QM8l623AouM
S07	English-Chinese	President Biden: https://www.youtube.com/watch?v=FugQNYtbyz0

seven projects on omissions in SI using Napier's cognitive framework met the validity criterion and were thus selected for the current research. Data from these seven projects on omissions and the causes for omissions as detailed in the students' retrospective analyses are the data for the current research. Among them, one is interpreting from English to Italian, one from English to Spanish, one from English to French, and the rest from English to Mandarin Chinese. The students in question all interpreted into their mother tongue. Table 5.1 presents information on language pairs, interpreting direction and the speeches sourced by the seven students who chose to examine their omissions by drawing on Napier's framework.

5 Data Analysis Results

5.1 Results from Analysis of Omissions

Tables 5.2 and 5.3 present the data of omissions found in the current study in accordance with Napier's categories and answer the first research question. For easy comparisons, the data from the current study are presented alongside Napier's in both tables.[2]

Table 5.2 Total omissions made by all subjects across all categories

Current study		Napier's study	
Omission categories	Number of omissions (percentage)	Omission categories	Number of omissions (percentage)
Unconscious	187 (26.23%)	Unconscious	92 (27%)
Conscious strategic	145 (20.34%)	Conscious strategic	87 (26%)
Conscious intentional	219 (30.72%)	Conscious intentional	61 (18%)
Conscious receptive	9 (1.26%)	Conscious receptive	52 (15%)
Conscious unintentional	153 (21.46%)	Conscious unintentional	49 (14%)
Total omissions	713	Total omissions	341

Due to S02's project design, only her omissions of interpreting in the second half of her chosen speech and her corresponding retrospections are used in the current study.

Table 5.3 Total and types of omission per subject

Current study

Omissions per subject per category	subject 1	2	3	4	5	6	7
Conscious strategic	11 (13.92%)	5 (4.31%)	18 (13.43%)	17 (47.22%)	41 (27.33%)	14 (26.42%)	39 (26.90%)
Conscious intentional	34 (43.04%)	22 (18.97%)	56 (41.79%)	11 (30.56%)	32 (21.33%)	20 (37.74%)	44 (30.34%)
Conscious unintentional	10 (12.66%)	13 (11.21%)	22 (16.42%)	2 (5.56%)	52 (34.67%)	7 (13.21%)	47 (32.41%)
Conscious receptive	9 (11.38%)	0	0	0	0	0	0
Unconscious	15 (18.99%)	76 (65.52%)	38 (28.36%)	6 (16.67%)	25 (16.67%)	12 (22.64%)	15 (10.34%)
Total (percentage)	99.99	100.01	100	100.01	100	100.01	99.99
Total number of omissions	79	116	134	36	150	53	145

Napier's study

Omissions per subject per category (in %)	Subject 1	2	3	4	5	6	7	8	9	10
Conscious strategic	32.3	14	18	31.5	16.5	26.8	30	31	24.5	33.5
Conscious intentional	26.5	30	16	17.5	16.5	6.7	24	7	17.5	9
Conscious unintentional	14.7	10	9	19.5	28	16.5	12.5	17.5	13.5	12
Conscious receptive	3	22	20.5	12	22.5	20	12.5	10	13.5	15.5
Unconscious	23.5	24	36.5	19.5	16.5	30	21	34.5	31	30
Total (%)	100	100	100	100	100	100	100	100	100	100
Total (number of omissions)	(34)	(54)	(44)	(41)	(18)	(30)	(33)	(29)	(29)	(33)

Table 5.2 shows that like Napier's research subjects, those in the current study made all of the five types of omission in their interpreting. This indicates that interpreters, whether in training (as in the current study) or experienced (as in Napier's study), all make omissions.

On the other hand, compared with Napier's subjects, those in the current study had fewer conscious strategic omissions (20.34 percent vs. 26 percent) but many more conscious intentional omissions (30.72 percent vs. 18 percent) and conscious unintentional omissions (21.46 percent vs. 14 percent). It is also noticeable that conscious receptive omissions in the current study occurred less frequently than they did in Napier's study. The fact that the subjects for the current study are all interpreting trainees may explain the relatively lower rate of occurrence of conscious strategic omissions and the higher rates of conscious intentional and conscious unintentional omissions: since they are being trained, they might not be confident in actively employing conscious strategic omission to achieve effectiveness of communication and their limited cognitive capacity might force them to omit either intentionally or unintentionally. However, it was surprising that the current study generated much fewer conscious receptive omissions. Further examination of the triggers as reported in the next section reveals something very interesting in this regard that I believe will also have implications for interpreter training.

Table 5.3 shows greater variations in the occurrence of omissions between subjects in the current study than in Napier's. For instance, the rate of unconscious omissions in the current study fluctuates between 10.34 percent and 65.52 percent, whereas this rate only fluctuates between 16.5 percent and 36.5 percent for Napier's participants. For another instance, the rate of conscious strategic omissions can be as low as 4.31 percent or as high as 47.22 percent in the current study, whereas the figure for Napier's study is respectively 14 percent and 33.5 percent. Again, the fact that the participants in the current study are trainees is the likely explanation for this tendency. However, the occurrence of conscious receptive omissions in the current study was attributed to just one participant while in Napier's study all participants had such incidents. This made it very important to investigate the reasons for these omissions.

5.2 Results from Analyzing the Triggers of Omissions

Data on the triggers of omissions were collected from the examples provided by each of the research subjects when they tried to illustrate the types of triggers for their omissions, so this part of the current study is of a qualitative nature. In total, the following seven causes led the research subjects to omit and provide answers to the second research question for the current study.

Type 1 trigger: redundancies, unnecessary repetitions, false starts or restarts and fillers on the speaker's part, and rendering considerations due to target language/culture

Example 1

> **Speaker:** To become that Britain where a thriving economy drives up living standards and creates greater security and opportunity for everyone [. . .] we need education to be the key that unlocks the door to a better future. Through education, we can become a country where everyone, from every background, gains the skills they need to get a good job and live a happy and fulfilled life.
>
> **Interpreter:** Per diventare quella Gran Bretagna dove l'economia guida gli standard di vita e crea grande sicurezza e opportunità per tutti [. . .], noi

abbiamo bisogno di un sistema scolastico che sia la chiave che apra le porte ad un futuro migliore.

In this example, the student completely omitted the last sentence of the ST. According to her, this is because she felt the sentence "was repetitive and redundant," because "[t]hroughout the speech, Theresa May [mentioned] repeatedly the fact that through education the United Kingdom can become a country where everyone gets the skills they need to do the job they want and live happily." By omitting, the student says, "I avoided burdening the speech with a piece of information that had already been said, and I also made up for the time that I had previously lost and resumed the rhythm of the Prime Minister."

Example 2

> **Speaker:** I'm honored to be here with you today because, let's face it, you accomplished something I never could.
>
> **Interpreter:** 我非常荣幸能够来到这里，因为你们完成了我从来没有完成的事情。

In this example, the student omitted "let's face it." According to her, expressions like "you see," "I know," and "let's face it" are "all empty gap fillers." The speech in question is a commencement speech given by Mark Zuckerberg at Harvard University. In the student's view, it is not as formal as government speeches, "so the speaker would use some informal words including empty fillers to allow a moment to pause and to connect the two sentences more naturally. However, these gap fillers have no meanings at all. They would not affect communications, so they are redundant. . . . Therefore, these empty fillers were omitted to avoid redundancy."

The decision by all the research subjects to omit because of redundancy issues in a source speech aligns well with Napier's category of omissions as a conscious strategy and was viewed by the subjects as a technique instead of a mistake. On top of this, some students also chose to omit because of redundancies for a given target language/culture, as illustrated in the following example.

Example 3

> **Speaker**: in order to defeat this evil ideology.
>
> **Interpreter**: pour pouvoir combattre et vaincre cette idéologie.

In this example, the interpreter did not render the word "evil," "as in French adding a description to the ideology, which is already known to be evil by its previous descriptions, would sound somewhat unusual." In her retrospection, the interpreter said, "I still feel strongly about this decision, as even in hindsight, none of the potential translations I can think of seem to fit the SS intended effect (e.g., 'idéologie du mal/du diable/néfaste'), as they either sound redundant or exaggerated."

This finding suggests that while actively seeking to achieve effective communication, interpreters not only actively analyze a source speech for redundancies but also try to analyze the target language or culture.

Type 2 trigger: comprehension problems on the interpreter's part
Example 4

>**Speaker**: When I was in Dublin and when I was 21 at the Gate Theatre in Dublin, I was doing Long Day's Journey into Night there, they spoke to me about doing a young 30 Hamlet [...]
>**Interpreter**: 我当时二十一岁，在都柏林，他们跟我说可不可以做一个新的哈姆雷特 [...]

In the interpretation, the interpreter failed to interpret "Gate Theatre" and "Long Day's into Night." She recalled that "I had never heard of the two names before and felt so confused the moment I heard them out of his mouth that I did not respond in time to interpret them.... In hindsight, the omission could have been avoided, if I did my research more thoroughly on the speaker's bio in the preparation stage."

Example 5

>**Speaker**: As luck would have it, Priscilla was at that party with her friends.
>**Interpreter**: 但是呢当时Priscilla 和她的朋友在那个聚会上。

In this example, the interpreter did not understand "As luck would have it." As a result, she "had to omit the whole [clause] to continue with my interpreting of the following part, but the entire simultaneous interpreting performance was impacted."

Type 3 trigger: production problems on the interpreter's part
Example 6

>**Speaker**: You know, today, our society spends more than 50 times as much treating people that are sick as we invest in finding cures so people don't get sick in the first place.

Interpreter: 那么今天我们的社会花很多的钱来治疗病人，而不是去研究治疗的方法。

In this example, the trigger for the omission of "more than 50 times as much" is the complex syntax "as ... as ..." in combination with the two V-ing constituents. The student reported that because of this contextual complexity, the comparative structure, as much as it was easy to understand, was hard to deliver in Chinese, and that therefore she chose to omit to save some processing capacity.

Example 7

Speaker: How about Lowell? (Cheering) I know you guys found community because you literally live right on top of each other. (Laughter) And Mather?

Interpreter: Lowell 呢？我知道你们有社区。Mather 呢？

In this example, the speaker was joking. The student reported that she found it hard to interpret jokes and humor. "I did not quite understand the jokes Zuckerberg made in his speech, so I had no choice but to omit." The student was also aware that because of such omissions, "the expected communication between the speaker and the listeners has not been well achieved as well."

Example 8

Speaker: Not more likely than their sisters who were growing up in the same households, parented by the same mothers who were struggling in the same social economic conditions.

Interpreter: No más propensos que sus hermanas quienes crecieron en la misma casa que ellos, con las mismas madres, con las mismas dificultades económicas.

Here, the speaker was arguing against the belief that boys are more likely to suffer from disadvantages than their female peers. The word "parented" was omitted. According to the interpreter, "I could not think of the equivalent in Spanish."

Type 4 trigger: improper allocation of attentional resources on the interpreter's part

Example 9

Speaker: Well it came from the idea that Rob and I would like to work with each other.

Interpreter: 是这样的，这源自于一个想法就是罗伯和我一起合作。

In this case, the speaker was introducing the origin of the idea of this reproduction, which was that the director and he wanted to work together. The omission of "would like to" is unintended. But what happened, as reported here, which led the interpreter to omit, was:

> At first, I heard the sentence starting with "it came from the idea that," and decided to wait for the sentence to be finished because apparently there must be something after "that." After finishing listening to this part, I started to render the information I received, but at the same time still was listening to the speaker as demanded by simultaneous interpreting. In retrospect, I found that this omission was a result of inappropriate allocation of available processing capacities between Efforts (Gile 2009). Specifically, I directed too much attention to the listening of the next part, and thus did not leave enough capacity to produce the previously heard segment of the source speech, which led to an omission.

Type 5 trigger: saturation/overload of cognitive capacity

Example 10

> **Speaker**: In just one year more than three in four U.S. Millennials donated to charity and more than seven in ten raise money for another one.
>
> **Interpreter**: 那么在一年里面，超过四分之三的美国人发起了捐款，有十分之七的人会帮人家筹款。

In this case, "more than" was omitted in its second occurrence in the speaker's speech. The interpreter reported that she was unconscious of the omission. In her words, this is because "the speaker was too fast on this part and nearly all my mental energy was employed to keep up with the speaker's pace and process the numbers in the sentence (which are one of my biggest weaknesses in interpreting). As a result, I could not recall hearing it or if [I interpreted] it at that time."

Type 6 trigger: failure sequence

Example 11

> **Speaker**: capping hundreds of thousands of literally orphan oil and gas wells that need to be cleaned up because they're abandoned.
>
> **Interpreter**: 并且用成千数百的 ... 那些被废弃的油矿等，他们需要被清洁，因为他们已经被放弃了。

In this example, the student omitted "literally" and "gas wells" in her interpreting. Her analysis of what in the interpreting process led to the omissions is as follows:

Notice that the word "literally" was omitted. This word is not hard to understand at all, and the literal translation is "逐字的" or "真实的," but it does not carry the sense when it is used as an English expression. The original text says "literally orphan oil," the word "literally" is used to describe "orphan," and without successfully rendering the word "literally," the "orphan" thus cannot be translated literally as "孤儿" either. Several decisions were made within seconds, the mental processing capacity was easily saturated, which naturally led to further omission of the "gas wells" because no extra capacity could be allocated to decipher this phrase. For this kind of situation, short term preparation couldn't help much. Instead, the interpreter should form the habit of finding equivalence in all aspects of languages, including everyday conversations.

This case therefore illustrates what Gile (1995) and Gumul (2018) categorize as failure sequence where "[b]ecause of the time pressure inherent in SI, the way one segment is processed affects the availability of processing capacity for handling further incoming segments"(Gumul 2018: 23). The example is a case where one omission leads to another. The following example is a case where a different issue led to an omission in a failure sequence.

Example 12

> **Speaker**: In the broader international community funding for women's rights sometimes has been framed as modernisation. Just a little beyond civilisation. Sometimes through the saviour lens.
> **Interpreter**: En la comunidad internacional, la financiación para los derechos de la mujer se enmarcó como "modernización." Sólo un poco más allá que la civilización.

Here, the interpreter omitted "Sometimes through the saviour lens" in a passage where "the speaker critically points out that women's rights even need to go through God's test and approval." She recalled that "I do not recall hearing this part, which is largely due to a lack of focus. In previous lines, I had to face a difficult passage, failing to interpret adequately, which explains why my focus clearly weakened." The interpreter recalled that this is "only one example of many" where "how cognitive overload hindered my rendition and lead me to commit unintentional omissions."

Type 7 trigger: interference of surroundings
Example 13

> **Speaker:** So, by focusing on these four key priorities, making tertiary education accessible to all, promoting choice and competition in the sector,

> [. . .] we can give every young person access to an education that suits their skills and aspirations. One which opens up possibilities for their future and helps them into a rewarding career.
>
> **Interpreter:** Quindi focalizzandoci su quattro priorità fondamentali, ovvero, rendere il sistema di istruzione universitaria accessibile a tutti, promuovere la scelta e la competizione nel settore, [. . .] possiamo dare a tutti giovani la possibilità di accedere ad un'istruzione che sia adatta alle competenze e alle loro aspirazioni.

According to the interpreter, here in this example, "[t]he first sentence was dense of information and unfortunately, because of my voice, I did not hear very well the next one," hence its omission. In Napier (2004: 125), receptive omissions happen "due to (reported) poor sound quality." While the reported poor sound quality in Napier is from the external environment, in the current study, what led to the poor sound quality was found, for the first time, to be the interpreter's own voice, which drowns the speaker's or in the student's words is "too high to overwhelm that of the speaker and consequently I do not understand well what is said."

6 Conclusions and Discussions

This chapter reported the findings from studying spoken-language interpreting trainees' omissions in their simultaneous interpreting and their retrospective examination of what caused them to make omissions. Although omissions in spoken-language interpreting have been known in relevant literature, no study has attempted to capture their full picture, especially from a cognitive perspective. The current study is the first of such attempts and compared with most relevant research reported in the literature, it explores a relatively large volume of data. The data on omissions from a cognitive point of view show that, just like sign language interpreters, spoken-language interpreters also make five types of omissions. The data from the retrospective reports reveal seven types of triggers for omissions, ranging from the recognition of a source speaker's ineffectiveness, the interpreter's comprehension and production difficulties, the interpreter's cognitive loads, to external environmental factors. The current study has provided empirical evidence for the existence of all five types of omissions, with some being clearly errors (which has often been under scholarly discussion) whereas some helping facilitate interpreting quality (which has not been studied previously in spoken-language interpreting). Together with Napier's study, the current study has therefore expanded our understanding of omissions. Additionally, the current study has for the first time identified interpreters' own voice as an external factor leading to receptive omissions. Whereas this factor may not be observable among professional interpreters (e.g., those in Napier's study), this was observed to happen in interpreting students. This finding, along with the remaining findings from the current study, will have implications for interpreter training. For example, interpreting trainers may develop guidance and strategies for how to do advance preparation, how to improve source and target language proficiency, how to improve attention allocation, and how to adjust interpreters' voice quality. As Gile states,

> [b]y concentrating on the *reasons* for errors or good choices in Translation rather than on the specific words or language structures selected/produced by the students, teachers devote most of their effective teaching time to Translation *strategies*, *tactics* and *skills* which can be generalized, and lose little time dealing with Translation solutions to specific words and structures in the source Text from which extrapolations can be more problematic. (2009: 15)

Secondly, both omissions and their triggers in the current study are identified from students' self-monitoring. The students' retrospective reports show a good depth of understanding of the interpreting issue at both a theoretical and a practical level, thus contributing to raising interpreting students' awareness. This will help them improve their interpreting learning and interpreting quality. I hope the current study will encourage more interpreting students to conduct self-monitoring in order to "update and develop competences and skills through personal strategies and collaborative learning" (EMT 2022: 10).

Thirdly, subject to further investigation, the current study may potentially contribute to theorization of the simultaneous interpreting process. The retrospective reports by students show interpreters' awareness of risks as termed by Pym (2008) when they made the decisions to omit. I argue that the risk analysis effort on the part of the interpreter is part of the Coordination Effort in Gile's Effort Model. Whereas experienced interpreters may be better at risk analysis for omissions, trainees may need guidance in how to draw upon contextual factors surrounding a speech so as to make better decisions regarding high- and low-risk omissions.

An interesting point raised in the current study concerns the labels "conscious strategic omissions" and "conscious intentional omissions." Unlike previous studies, both the current study and that by Napier (2004) show that omission is not a passive technique but can be an active decision made by interpreters in their effort to produce good interpreting quality. The categories "conscious strategic omissions" and "conscious intentional omissions" are clear evidence for such efforts, and both can thus be understood as "strategies," although they differ in that the former type of omission is not error whereas the latter type is. As one of the research subjects noted:

> it is worth mentioning that although sometimes omissions fall under category of "conscious intentional omissions" and indeed cause loss in meanings, the effect on the final interpretation is minimal, and if giving up this word can guarantee the meaning of the whole sentence is correct, it can be viewed as a strategy to some extent.

I agree with this view and believe future studies may modify the labelling to distinguish between an effective strategy and an intended coping technique. Nonetheless, I believe Napier's categories help reveal from a cognitive point of view significant details of the interpreting process surrounding omissions.[3]

Finally, the current study is not without limitations. Like most existing studies reviewed earlier, the sample size is modest, and then there is the imbalance in the number of language pairs assessed. Both are due to the naturalistic nature of the study itself as it was not conducted under controlled conditions. Despite these, I hope the study will encourage more similar studies to come, more language pairs for examination, and more importantly will encourage more similar reflective learning on the part of future interpreting trainees. Additionally, the data source is dissertation, an important piece of work assessed for a postgraduate degree. The nature of the work being an assessment may affect the range of student reflections, though the students on the dissertation module had all the freedom to study their interpreting issue(s) and reflect on their performance.

Notes

1 Unless otherwise stated, this word with the capitalized "t" is used to refer to both translation and interpreting.
2 In Tables 5.2 and 5.3, the data source for Napier's study is respectively Table 1 and Table 2 of Napier (2004), cited with permission of the publisher.
3 But see Zhong (2020) where the other three types of omission are subsumed together and labeled as errors instead.

References

Ahrens, B. (2017), "Interpretation and Cognition," in J. W. Schwieter and A. Ferreira (eds.), *The Handbook of Translation and Cognition*, 445–60. Hoboken: Wiley Blackwell.

Altman, J. (1994), "Error Analysis in the Teaching of Simultaneous Interpretation: A Pilot Study," in S. Lambert and B. Moser-Mercer (eds.), *Bridging the Gap: Empirical Research in Simultaneous Interpretation*, 25–38, Amsterdam and Philadelphia: John Benjamins Publishing.

Angelone, E. (2012), "The Place of Screen Recording in Process-Oriented Translator Training," *Rivista Internazionale di Tecnica della Traduzione*, 14: 41–56.

Angelone, E. (2015), "The Impact of Process Protocol Self-analysis on Errors in the Translation Product," in M. Ehrensberger-Dow, B. Englund Dimitrova, S. Hubscher-Davidson, and U. Norberg (eds.), *Describing Cognitive Processes in Translation*, 105–23, Amsterdam, Netherlands ; Philadelphia: John Benjamins.

Barik, H. C. (1971), "A Description of Various Types of Omissions, Additions and Errors of Translation Encountered in Simultaneous Interpretation," *Meta*, 16(4): 199–210. https://doi.org/10.7202/001972ar

EMT (European Master's in Translation) (2022), "European Master's in Translation - Competence Framework 2022." https://commission.europa.eu/system/files/2022-11/emt_competence_fwk_2022_en.pdf (accessed October 2022).

Ericsson, K. A. and H. A. Simon (1984/1993), *Protocol Analysis: Verbal Reports as Data*, Cambridge, MA: MIT Press.

Ferreira, A. and J. W. Schwieter (2017), "Translation and Cognition: An Overview," in J. W. Schwieter and A. Ferreira (eds.), *The Handbook of Translation and Cognition*, 3–17, Hoboken: Wiley Blackwell.

Gile, D. (1995), *Basic Concepts and Models for Interpreter and Translator Training*, Amsterdam: John Benjamins Publishing.

Gile D. (1999), "Testing the Effort Models' Tightrope Hypothesis in Simultaneous Interpreting – A Contribution," *Hermes*, 23: 153–72.

Gile, D. (2009), *Basic Concepts and Models for Interpreter and Translator Training*, Amsterdam: John Benjamins.

Gile, D. (2011), "Errors, Omissions and Infelicities in Broadcast Interpreting: Preliminary Findings from a Case Study," in C. Alvstad, A. Hild, and E. Tiselius (eds.), *Methods and Strategies of Process Research: Integrative Approaches in Translation Studies*, 201–18, Amsterdam and Philadelphia: John Benjamins Publishing.

Gumul, E. (2018), "Searching for Evidence of Gile's Effort Models in Retrospective Protocols of Trainee Simultaneous Interpreters," *Między Oryginałem a Przekładem*, 24(42): 17–39. https://doi.org/10.12797/MOaP.24.2018.42.02

Hansen, G. (2006), "Retrospection Methods in Translator Training and Translation Research," *Journal of Specialised Translation*, 5: 2–41.

Jääskeläinen, R. (2017), "Verbal Reports," in John W. Schwieter and Aline Ferreira (eds.), *The Handbook of Translation and Cognition*, 211–31, Hoboken: Wiley Blackwell.

Jakobsen, A. L. (2014), "The Development and Current State of Translation Process Research," in E. Brems, R. Meylaerts, and L. van Doorsler (eds.), *The Known Unknowns of Translation*, 65–88, Amsterdam and Philadelphia: John Benjamins Publishing.

Korpal, P. (2012), "Omission in Simultaneous Interpreting as a Deliberate Act," in A. Pym and D. Orrego-Carmona (eds.), *Translation Research Projects 4*, 103–11, Tarragona: Intercultural Studies Group.

Lambert, J. (2022), Cardiff University, personal communication on external examination.

Li, C. (2010), "Coping Strategies for Fast Delivery in Simultaneous Interpretation," *The Journal of Specialised Translation*, 13: 19–25.

Muñoz Martín, R. (2017), "Looking Toward the Future of Cognitive Translation Studies," in John W. Schwieter and A. Ferreira (eds.), *The Handbook of Translation and Cognition*, 555–72, Hoboken: Wiley Blackwell.

Napier, J. (2004), "Interpreting Omissions: A New Perspective," *Interpreting*, 6(2): 117–42. https://doi.org/10.1075/intp.6.2.02nap

Pym, A. (2008), "On Omission in Simultaneous Interpreting: Risk Analysis of a Hidden Effort," in G. Hansen et al. (eds.), *Efforts and Models in Interpreting and Translation Research: A Tribute to Daniel Gile*, 83–105, Amsterdam and Philadelphia: John Benjamins Publishing.

Zhong, H. (2020), "An Observational Study of Simultaneous Interpreting: Towards a Thick Description of Norms with Regard to Omission," in *Interdependenzen und Innovationen in Translation und Fachkommunikation: Interdependence and Innovation in Translation, Interpreting and Specialised Communication*, 187–203, Berlin: Frank and Timme GmbH.

6

Interpreting as Communicative and Sociocultural Interaction

Binhua Wang

1 A Critical Overview of the Cognitive Approach to Interpreting Studies

Since the 1960s, interpreting has often been investigated from the cognitive approach. Cognitive processing has always been a major focus in interpreting studies. To experimental psychologists, cognitive psychologists, and psycholinguists, interpreting offers many fascinating elements that an object of study can provide: it is bilingual processing, in which the interpreter performs language comprehension and language production in real time; it is also extreme language processing because both comprehension and production have to be completed immediately due to the time constraints in interpreting; and the process is natural and authentic to an extent that few artificial experiments can simulate. Even in recent years when the computer has become smarter with artificial intelligence, people would still wonder at the "amazing brains of the real-time interpreters." As a *BBC Future* special column journalist observed in his article, "The world's most powerful computers can't perform accurate real-time interpreting of one language to another. Yet human interpreters do it with ease. [. . .] Executing it required versatility and nuance beyond the reach of the most powerful computers. It is a wonder that her brain, indeed any human brain, can do it at all" (Watts 2014).

The cognitive approach to interpreting studies was first initiated by psychologists in the 1960s and 1970s, who explored the cognitive process in interpreting from the interdisciplinary vantage of experimental psychology. For example, Oléron and Nanpon (1965) measured ear-voice span (EVS) between speakers and interpreters in experiments. Goldman-Eisler (1967)examined simultaneity of comprehension and production in simultaneous interpreting. Gerver (1971) related errors to speech rates of the input in simultaneous interpreting and shadowing. Their studies, though later were criticized for lacking ecological validity, were picked up again by researchers in the experimental paradigm with renewed experimental tools in recent years.

In the 1990s interpreting studies in the cognitive approach were represented by Daniel Gile's works on cognitive management in interpreting. In his seminal book on interpreter and translator training he proposed the "Effort Models" about the interpreting process (Gile 1995), which can be summarized as follows: in simultaneous interpreting the cognitive efforts that need to be managed include listening and analysis effort, short-term memory effort, production effort, and coordination efforts; in Phase 1 of consecutive interpreting the cognitive efforts that need to be managed include listening and analysis effort, note-taking effort, and coordination effort; in Phase 2 of consecutive interpreting the cognitive efforts that need to be managed include remembering effort, note-reading effort, and production effort. As operational requirements of the effort modules, during the interpreting process the cognitive capacity requirement of any single effort or the total requirement of all the effort modules must not exceed the cognitive capacity availability of any single effort or the total availability (Gile 1995: 169–80). Later, Gile proposed the "tightrope hypothesis" about cognitive management in interpreting, which highlighted that "for most of the time, interpreters work near saturation level [of their cognitive capacity]" (Gile 1999). These models still await more evidence from empirical testing about management of cognitive efforts in the interpreting process because they are theoretical or hypothetical models.

In the past few decades after the initial explorations of the experimental psychologists in the 1970s, the psycholinguistic and behavioral approaches have continued to date with an interest in simultaneous interpreting specifically (e.g., Moser 1978; Fabbro and Darò 1995; Fabbro and Gran 1997; Lambert and Moser-Mercer 1994; Dong and Wang 2013; Dong and Lin 2013) and bilingual language processing in general (e.g., Macizo and Bajo 2004; De Groot and Christoffels 2006). A common feature in these approaches is breaking down the overall cognitive process of interpreting into component tasks so as to analyze and understand the cognitive processes involved. Most attention has focused on the following component tasks such as auditory speech processing, working memory, syntactic parsing, meaning assembly, articulatory suppression, and so on. The main results of these studies are cognitive models of the interpreting process, which have been developed to describe the temporal flow and sequence of processes in interpreting. For example, Moser's (1978: 355) complex "processing model of simultaneous interpreting" hypothesized the temporal flow of all the cognitive components of simultaneous interpreting. Macizo and Bajo's (2004) proposed the "vertical-approach" model, which depicted the vertical sequence of processes involved in translation and interpreting, including the processes of linguistic input, lexical, syntactic, and discourse in understanding the source language (SL) and through the link of "abstract" proceeding to the processes of lexical, syntactic, discourse, and linguistic input in production of the target language (TL); they also proposed the "horizontal-approach" model, in which they argue that code switching happens at lexical, syntactic, and discourse levels across the understanding and the production stages. Dong and Wang (2013) proposed two hypotheses about the time order of comprehension and production in interpreting and how they are different from general language processing, which were tested in Dong and Lin (2013). They are: (1) the hypothesis of "parallel processing" at the stage of SL comprehension, which posits that in interpreting SL comprehension is usually accompanied by the parallel processing of TL reconstruction and that TL reconstruction during SL comprehension merges with SL deverbalization through the function of incremental processing; (2) the hypothesis about TL production, which posits that TL production is mainly meaning driven, though it may sometimes be construction driven.

In recent years thanks to the advancement of research equipment in neuroscience, such as eye tracker and neuroimaging fMRI, it has become possible to observe more directly the "black box" of the interpreters' brain, which helps to reveal the neurobiological foundation of the cognitive process in interpreting. For example, Elmer, Jänggi, and Jäncke (2014) found that processing demands upon cognitive, linguistic, and articulatory functions promote grey matter plasticity in the multilingual brain of simultaneous interpreters; Hervais-Adelman et al. (2015) revealed the neural basis of extreme language control through functional magnetic resonance imaging (fMRI) of simultaneous interpreting. It is particularly interesting to look at the large-scale neuroscience study of novice interpreters that was carried out by Hervais-Adelman's team (Hervais-Adelman et al. 2015), which used fMRI to observe the relative levels of brain activation during task performance of simultaneous interpreting in comparison with shadowing. It identified simultaneous interpreting cerebral activation in the basal ganglia, which are subcortical structures that form the basis of our ability to select, plan, learn, and execute actions and have been found to play a significant role in higher cognitive functions such as motivation and decision-making. This study reveals the neural basis of extremely rapid decision-making in simultaneous interpreting.

In summary, the cognitive approach to interpreting studies has focused on the cognitive operation, management of cognitive load/efforts in the interpreting process, and their neurophysiological foundation. In this approach some researchers proposed hypothetical models about cognitive operation of the interpreting process or about management of cognitive load/efforts; other researchers conducted experiments with simulated or decontextualized tasks to test hypothesis about cognitive processing in interpreting.

2 Necessity of Going Beyond the Decontextualized Cognitive Approach—as Seen from Real-Life Examples in Interpreting

As rightly pointed out by Linell (1997: 52), studies on human communication are dominated by the alternatives of two basic models, that is, the conduit model and the social-interactionist model. The former model is monological and views the interpreter as only a recipient of what the speaker says and a conduit of information transfer. The latter model is dialogical and views the interpreter as coparticipant of the interlocution and interpreting as interaction in the communicative situation and the sociocultural contexts. As seen from real-life events mediated by interpreting, interpreting is much more than cognitive operation and management of cognitive load/efforts. Interpreting is conducted for the purpose of ensuring cross-lingual, cross-social, and cross-cultural communication between monolingual interlocutors that are separated by the language barrier. Whether such communication is accomplished successfully or unsuccessfully relies not only on whether the interpreter can complete the cognitive process of interpreting but also on the communicative and sociocultural interaction coparticipated by all the parties (e.g., the source-language speaker, the interpreter, and the target-language speaker) (ref. Linell 1997: 55).

For example, in business interpreting and in diplomatic interpreting in the language combination between English and Chinese, a typical scenario that almost every interpreter would experience is receiving the guest or the guest delegation in the airport, in which if the host is Chinese, they would always greet the guests with "您一路辛苦了" [Literal gloss: You must be very tired on your way.]. However, if the sentence is interpreted literally as "You must be very tired on your way," the guests from the Western culture would get offended because they don't want to be seen as weak physically. The intended meaning of the

Chinese sentence, however, is to show hospitality and care of the host, which is a typical greeting frequently used when receiving guests in Chinese culture. In this scenario the interpreter needs to take into account of the communicative function and sociocultural interaction so as to render the sentence into a greeting "Have you had a nice flight?," which has the same intended meaning as the original. Therefore, translating the sentence into English and completing the cognitive process of interpreting is far from achieving the goal of the interpreting task.

Communicative and sociocultural interaction is an obvious and typical feature for liaison/dialogue/community interpreting, but it is worth noting that it is equally important to conference interpreting. Many similar examples can be found in headline international news reports. For example, on March 8, 2014, the Malaysia Airlines Flight MH370, with 239 people on board, was en route from Kuala Lumpur to Beijing when air traffic control lost contact with it. The disappearance of the plane became breaking news that were widely reported worldwide. After searching for sixteen days, on March 24, 2014, Malaysian prime minister Najib Razak held a press conference, which was broadcast live by the China Central TV in Beijing and the Phoenix TV in Hong Kong, which was simultaneously interpreted from English into Chinese by two separate interpreters, respectively, for each TV channel. In this press conference the Malaysian prime minister made an important statement about MH370: "I must inform you that, according to this new data, Flight MH370 **ended** in the southern Indian Ocean." (The boldface is added by the author for emphasis, as in other examples below.) And both interpreters, in spite of the fact that they did their interpreting independently in two different cities (one in Beijing and the other in Hong Kong), chose to interpret the sentence "Flight MH370 **ended** in the southern Indian Ocean" into "马航MH370坠毁于南印度洋" [Literal gloss: Flight MH370 **crashed** in the southern Indian Ocean.]. This prompted many protests in China and in Chinese (social) media disputing the prime minister's hasty conclusion that the plane was "crashed." He consequently had to make another official statement to clarify that he had never concluded that the plane actually "crashed" (坠毁). This example shows an extreme case that an interpreting decision of the simple word, "ended," which is not cognitively challenging for the interpreter, can have serious consequences in the social and communicative context.

More recently in July 2021, a phrase within the following sentence in a speech made by the Chinese president in his address to the celebration on the 100th anniversary of the Chinese Communist Party, which was interpreted into English, became an international media headline.

The speech text in Chinese: "中国人民从来没有欺负、压迫、奴役过其他国家人民，过去没有，现在没有，将来也不会有。同时，中国人民也绝不允许任何外来势力欺负、压迫、奴役我们，谁妄想这样干，必将在14亿多中国人民用血肉筑成的钢铁长城面前碰得头破血流！"

[Literal gloss: The Chinese people have never bullied, oppressed or subjugated people of any nations—have never been in the past, are not doing so now and will never do in future. Also, the Chinese people do not allow any foreign forces to bully, oppress or subjugate us. Anyone who tries to do so will find their head broken and blood flowing against the Great Wall of steel built with the flesh and blood of more than 1.4 billion Chinese people!]

The sentence was rendered in English by *New York Times* and *BBC News* as follows:

New York Times: "The Chinese people will never allow foreign forces to bully, oppress or enslave us. Whoever nurses delusions of doing that will **crack their heads and spill blood** on the Great Wall of steel built from the flesh and blood of 1.4 billion Chinese people."[1]

BBC News: "We will never allow anyone to bully, oppress or subjugate China. Anyone who dares try to do that will **have their heads bashed bloody** against the Great Wall of Steel forged by over 1.4 billion Chinese people."[2]

According to David Rennie, *The Economist*'s Beijing bureau chief and columnist, who knows the Chinese language and China well, those were not accurate renditions of the phrase used in the original Chinese speech. As he observed:

"This shouldn't be hard [to understand]: A) some Chengyu [idioms] sound more aggressive to foreign ears; B) it's risky to use a violent-sounding one in a line about foreigners. As a thought experiment, Trump loved to say rivals 'choked like a dog.' If he'd used that about Xi, what would China reax be?"[3]

Actually, the phrase "头破血流" is one of those Chinese idioms that have lost their literal meaning in daily usage over the years. To Chinese ears it emphasizes the meaning of "total failure" in this context, rather than the literal meaning "head skull broken and blood flowing." Just like another idiom used widely in Chinese "粉身碎骨，在所不辞": rather than its literal meaning "Even my body and bones will need to be crushed and smashed, I will not flinch," it is used to express a sense of determination in conquering difficulty.

Therefore, the on-site interpreter interpreted President Xi's sentence as: "We will never allow anyone to bully, oppress or subjugate us. Anyone who would attempt to do so will **find themselves on a collision course** with a great wall of steel forged by over 1.4 billion Chinese people."

From these examples, it is clear that on top of complex operation of cognitive processes and management of cognitive efforts, interpreting also requires mediation of meaning taking into account of communication and sociocultural interaction. This transition of mindset is necessary and important because the interpreter can easily be seen as a "conduit" in interpreting when the qualified interpreter often fulfils the job of bridging cross-lingual and cross-cultural communication successfully. The speaker and audiences from different languages and cultures communicate through the interpreter so smoothly that people tend to neglect the various complex facets involved in interpreting. Just like the general public who always assume that everything just flows via the interpreter from the speaker to the listener and across language and cultural barriers easily, it seems that many researchers in the tradition of cognitive approach only focus on how intriguing the interpreter can manage to juggle with so many cognitive "balls"—listening, analysis, memorizing, note-taking, and speaking in another language—and can do so under the time constraint within split second after hearing the source speech. This might also explain why so many efforts in interpreting studies have been devoted to cognitive processing during the past several decades.

3 The Communicative Situation and Sociocultural Context as Major Variables Shaping the Interpreting Performance and Product

Although during the past several decades the mainstream efforts in (conference) interpreting studies have focused on cognitive operation and management in the interpreting process, they have not covered all the grounds about interpreting. While the cognitive process is pivotal in interpreting and has always been perceived as most intriguing by researchers in interpreting studies and beyond, it is important to be aware that the interpreting performance and product are shaped by a combination of multiple variables, including not only cognitive processing under the on-site cognitive conditions (or input variables) and the interpreter's interpreting competence but also interpreting strategies and norms adopted in the communicative situation and sociocultural context, as shown in Figure 6.1, which is adapted from Wang (2012).

As demonstrated in Figure 6.1, in real-life practice interpreting is conditioned and contextualized in a much more complex manner than assuming that the

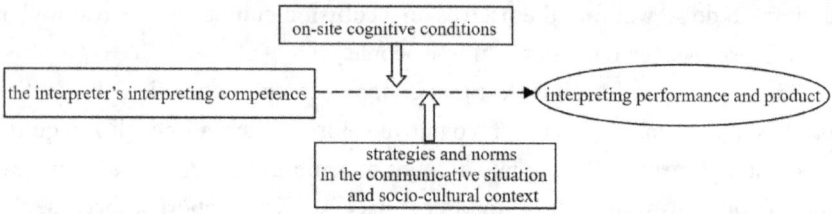

Figure 6.1 Major variables shaping the interpreting performance and product.

interpreting performance or product is just the realization of the interpreter's interpreting competence, with cognitive processing skills at the core, which underlies the logic of research design in most cognitive processing studies. According to that simple hypothesis, if any problem occurs in the interpreting process or if the interpreting product is problematic, these can largely be attributed to the deficiency in interpreting competence, particularly to issues with cognitive processing. However, in real-life practice, interpreting is much more complex because it involves more variables than the interpreting competence. In real-life interpreting tasks, problems still occur even if the interpreter is a qualified one with adequate interpreting competence, which can often be attributed to other variables such as the on-site cognitive conditions and interpreting strategies to cope with them. For example, the speech might be delivered by the speaker so fast that it is not possible for the interpreter to capture and memorize all the details or to speak equally fast even if he or she can manage to catch and capture most information from the speaker. In this case, an experienced interpreter would always resort to the strategy of compression and omission. This strategy must be employed not only to cope with the cognitive overload caused by the fast speech but also with legitimate consideration of maximizing communication effects by keeping the gist and main information intact while sacrificing minor details and trivial redundancies.

4 Interpreting as Communicative and Sociocultural Interaction

Also demonstrated in Figure 6.1, real-life interpreting is conditioned and contextualized by the communicative situation and sociocultural context, which often requires employment of interpreting strategies and adoption of norms in interpreting. This can explain why in the real-life interpreting the interpreter would violate the norms prescribed by associations of interpreters that "interpreters and translators do not alter, add to, or omit anything from the content" (AUSIT Code of Ethics and Code of Conduct[4]) and adopt the strategies of elaboration, addition, compression, and even omission. That is because interpreting strategies should be adopted not only for cognitive processing but also for communicative and sociocultural interaction.

The following framework can be used for analyzing mediation in interpreting communicative and sociocultural interaction (Figure 6.2), as translated and adapted from Wang (2019), which summarizes the various aspects of mediation that interpreters need to make in interpreting.

As shown in Figure 6.2, while doing interpreting interpreters not only render the speech from the monolingual speakers in the source language to the target language for the monolingual audience but also need to mediate the discourses in order to make it comprehensible to the audience. Interpreters also need to mediate the communicative interaction between the speakers and the audience, which is particularly evident and explicit in managing turn-takings and participation framework in dialogue interpreting (Wadensjö 1998: 93). In addition, they also need to mediate the interaction of social and cultural conventions between the two monolingual sides from different social and cultural contexts, which often make their words susceptible to misunderstanding. Also, as part of the social interactions, interpreters often need to mediate the power relations between the interlocutors. There are various types of interpreting settings where asymmetrical power differential necessitates mediation in interpreting. For example, in press conference interpreting, the speakers/principals are always influential senior politicians whereas the audiences are just journalists and ordinary citizens; similarly, in business interpreting, one side may be powerful executives and managers but the other side might be ordinary business clerks;

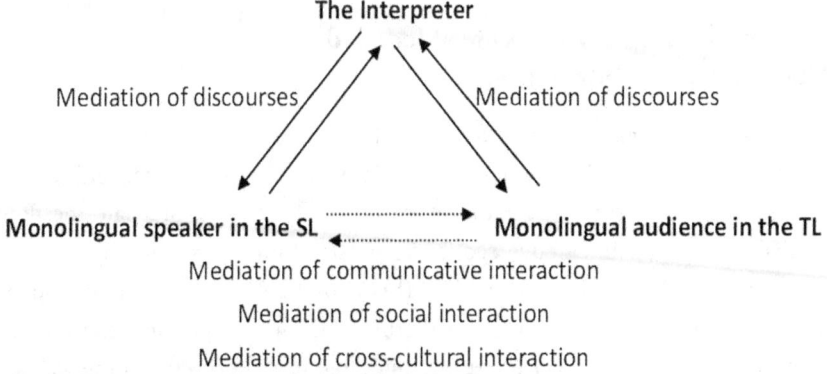

Figure 6.2 A framework for analyzing mediation in interpreting.

in asylum hearing interpreting, one side is government officials who have the power to decide the fate of the asylum seekers but the other side is powerless refugees.

Mediation of discourses in interpreting is more obvious than the other aspects of mediation because interpreting is primarily and explicitly an act of interlingual processing of the source-language discourse and the target-language discourse. According to Sergio Viaggio, a veteran conference interpreter who had served the United Nations for over thirty years, "every act of translation is, at the same time, an act of mediation" (Viaggio 2006: 121). Interlingual mediation in interpreting and translation, as pointed out by Viaggio, is evident in "achieving a specific relationship, not between 'texts' or 'utterances', but between what the original speaker means to have understood and what the mediator's interlocutor finally understands. The relationship that counts, then, is not between signs but rather between mental representations" (Viaggio 2006: 7). A vivid example about mediation of discourses in interpreting is from André Kaminker (1888–1961). Kaminker is known to be one of the first-generation interpreters in modern history, who was known for his legendary photographic memory and could reproduce a speech as long as one hour in a different language without notes in interpreting. When he was chastised at the League of Nations for not providing a faithful consecutive target language rendition of a diplomat's speech, Kaminker responded: "Monsieur, je n'ai pas dit ce que vous avez dit, mais ce que vous auriez dû dire" ("Sir, I didn't say what you said but what you should have said") (Schweda-Nicholson 2009).

The other three aspects of mediation in interpreting, that is, mediation of communicative interaction, mediation of social interaction, and mediation of cross-cultural interaction, are expounded in the following subsections.

4.1 Interpreting as Interpreter-Mediated Communicative Interaction

When interpreting is viewed as "discourse-based interaction, the focus is on the status and role of the interpreter as a participant in the encounter and on the way s/he manages the discourse process—that is, acts to coordinate the flow of discourse in an interactive sequence that is jointly negotiated among the participants" (Pöchhacker 2016: 144). This is particularly explicit and evident when interpreters in dialogue interpreting, liaison interpreting, community interpreting, or public service interpreting often use interpreting strategies for communicative interaction.

Several previous studies have provided evidence in this regard. Wadensjö (1998: 93) found from the perspective of participation framework that interpreters would make three types of shifts in footing by acting as "reporter," as "recapitulator," and as "responder" of the interlocutors' discourse in communication. Angelelli (2004) found that interpreters' visibility and participation are not only evident in the linguistic co-construction of the discourse in interlocution but also essential in communication and facilitating communication. For example, they bridge cultural gaps as well as linguistic barriers; they establish trust between all parties in the conversation and help to create more power balance during the conversation (Angelelli 2004: 11).

Though conference interpreting is more monologic and less dialogic/interactant, communicative interaction and its effect are still important for conference interpreters. According to Wang's (2012) descriptive study based on a corpus of on-site press conference interpreting, though the institutional interpreters on the occasion of the high-profile press conferences of the Chinese Premiers (including both relatively slow speakers and relatively fast speakers) are supposed to follow the strictest rule of "do not alter, add to, or omit anything from the content" (AUSIT Code of Ethics and Code of Conduct[5]), all the seven interpreters who interpreted for the eight annual press conferences held in different years have been found mediating the discourse and communication. As reported by Wang (2012), five types of addition shifts were identified in the corpus, including: an average (across the seven interpreters in the eight press conferences) of thirty-nine shifts in cohesive addition, an average of sixty-seven shifts in elaboration and expansion of information, an average of thirty-eight shifts in explicitation of intended meaning, an average of twenty-seven shifts in synonymous repetition, an average of six shifts in addition of new information. Two types of reduction shifts were identified, including: an average of nineteen shifts in omission, and an average of eight shifts in compression of loose structures and redundancy. Additionally, correction shifts were identified in the corpus, with an average of six across the interpreters and conferences. Though in some cases these shifts might be attributed to cognitive management tactics (e.g., omission and compression to save time), most of these shifts (esp. addition and correction) were found to be strategies adopted by conference interpreters to facilitate the ease of communication between the speaker and the listener. They include explicitation of logic relations, specifying information content, explicit expression of discoursal meaning, and clarity and intelligibility through compression of loose structures and redundancy (Wang 2012). These strategies are adopted by conference interpreters to "maximi[se] the communication impact of the speech" (Gile 2009: 213).

4.2 Interpreting as Interpreter-Mediated Social Interaction

Interpreting is a venue for mediation of the social interaction between the interlocutors from different societies, in which interpreters are empowered with linguistic capitals as bilinguals, cultural capitals as people who are conversant with both cultures, and professional capitals in the working role of professional mediators (Inghilleri 2005). Some recent studies have provided evidence on how interpreters leverage their linguistic and cultural resources in interpreting to mediate social interaction.

Analyses conducted from the perspective of appraisal theory (which concerns the interpersonal function of language, e.g., attitude, stance, and engagement) or in the analytical approach of critical discourse analysis reveal systematic shifts of evaluative and attitudinal meanings in interpreted discourse, which are important indicators of social interaction. It is no exception in conference interpreting. For instance, based on an analysis into the corpus of on-site Chinese/English interpreting of the panel discussions in the World Economic Forum, Gao (2021) revealed that the Chinese interpreters, who are contracted to do interpreting for the conference, strengthened positive evaluations and mitigated negative evaluations in reconstructing the interpreted discourse about the Belt and Road Initiative by manipulating linguistic resources of appraisal through shifts of intensification and shifts of downtoning. Strengthening of positive evaluative meanings was achieved mainly through addition of positive attitudinal expressions, addition of intensifiers before positive evaluations, and upgrading degrees of positivity in the discourse (Gao 2021: 32). Mitigation of negative evaluative meanings was manipulated through neutralizing negative evaluation and omitting negative expressions (Gao 2021: 33). According to Gu (2019), interpreters also mediated "face" in triadic political communication, which is a core concept for cross-language social interaction. Viewing interpreter-mediated press conferences as a dynamic site of dialogized heteroglossia featured with bilingual discourses and ideological tug-of-war mediated by the interpreter, Gu (2019) analyses a corpus containing 280 questions asked by journalists in the Chinese Premiers' press conferences between 1998 and 2017. In the critical discourse analytical approach, the study interrogates the interpreters' agency in (re)constructing the Chinese government's image. It has revealed that the government-affiliated interpreters are found to actively engage in "facework" and image (re)construction, which is evident in their emphasizing and foregrounding the positive elements and in mitigating the negative elements for the government they represent.

What is particularly interesting is the use of paralinguistic semiotic resources in interpreter-mediated communicative and sociocultural interaction, which, in spite of its importance in meaning-making in interpreting, had not been examined in interpreting studies until most recently. Based on one recent PhD study (Gao 2020), interpreters in the panel discussion of World Economic Forum would use verbal resources to compensate for speakers' paralinguistic intensification. According to Gao (2020: 133), interpreters regularly adjusted their acoustic intensity in interpreting paralinguistic emphases (perceived as the level of intonation changes, loudness, and speech rate and measured as pitch range, intensity, and duration). The quantitative analysis indicates correlation between the speaker's paralinguistic emphases and the interpreters' verbal compensation (Gao 2020: 130).

4.3 Interpreting as Interpreter-Mediated Cross-Cultural Interaction

According to Hatim and Mason (1997), interpreting is "an act of communication which attempts to relay, across cultural and linguistic boundaries" (Hatim and Mason 1997: 1). Interpreting is not only a means to bridging language gaps but also a venue for mediating cultural differences and cultural conflicts, of which issues span much beyond the proper rendition and (un)translatability of culture-specific items. More frequently, the mediation of cross-cultural interaction in interpreting deals with cultural conventions and norms, which are much more implicit, delicate, and complex.

In mediating the cross-cultural interaction between the monolingual interlocutors from different cultures in interpreted events, the interpreter's knowledge and understanding about the content, the conventions, and norms of the source and target cultures play an important role in the accomplishment of meaningful and purposeful interaction. Cultural differences would constitute "intercultural noise in interpreting" (Chen 2007) that might hamper cross-cultural communication between the monolingual interlocutors, which is why Chen (2007) calls them "noise." According to Chen (2007), there are two types of intercultural noise disturbing the process of interpreting, including: (1) risk of misunderstanding due to the cultural factors contained in the source language, source paralanguage, and source kinesics from the source-language speaker and (2) risk of misunderstanding due to the social, cultural, and situational context of the interpreting-mediated event. Chen (2007) used a typical example in Chinese to explain this.

由于本人学识浅薄，加之准备不充分，所讲之处肯定多有疏漏和不妥，请大家包涵。

[Literal gloss: Due to my limited knowledge and insufficient preparation, there must be quite some oversight and errors in my speech. Everyone, please tolerate me.]

This is a type of common expressions used by Chinese speakers in ending their speeches after presentation. There is a tendency that Chinese speakers purposely degrade themselves in the speech as a token of modesty and humbleness, which are regarded as virtues in the Chinese culture (Chen 2007). However, it should not be rendered literally, which sounds absurd to the audience from Anglophone culture, who might understand the words literally that the speaker's knowledge on the topic is really limited and that the speaker doesn't even prepare for the speech sufficiently. If that happened, the speaker and their speech would be perceived rather negatively in cross-cultural communication. Therefore, to cope with such intercultural noise that would cause misunderstanding in cross-cultural communication, experienced Chinese interpreters would always render the sentence into "Thank you very much for your attention. I look forward to your comments on my speech." Although this is not faithful interpretation in its form or content, it is functionally equivalent to the intended meaning in the cross-cultural interaction.

To accomplish successful cross-cultural interaction in interpreting-mediated events, interpreters should not act as decontextualized translation machines, that is, simply perform the source-language listening comprehension and the target-language production instantaneously (as studies in the cognitive approach tend to focus on); they need to consider communicative and sociocultural factors on top of the existing cognitive undertaking. Only by integrating all these different approaches and factors are we able to fully understand the practice of interpreting. This can also explain why interpreting strategies, such as explicitation, specification (Wang 2012), adaptation, paraphrasing, generalization, simplification, and even omission (Chen 2007), are an integral part of reality in real-life interpreting.

5 Conclusion

This chapter has expounded the necessity of going beyond the decontextualized cognitive approach to interpreting studies. Based on the discussion about major variables shaping the interpreting performance and product, including the interpreter's interpreting competence, on-site cognitive conditions, and interpreting strategies and norms adopted in the communicative situation and sociocultural context, it has proposed a framework for analyzing communicative and sociocultural interaction in interpreting, which outlines that how interpreting can be studied as interpreter-mediated communicative interaction, interpreter-mediated social interaction, and interpreter-mediated cross-cultural interaction.

The implication of the transition from the cognitive approach to communicative and sociocultural interaction approach to interpreting studies lies primarily in highlighting the nature of interpreting as mediated human communication and interaction. It has particular relevance in the current climate when artificial-intelligence-enhanced machine interpreting, which is developed on the basis of the conduit model of interpreting, is claimed to be able to replace human interpreting. While it is useful to utilize latest technologies to enhance and empower cross-language communication, the complexity of (human) interpreting must not be underestimated and the entirety of various facets of interpreting must be fully captured in interpreting studies and beyond. What this chapter has discussed and proposed demonstrates the necessity and the rationale to go beyond the decontextualized cognitive approach in studying interpreting, which largely focuses on the internal process inside the interpreters' brain through experiments that simulate interpreting. To put it in another way, the exploration into the cognitive process itself should also be "situated," that is, to enhance the ecological validity in the experimental design and to enhance reliability of data analysis by taking into consideration of all the major variables shaping the interpreting product/performance.

Notes

1 https://www.nytimes.com/2021/07/01/world/asia/xi-china-communist-party-anniversary.html.
2 https://www.bbc.co.uk/news/world-asia-china-57648236.
3 https://twitter.com/DSORennie/status/1410799713788461060?ref_src=twsrc%5Etfw%7Ctwcamp%5Etweetembed%7Ctwterm%5E1410799713788461060%7Ctwgr%5E%7Ctwcon%5Es1_&ref_url=https%3A%2F%2Fwww.bbc.com%2Fzhongwen%2Fsimp%2Fworld-57703178.
4 The Australian Institute of Interpreters and Translators: https://ausit.org/wp-content/uploads/2020/02/Code_Of_Ethics_Full.pdf.

5 The Australian Institute of Interpreters and Translators: https://ausit.org/wp-content/uploads/2020/02/Code_Of_Ethics_Full.pdf.

References

Angelelli, C. (2004), *Medical Interpreting and Cross-Cultural Communication*, Cambridge: Cambridge University Press.

Chen, J. (2007), "Strategies for Abating Intercultural Noise in Interpreting," *Meta*, 52(3): 529–41.

De Groot, A. and I. Christoffels (2006), "Language Control in Bilinguals. Monolingual Tasks and Simultaneous Interpreting," *Bilingualism: Language and Cognition*, 9(2): 189–201.

Dong, Y. P. and J. X. Lin (2013), "Parallel Processing of the Target Language during Source-Language Comprehension in Interpreting," *Bilingualism: Language and Cognition*, 16: 682–92.

Dong, Y. P. and B. H. Wang (2013), "General vs. Interpreting-Specific Language Comprehension and Production: A Two-Stage Account of the Interpreting Process" (口译过程的两阶段解读——以一般语言理解和产出为参照), *Chinese Translators Journal* (中国翻译), 34(1): 19–24.

Elmer, S., J. Jänggi, and L. Jäncke (2014), "Processing Demands upon Cognitive, Linguistic, and Articulatory Functions Promote Grey Matter Plasticity in the Adult Multilingual Brain: Insights from Simultaneous Interpreters," *Cortex*, 54: 179–89.

Fabbro, F. and V. Darò (1995), "Delayed Auditory Feedback in Polyglot Simultaneous Interpreters," *Brain and Language*, 48: 309–19.

Fabbro, F. and L. Gran (1997), "Neurolinguistic Research in Simultaneous Interpretation," in Y. Gambier, D. Gile, and C. Taylor (eds.), *Conference Interpreting: Current Trends in Research*, 9–28, Amsterdam: John Benjamins Publishing.

Gao, F. (2020), "Interpreters' Ideological Positioning through the Evaluative Language in Conference Interpreting," Unpublished PhD diss., University of Leeds.

Gao, F. (2021), "From Linguistic Manipulation to Discourse Reconstruction: A Case Study of Conference Interpreting at the World Economic Forum in China," in B. H. Wang and J. Munday (eds.), *Advances in Discourse Analysis of Translation and Interpreting*, 24–39, Oxon and New York: Routledge.

Gerver, D. (1971), "Simultaneous Interpretation and Human Information Processing," Unpublished doctoral diss., Oxford University.

Gile, D. (1995), *Basic Concepts and Models for Interpreter and Translator Training*, Amsterdam and Philadelphia: John Benjamins Publishing.

Gile, D. (1999), "Testing the Effort Models' Tightrope Hypothesis in Simultaneous Interpreting – A Contribution," *Hermes. Journal of Linguistics*, 23: 153–72.

Gile, D. (2009), *Basic Concepts and Models for Interpreter and Translator Training*, Revised edition, Amsterdam and Philadelphia: John Benjamins Publishing.

Goldman-Eisler, F. (1967), "Segmentation of Input in Simultaneous Interpretation," *Journal of Psycholinguistic Research*, 1: 127–40.

Gu, C. (2019), "Mediating 'Face' in Triadic Political Communication: A CDA Analysis of Press Conference Interpreters' Discursive (re)construction of Chinese Government's Image (1998–2017)," *Critical Discourse Studies*, 16(2): 201–21.

Hatim, B. and I. Mason (1997), *The Translator as Communicator*, London: Routledge.

Hervais-Adelman, A., B. Moser-Mercer, C. M. Michel, and N. Golestani (2015), "fMRI of Simultaneous Interpretation Reveals the Neural Basis of Extreme Language Control," *Cerebral Cortex*, 25: 4727–39.

Inghilleri, M. (2005), "The Sociology of Bourdieu and the Construction of the 'Object' in Translation and Interpreting Studies," *The Translator*, 11(2): 125–45.

Lambert, S. and B. Moser-Mercer, eds. (1994), *Bridging the Gap. Empirical Research in Simultaneous Interpretation*, Amsterdam: John Benjamins Publishing.

Linell, P. (1997), "Interpreting as Communication," in Y. Gambier, D. Gile, and C. Taylor (eds.), *Conference Interpreting: Current Trends in Research. Proceedings of the International Conference on Interpreting: What Do We Know and How?* 49–67, Amsterdam: John Benjamins Publishing.

Macizo, P. and M. T. Bajo (2004), "When Translation Makes the Difference: Sentence Processing in Reading and Translation," *Psicologica*, 25: 181–205.

Moser, B. (1978), "Simultaneous Interpretation: A Hypothetical Model and Its Practical Application," in D. Gerver and H. W. Sinaiko (eds.), *Language Interpretation and Communication*, 353–68, New York and London: Plenum Press.

Oléron, P. and H. Nanpon (1965), "Recherches sur la traduction simultanée," *Journal de psychologie normale et pathologique*, 62: 73–94.

Pöchhacker, F. (2016), *Introducing Interpreting Studies*, 2nd ed., London and New York: Routledge.

Schweda Nicholson, N. (2009), "Review of Sergio Viaggio *A General Theory of Interlingual Mediation*," *Interpreting*, 11(1): 93–8.

Viaggio, S. (2006), *A General Theory of Interlingual Mediation*, Berlin: Frank & Timme.

Wadensjö, C. (1998), *Interpreting as Interaction*, London and New York: Longman.

Wang, B. H. (2012), "A Descriptive Study of Norms in Interpreting – Based on the Chinese-English Consecutive Interpreting Corpus of Chinese Premier Press Conferences," *Meta: Translators' Journal*, 57(1): 198–212.

Wang, B. H. (2019), "Conceptualizing Interpreting as Communicative Mediation. Is Interpreting only a Skill of Cognitive Processing?" (口译的交际协调论——兼论"口译只是认知处理技能吗？"), *Journal of Foreign Language Education* (外语教学), 40(1): 78–83.

Watts, G. (2014), "The Amazing Brains of the Real-Time Interpreters." https://www.bbc.com/future/article/20141117-the-ultimate-multi-taskers (accessed November 18, 2014).

Investigating Sight Translation via Eye Tracking

Monika Płużyczka

1 Introduction

In recent years, there has been growing interest in the mental processes involved in translation and interpreting, leading to an increase in experimental research in this field. This research has been facilitated by the rapid development of technology, particularly neuroimaging techniques, and greater access to research apparatus by researchers in the humanities. All of this has contributed to the ongoing development of cognitive translation studies. In this chapter, I present the results of selected eye-tracking experiments I conducted from 2011 to 2019.[1] Eye tracking involves tracking eye movements while the subject performs a translation task and analyzing particular eye movement parameters. The main assumption of such research is that eye movement parameters are indicators of cognitive load and (to some extent) of specific mental processes. I will particularly focus on the possibilities of verifying and complementing assumptions about mental modelling of translation activity by interpreting the results of eye-tracking experiments in the context of well-known theoretical mental models.

2 Exploring Mental Processes in Translation Studies

Interest in the mental processes engaged in translation[2] does have a quite long history. The first article on the subject, to the best of my knowledge, was published in 1910 by Gabriele von Wartensleben (Olalla-Soler, Aixela, Rovira-Esteva 2020) and is titled "Beiträge zur Psychologie des Übersetzens" (*Contributions to the*

Psychology of Translation). Some scholars (e.g., Muñoz Martín and Martín de León 2020) date such research as far back as the late nineteenth century (e.g., research on single-word translation). However, it is only since the 1960s that we have seen more interest in the mental side of translation. This interest has grown out of the creation of theoretical and empirical foundations of cognitive psychology in the 1950s and 1960s as well as the definition of a theoretical and research framework for psycholinguistics (Osgood and Sebeok 1954). Eva Paneth, in her MA thesis in 1957, examines conference interpreting in practice based on observational and training methods in select schools for interpreters. In 1962, van Hoof publishes his work "Théorie et pratique de la traduction" (*Theory and Practice of Translation*). Pierre Oléron and Hubert Nanpon, in their publication "Recherches sur la traduction simultanée" (*Research on Simultaneous Translation*) from 1965, compare the speed of original and interpreted presentation, the delay of interpretation, and the number of words added and omitted. Barik, in 1969, in his unpublished PhD thesis, compares interpreting output, respectively, by professionals, students, and amateurs (Barik 1969). Gerver, in 1971, investigates the effects of noise on the performance of simultaneous interpreting and examines verbal and temporal aspects of their output. However, all this research focused on analyzing the translation product (mainly interpreting output) and translation activities, and one could only make assumptions about certain processes occurring in the translator's brain. A breakthrough in process research was the introduction in the 1980s of so-called think-aloud protocols (TAPs) in translation studies (see Krings 1986; Gerloff 1988; Lörscher 1987, 1991; Kussmaul 1991, 1995). TAPs were used in conjunction with other prevalent methods of the time such as introspective and retrospective questionnaires and audio and video recordings. They allowed "insight" into the translator's thought processes as the subjects were supposed to verbalize what they were thinking about while translating. This was an important step forward even though it provided only fragmentary knowledge about the mental processes involved because test subjects reported solely on conscious processes, usually decision-making processes. Moreover, TAPs have tended to give a picture of the participants' subjective perception of the task alone, and this may differ from the objective (often unaware) difficulties they encounter. Moreover, subjects decide on which aspects of the task they wish to report. Nevertheless, TAPs represented a major step forward in understanding what goes on in the translator's mind, and this period is often regarded as the beginning of the study of mental processes in translation studies. Since that time, translation studies scholars have used, in addition to the protocols mentioned earlier, such online methods as video, audio, key logging, dialogue protocols, eye tracking, electroencephalography, and various neuroimaging methods (PET, MRI, EPI). In recent years, research involving the use of the eye-tracking method has intensified, aided by the availability of specialized research equipment, which is well suited to conducting research on text perception, including translational processing of text. The possibility of overlaying an image of eye movement patterns on text read by subjects allows us to obtain information about their perception. Moreover, due to the extraction of individual values for specific eye movement parameters, we can obtain information about the involvement of certain mental processes in the performed task.

3 Mental Models of Translation

The interest in mental processes and their study resulted in the theoretical mental modelling of the translation act, that is, a schematic representation of the mental processes involved in translation. One of the first mental models of translation was introduced by Danica Seleskovitch as the *théorie du sense*, later called the Interpretive Theory of Translation, developed with Mariane Lederer (see Seleskovitch 1968, 1975; Lederer 1981, 1994; Seleskovitch and Lederer 1984). They identified the main mental processes involved in both oral and written translation as understanding sense, deverbalizing/conceptualization, and reexpressing/reformulating.

In 1980, R. K. Min'âr-Beloručev presented his perspective on the mental modelling of the translation process. In his publication, he regards several mental mechanisms to be the most important in translation activity:

1. source text perception,
2. memorizing,
3. "switching" from one language to another,
4. formulating a translated text,
5. the synchronization of translation operations.

According to R. K. Min'âr-Beloručev, all aforementioned mechanisms operate under various mental conditions. These conditions could be:

(a) a large memory load,
(b) aural text reception only,
(c) obtaining a written text,
(d) the synchronization of the abovementioned processes.

Another well-known model (most discussed in translation studies by far) was proposed by D. Gile and is called the Effort Model. In this model, the act of translation (which can be called interpreting here, because he includes sight translation in interpreting) is described in terms of the mental efforts required. Mental effort is a generalized term, indicating a series of mental processes connected to each other. Gile proposed separate models for simultaneous interpretation (1983), consecutive interpretation (1990), sight translation (1995), and simultaneous interpretation with text (1995). As he points out, modelling was a result of his observation of the difficulties faced by interpreters during simultaneous interpretation. His analysis of these difficulties led him to conclude that interpreting as such takes place during various cognitive operations that are performed in the context of mental processing capacity limitations. These difficulties include a source-language utterance that is produced too fast, a large amount of specialized vocabulary of source language speeches, and also such items as proper names, terms, numerals, and specific regional pronunciation. Gile (2009) stresses that if the interpreter does not have enough mental skills to process information, the cognitive balance between the efforts will be violated and result in the deceleration of the interpreting process and/or the occurrence of mistakes. He adds that an interpreter should have adequate processing capacity for each effort so that the process of listening, reading, or producing is not disrupted.

Another mental model worth mentioning is the psycholinguistic model of R. T. Bell (1991). In this model, the translation is seen in categories of processing information and it posits the use of short-term and long-term memory for "decoding" the source language and "encoding" it into the target language. More precisely, it assumes the existence of such operations as visual recognition of words in a text, syntactic and lexical analysis, and semantic and pragmatic processes for the purpose of generating a semantic representation supported by organization and planning.

In the psycholinguistic model of Kiraly (1995), the translator's mind is regarded as an information processing system. Translation is the result of interactions between intuitive and controlled processes of using linguistic and extralinguistic information. The model assumes the existence of:

1) information sources which cover:
    a) long-term memory—cultural, physical, social schemata, translation-related schemata and discourse frames, lexico-semantic knowledge, and morpho-syntactic frames,
    b) a stimulus in the form of the source text,

    c) external resources such as databases, native users of the language, and source literature.
2) the intuitive centre/workspace;
3) the controlled processing centre.

Kiraly proposes singling out an intuitive (or relatively uncontrolled) workspace where information from long-term memory is integrated (without conscious control) with information from the source text and external resources. On the other hand, controlled processes are involved when it is impossible to solve a problem automatically out of intuitive processing. In such a case, the controlled processing center is activated, and an appropriate translation strategy is selected and applied. If, in turn, an inappropriate strategy is chosen, the problem is directed back to the intuitive space, where it is either solved or, if a final solution is not possible, an initial translation is offered. If the problem cannot be solved at all, the procedure starts again.

There have also been other mental models proposed by translation studies scholars where the authors attempted to explain what is happening in the "black box" of the translator (see Wilss's model of 1996 or Gutt's model of 1991). Although all models or schemas reduce the complexity of the mental activity of the translation act, they enable us to better understand the complex phenomenon of translation. Models and schemas also—through mentioned simplifications—facilitate the discourse on the subject. With current technological capabilities, these general theoretical models can be empirically verified and complemented. This article will consider whether these models still have relevance and rationale.

4 Sight Translation as a Specific Type of Translation

The focus of my research interests for a long time has been sight translation. It is a very demanding translation process and one that for many years has had little attention paid to it. When it has, there have been problems classifying it due to its hybrid nature (visual input and audial output). Some scholars (e.g., Lambert 1988; Seleskovitch 1983) treat it as written translation, assuming that its first "stage" (as they call it), that is, reading, corresponds with the first stage of written translation. Others (e.g., Herbert 1952a; van Hoof 1962; Percival 1983; Dejean Le Féal 1981; Gile 1983, 1995; Lambert 1991; Kutz 2002; Żmudzki 2015 et al.) focus on the audial "target text production stage," which they contend places sight translation in the same category as interpretation. These early theories and reflections were interspersed with concepts of recognizing sight translation as a hybrid form combining features of written translation and interpretation (see Moser-Mercer 1997/2002). Some awarded sight translation the status of an intermediary form with an indeterminate attribution (see Feldweg 1996; Kalina 2003; Pöchhacker 2004). Finally, there are also scholars who consider sight translation to be a separate type of translation, neither an intermediate nor a hybrid. This latter case was particularly true of Russian scholars (see Barhudarov 1975; Minyar-Beloruchev 1980) and is the view that I share.

I treat sight translation as *a separate/distinct type of translation*, neither as a type of written translation, nor as a type of interpreting, nor as a hybrid translation combining the features of written translation and interpreting. In this chapter, I have presented arguments supporting my hypothesis, along with study results. In my opinion, the mental processes that occur are specific to this type of translation only. This is due, in part, to not only the different output and input channels involved but also the simultaneous overlap of all operations, which requires a very large coordination/control effort. I distinguish in sight translation at least the following main operations, most of which occur simultaneously:

(a) reception of a signal in the form of a graphic sign,
(b) reconstruction of the meaning based on the utterance formulated in the source language (SL),
(c) retaining necessary information in memory, i.e. memorizing,
(d) long-term memory scanning to find expressions in the target language (TL) that correspond with the meaning expressed in SL,
(e) expression of internalized sense in the form of a target-language audial text,
(f) the translator's control over possible immediate self-correction,
(g) and most importantly, the process of coordinating all these operations, and of managing language control.

I deliberately use such words as "operations" and "processes" rather than "stages" (although the latter expression is used in the relevant literature) because the word "stages" suggests, or at least may suggest, a sequence of events. However, these processes occur simultaneously or overlap.

Sight translation can take place either with preparation (when the translator is allowed to read the text beforehand) or without preparation (the translator starts translating straight away, without having read the text beforehand, i.e., without so-called pretranslational reading). In this article, I present studies on the second type of sight translation,—that is, sight translation without preparation.

In the mental models presented earlier, sight translation was analyzed in both Gile's and Min'âr-Beloručev's models. Gile (1995, 2009) characterizes sight translation in terms of mental efforts. He presents the efforts involved as follows: reading effort + memory effort + speech production effort + coordination. He did not provide a detailed description of these efforts. And the concept of "reading effort" is very general. After all, a reading effort also occurs in written translation or simply in the process of reading. And yet it differs quite significantly in all these processes. This should therefore be indicated or explained. Moreover, Gile (1995) did not at first include memory effort in sight translation, which was a significant oversight. He only integrated it into the sight translation model in 2009 after the publication of Agrifoglio (2004), adding, however, that it is only a short-term memory effort, which I cannot quite agree with.

Min'âr-Beloručev (1980) considers the level of complexity of sight translation very high due to the number of factors that hinder mental operations during translation. He points out that if the conditions in which mental mechanisms operate are difficult, then translation requires more mental effort, so it evokes a greater cognitive load. For example, the method of conducting translation operations (be it consecutive or simultaneous) requires a different kind of engagement of the translator's mental resources. He considers sight translation a very difficult (mentally demanding) type of translation (6 points out of 7 on the difficulty scale), making it almost as difficult as simultaneous interpretation (7 points out of 7 on the difficulty scale). He lists the difficulties as visual information reception, switching from one language to another within a limited amount of time, oral production of translation, and a simultaneous order of operations as difficult conditions in which sight translation is performed.

5 Research Objectives

The purpose of my research was to investigate the process of sight translation, especially the mental processes involved. This research has enabled the verification and completion of previous mental models of sight translation.

The research questions were:

(a) What is the (level of) cognitive load during sight translation?
(b) Can it be assessed with the help of eye-tracking parameters?
(c) Are selected eye-tracking parameters reliable in evaluating cognitive load on every unit of analysis?

(d) What mental processes can be distinguished by using eye tracking (and is it at all possible)?
(e) What is the visual perception during sight translation and how does it differ from reading for comprehension?

In all experiments, a triangulation of methods was applied: eye tracking, video recordings, product (target text) analysis, and, in one of the experiments, an additional detailed analysis of the types of mistakes made by participants during sight translation.

The task of the experimental group was to sight translate, whereas the task of the control group (homogeneous with the experimental group) was to read a text for comprehension. The experiment was designed this way for several reasons.

Firstly, it allowed an assessment of how much cognitive load is involved during sight translation. The hypothesis was that sight translation is mentally demanding, that is, the level of cognitive load is very high. Studying this issue, I wanted to verify Min'âr-Beloručev's and Gile's assumptions regarding the difficulty of sight translation. As there are no fixed levels of eye-tracking parameters that indicate high cognitive load, I compared two processes that differ considerably in terms of the requirements for the mental effort invested. I chose "reading for comprehension" in the native language (as a control process), which by assumption requires low mental effort, and sight translation (as an experimental process), which requires—as I hypothesized—a high level of mental effort and cognitive load. Measuring the size of the difference in parameter results made it possible to assess how difficult sight translation is, that is, how much cognitive load is involved when sight translation is performed.

Secondly, comparing processes with such prominent differences in cognitive demands allowed me to also verify which eye-tracking parameters are the most reliable in estimating cognitive load. I assumed that parameters that showed a large difference in cognitive load would prove to be reliable. I examined parameters that are reported in the literature to be indicators of cognitive load, and there are numerous, which seemed suspicious and overly optimistic. Therefore, I hypothesized that not all eye-tracking parameters reported in the literature are reliable indicators of cognitive load and are not reliable to the same degree. I verified the parameters: dwell time, fixation count, and revisits, which I was assuming would be reliable. I also checked pupil dilation and average fixation, which are also given as indicators of cognitive load but which I hypothesized might prove unreliable. I first checked the mentioned parameters at the level of the whole text (these will be presented in this article) and then at the level of paragraphs, sentences, and words in one task (sight translation). These results will be presented partially on the example of paragraphs due to limited space in the article. To my knowledge, such extensive testing of eye-tracking parameters, and, moreover, testing them on differently sized units of analysis in a single task, has not yet been carried out (and almost certainly had not been prior to the first experiments I began in 2011).

Third, sight translation involves a series of mental operations. Gile (2009) lists the first as reading for comprehension. However, in my opinion, during sight translation, separating the source text reception process (reading for comprehension) from the target text production can be done only at an analytical level because in practice the processes take place almost concurrently. Reflecting on the nature of sight translation, I have concluded that it is necessary to test whether the processes of reading for comprehension and sight translation are similar at all, for they would need to be if the former is to be considered the first phase of the latter. Thus, I developed the hypothesis that in sight translation a different kind of reading occurs, not reading merely for comprehension but reading for translation. In 1993, Shreve with coauthors published the article "Is there a special kind of 'reading' for translation?: An empirical investigation of reading in translation process." They hypothesize that if reading for comprehension is embedded in a translation task, quantitative measures of the reading process will indicate the influence of the translation task. They conducted an empirical study in which they compared three groups of participants who read a text with different aims: comprehension, paraphrasing, and translation. The performance of the groups differed not only in the amount of time taken to complete the task but also in the problems that they identified during the task. The conclusion was that the translation task does affect reading and there is, at some level, "reading for translation." I, therefore, assumed that reading for comprehension would be a good reference process to use to detect how it differs from reading for sight translation. This assumption would enable me to provide empirical evidence to propose naming the phase (or element) of sight translation "reading for translation" rather than "reading for comprehension." I have found no other eye-tracking studies that deal with this research problem.

6 Experimental Design

The source text (the stimulus) was a press article on politics in the Polish language. This text was carefully selected to ensure it included various potential translation problems (leading to additional cognitive load). Two groups were formed: an experimental group tasked with performing sight translation and a control group tasked with only reading the text and then answering comprehension questions. The data consisted of thirty-six recordings: eighteen in the experimental group and eighteen in the control group, selected from an initial fifty-three recordings. The recordings that I had to reject were mainly recordings of participants with a very high level of visual impairment and who were wearing glasses. It was necessary to reject these recordings as the scan paths were affected by these factors and were abnormal. Also rejected were recordings during which decalibration occurred and the fixations did not fall exactly on the words or over them.[3]

Eye movement parameters that were analyzed: dwell time, fixation count, revisits, average fixation, and pupil dilation. The statistical analysis was divided into four parts to also check the reliability of selected parameters on different sizes of units of analysis. First, all parameters were analyzed on the level of the whole text and then on the level of paragraphs. They were next analyzed on the level of individual sentences of the text and finally on the level of words (see detailed results: Płużyczka 2015). In this article, I will present mainly the results collected at the whole text level because I will focus on the differences occurring while reading for comprehension and while sight translating. At the level of the whole text, additional parameters included time spent on task and spatial saccadic movements; I identified these while researching cognitive load, and to my knowledge, they have not been previously identified in translation studies.

All experiments were carried out in the Laboratory of Experimental Eye Tracking Linguistics (LELO) in the Institute of Specialised and Intercultural Communication at the Faculty of Applied Linguistics of the University of Warsaw. The laboratory is located in a separate, acoustically isolated room. Studies were carried out in similar lighting conditions.[4] Lighting was controlled because of its effect on pupil diameter, which was one of the analyzed parameters. During the study, only the experimenter and individual participants were present in the room.

7 Measuring Cognitive Load with Eye-Tracking Parameters

In the following, I will present the results of the eye-tracking experiments using eye movement parameters reported in the literature as indicators of cognitive load, that is, dwell time, fixation count, revisits, average fixation, and pupil dilation. An additional parameter I have taken into account is the total reading time, which is not always equivalent to the dwell time parameter.

7.1 Total Reading Time

In the experimental group, the total reading time refers to the total time of text reception during sight translation (ST), that is, the total time taken to perform the task (in this type of translation, reception and production occur nearly simultaneously). In the control study, the time of task performance was the total time of text reception while reading for comprehension (RC). It can be assumed that the longer the task lasts, the higher cognitive load it causes.

When reading for comprehension (RC), the time of the task was on average 1.30 minutes, and while sight translating (ST) it was 4.14 minutes. Student's t-test showed that the differences were statistically significant: $t\,(21.986) = 8.967$; $p < 0.001$, Cohen's $d = 2.989$. The time to perform the task during ST was almost three times longer than during RC (see Table 7.1).

Table 7.1 Descriptive Statistics for Total Reading Time

Group	N	Mean (sec.)	Standard Deviation (sec.)
RC Group	18	90 sec. (1 min. 30 sec.)	24775.98
ST Group	18	254.27 sec. (4 min. 14 sec.)	65532.68

7.2 Dwell Time

Dwell time is the sum of all fixations and saccades on a particular area of interest (AOI) divided by the number of test subjects. Renshaw et al. (2004a, 2004b) claim that the scan paths and dwell time are crucial factors in measuring cognitive load: the longer the scanning lasts, the more difficult the assigned task turns out to be for the test subject.

The average dwell time during sight translation is nearly 2.5 times greater than during reading for comprehension (see Table 7.2). Student's t-test for independent samples showed that the differences were statistically significant: $t\,(21,763) = 6.96$; $p < 0.001$; Cohen's $d = 2.321$.[5] Dwell time during sight translation was on average 3.20 minutes while during reading for comprehension it was 1.28 minutes. Therefore, the time required to complete the sight translation task indicates the demand for a much higher level of cognitive load to perform it.

Table 7.2 Descriptive Statistics for Dwell Time

Group	N	Mean (ms)	Standard Deviation (ms)	Standard Error of Means (ms)
RC Group	18	77115.71 (1.28 min.)	24775.98	5839.75
ST Group	18	192133.11 (3.20 min.)	65532.68	15446.20

When comparing total reading time with dwell time while reading for comprehension, we see that the difference between the values of these two parameters is minor, but this difference is substantial while reading for sight translation. The total reading time during sight translating was 4.14 minutes, and the dwell time in sight translation (i.e., the registered time of all fixation and saccades on the text) was only 3.20 minutes. That is, on average, for 3.20 minutes eye tracker recorded eye movements on the text even though the entire process took 4.14 minutes. That means that participants were not looking at the text (i.e., not at the monitor) for nearly one minute, and if they were not looking at the text, the eye tracker could not register their eye movements. I will return to this topic later when discussing "spatial saccadic movements." The results regarding spatial saccadic movements turned out to be significant, as they indicate the involvement of memory processes and a high cognitive load.

7.3 Fixation Count

This parameter is frequently used in eye-tracking research. According to A. Duchowski (2007), its value is directly proportional to the intensity of cognitive load.

There were statistically significant differences in the average fixation count at the whole text level between sight translation and reading for comprehension: $t(34) = 5.381$; $p < 0.001$; Cohen's $d = 1.7935$. During sight translation, there were on average 643 fixations registered on the text while during reading for comprehension there were 339. Fixation time nearly doubled during sight translation, which would also indicate a much greater (at least double) cognitive load required (see Table 7.3).

Table 7.3 Descriptive Statistics for Fixation Count

Group	N	Mean	Standard Deviation	Standard Error of Means
RC Group	18	339.05	105.15	24.78
ST Group	18	643.94	216.18	50.95

7.4 Revisits (Refixations)

This denotes the number of repeated glances registered on a particular AOI occurring after the first recorded fixation on it. We usually take into consideration the average revisits count, which is the sum of all revisits to a AOI divided by the number of test subjects for whom at least one fixation was registered.

The largest differences found between the compared processes were obtained for this parameter. During sight translation, the average number of revisits was sixty-five, while during reading for comprehension it was eight. Student's t-test for independent samples showed that the differences were statistically significant: $t(34) = 5.381; p < 0.001$; Cohen's $d = 2.177$ (see Table 7.4).

Table 7.4 Descriptive Statistics for Revisits

Group	N	Mean	Standard Deviation	Standard Error of Means
RC Group	18	18.61	8.05	1.89
ST Group	18	65.16	29.14	6.87

The number of revisits during ST was more than four times higher than that recorded during RC. This may mean that the number of revisits is the most representative indicator of the level of cognitive load. Multiple revisits occur during translation tasks because the translator cannot immediately find an equivalent for a word encountered, and that word is revisited until an equivalent is found. This was confirmed by listening to the translation recordings along with the scan path videos. The subjects returned to the text elements they had translational difficulties with.

7.5 Average Fixation

Average fixation is the sum of the "average fixation time" per subject registered on a particular AOI, divided by the number of subjects who fixated on it. Average fixation is considered in the related literature an indicator of conscious information processing and therefore, to a certain extent, a cognitive load indicator as well. The longer the average fixation, the more difficult the task (see Yarbus 1965; Renshaw 2004a, 2004b; Just and Carpenter 1980; Duchowski 2007). The more complicated a text is, the longer the average fixations are, spanning between 200 and 260 ms when reading specialized text (Rayner and Pollatsek 1989).

The average fixation during sight translation was 246 ms and during reading for comprehension it was 198 ms (see Table 7.5). Student's t-tests for independent

Table 7.5 Descriptive statistics for average fixation

Group	N	Mean (ms)	Standard Deviation (ms)	Standard Error of Means (ms)
RC Group	18	198.6098	33.49716	7.89536
ST Group	18	246.5376	55.36439	13.04951

samples showed that the differences between the groups were statistically significant: $t(34) = 3.142$, $p = 0.003$, Cohen's $d = 1.047$. This parameter also confirms a much higher cognitive load during sight translation.

7.6 Pupil Dilation

Pupils react not only to stress and emotions (Siegle et al. 2003) but also to the cognitive effort that is necessary to face a difficult task (Kahneman 1973; Matthews et al. 1991). So far, studies using the pupil dilation parameter and linking it to mental effort have mainly been conducted in solving arithmetic problems (see Ahern and Beatty 1979), linguistic processing (P. Wright/D. Kahneman 1971), short-term memory tasks (Kahneman, Onuska, and Wolman 1968; Kahneman and Beatty 1966), attention tasks (Hoeks and Levelt 1993), and reading (Just and Carpenter 1993). There have been very few studies done that look at pupil dilation during translation (Hyönä, Tommola, and Alaja 1995). The results of my experiments showed significant differences in pupil size during the two analyzed processes. Student's t-test for independent samples showed that the differences were statistically significant: $t(34) = 4.858$; $p < 0.001$; Cohen's $d = 1.619$. In the group that performed ST, the average pupil diameter was 4.15 mm, while in the group that was given the task of RC it was 3.42 mm (see Table 7.6).

Table 7.6 Descriptive statistics for pupil dilation

Group	N	Mean (mm)	Standard Deviation	Standard Error of Means
RC Group	18	3.42	0.27	0.06
ST Group	18	4.15	0.57	0.13

The pupil diameter was on average 0.72 mm larger during sight translation. Cohen's d indicates a very substantial effect size. This parameter also confirmed that participants who sight translated had to deal with a much higher cognitive load than those who had read for comprehension.

Interestingly, when analyzing smaller units of text in one task, pupil diameter turns out to be unreliable in assessing cognitive load. I have noticed this unreliability for all smaller units of analysis: paragraphs, sentences, and words within one task. We cannot capture significant differences between paragraphs/sentences/words to measure which one was the most difficult for subjects. Below I illustrate this by showing pupil dilation values, which were not very different between paragraphs (although the second paragraph was the most difficult to translate) (See Figure 7.1), and the values of the parameter "fixation count," which reliably indicated the most difficult paragraph (See Figure 7.2):

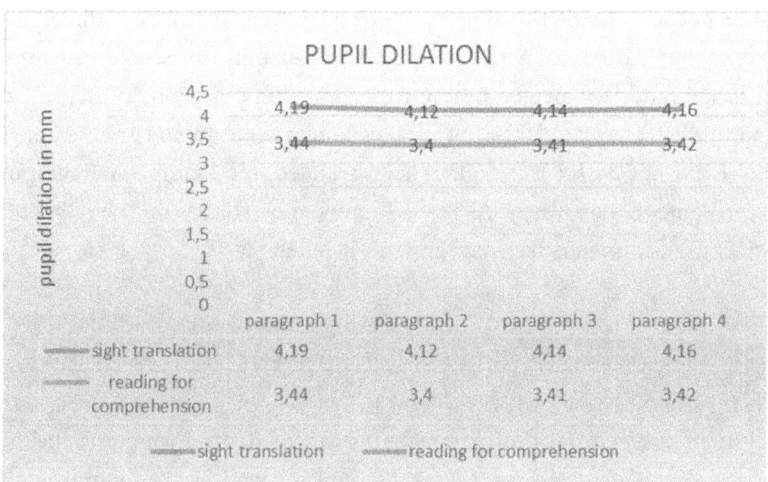

Figure 7.1 Pupil dilation data on paragraphs.

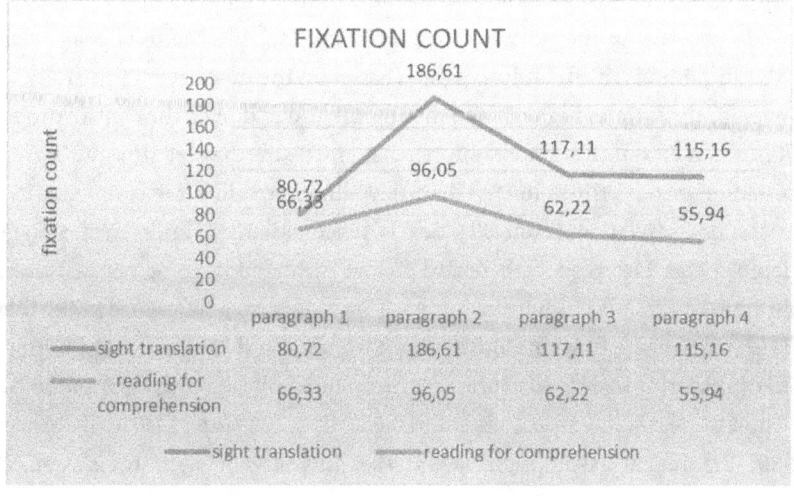

Figure 7.2 Fixation count data on paragraphs.

The differences in pupil dilation were minimal between smaller units of analysis, so they could not be used to indicate which part of the text was most difficult to translate (see more: Płużyczka 2020). In other words, verifying the reliability of eye-tracking parameters in estimating cognitive load showed that the pupil dilation parameter is reliable when comparing two tasks with each other but is no longer reliable when comparing smaller units of analysis (e.g., paragraphs) in one task.

In searching for reasons for this unreliability, I came to the conclusion that they are biologically determined and related to the specifics of the autonomic nervous system. When the sympathetic part of this system activates the fight or flight response during a threat, danger, stress, or high cognitive load, our body, including pupil dilation, acts immediately. Returning to a state of calmness takes longer and is managed by the parasympathetic nervous system. That is, the pupil dilates very quickly, but it takes longer for it to constrict again. This is why I did not detect large differences between, for example, paragraphs or between sentences or words. As far as I know, such studies on the reliability of eye-tracking parameters have not previously taken place.

8 Discussion of the Eye-Tracking Parameters Results

Analysis of the eye-tracking parameters confirmed my hypothesis that sight translation is related to a great level of cognitive load even though the visual stimulus in the form of a source text is always present. All parameters obtained very high values in comparison with the control process. Assuming that the values of selected eye movement indicators primarily reflect the level of involvement of mental processes in the task, one may presume that the cognitive load during sight translation is several times higher (based on the outcome of this study, it is on average three times higher) than the cognitive load during the control process, that is, when reading a text for comprehension. The mean dwell time during sight translation was 2.5 times longer than that during reading for comprehension, and the mean fixation count was nearly twice as large. However, the biggest difference was observed with regard to the mean number of revisits; during sight translation, it was 3.6 times higher. There was also a difference in the mean duration of average fixations; during sight translation it was about 48 ms longer. Moreover, during sight translation, the mean pupil dilation was 0.73 mm wider.

Thus, these results empirically confirmed Gile's (2009) and Min'âr-Beloručev's (1980) theoretical assumptions about the difficulty of sight translation. All selected parameters examined at the level of the whole text as a unit of the analysis proved to be reliable. However, when comparing smaller units of the text in one task, some parameters (e.g., pupil dilation) turn out to be unreliable (see Płużyczka 2020), which I have outlined earlier using paragraphs as an example. This demonstrates certain limitations of the pupil dilation parameter.

9 Specificity of Text Perception in "Reading for Sight Translation"

The differences in text perception in the two analyzed tasks, namely reading for comprehension and sight translation, are best illustrated by the scan paths (Figure 7.3.). Fixations[6] are marked as circles, and their duration is directly proportional to the size of the circle's diameter. Saccades,[7] which are marked as straight lines, occur when the gaze goes from one fixation to another or when it revisits a text element that had been previously fixated on. In Figure 7.3, the selected scan paths illustrate the differences in perception between the two tasks.

During sight translation, there is a high frequency of fixations, and many were long lasting, and these are an indicator of a very high cognitive load during task performance. The registered fixations were usually concentrated in the middle of the text (the second paragraph), which had been adapted in such a way as to include the most translation difficulties. For some participants, lateral text areas were within the so-called peripheral vision field. Several regularities regarding saccades also occurred: the saccadic movement was much more irregular than in reading for comprehension; there were many regressive saccades as well as vertical and oblique ones. There were also lateral upward (less often lateral downward) saccades that went beyond the text. They will be the subject of the next section.

During reading for comprehension, there were clearly fewer fixations and their duration was shorter than those during sight translation. The duration of fixations during reading for comprehension did not vary greatly. The saccadic movement was consistent, most of the saccades were horizontal, and few spatial saccadic movements were recorded during this process.

Scan paths clearly illustrate the differences in perception between the two tasks. This suggests that **we should not treat text reception during sight translation as "reading for comprehension," so I propose to distinguish it as "reading for translation."**

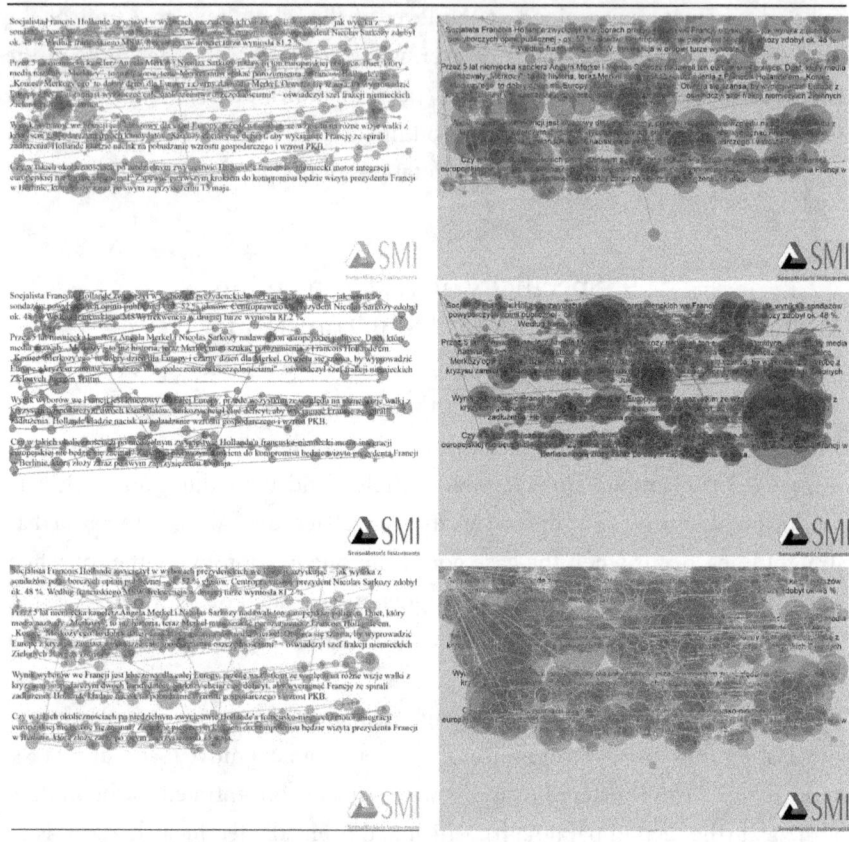

Figure 7.3 Scan paths of reading for comprehension (column 1) and sight translation (column 2)

10 Detection of Particular Mental Processes, Long-Term Memory, and Saccadic Movement

During pilot experiments with the eye tracker Tobii T120, which I conducted in 2011 and 2012, I had already noticed that some saccades deviated away from the text while translating. I called them "spatial saccadic movements."[8] These are saccades that point beyond the text and the monitor. It should be assumed that the subjects were fixating their gaze on something other than the monitor (text), but since the eye tracker only records gaze directed at the monitor, the locations of fixations beyond the text were not identified (indefinite space). For this reason, I called them "spatial saccadic movements." I present the results regarding spatial saccades since, to the best of my knowledge, this type of saccades has not previously been distinguished in eye-tracking research as a parameter of cognitive load, nor have they been at all analyzed in linguistics and translation studies. Rather, they have been the subject of psychological studies (although not any involving eye tracking).

In experiments on Tobii T120 (2011–13), I analyzed text perception during sight translation by native Polish speakers from their first language L1 (Polish) into their second (foreign) language L2 (Russian) and then from L2 into L1 (Płużyczka 2013). The test groups each consisted of seventeen students studying translation and interpreting at the Faculty of Applied Linguistics of the University of Warsaw. The stimuli were one-page source texts dealing with politics and economics (the first in L1, the second in L2). Participants sight translated the source text into their L2 (the first experiment) and then the second source text into their L1 (the second experiment). The hypothesis that translating from L1 into L2 would require a much higher cognitive load than translating from L2 into L1, which would result in higher levels of all selected eye-tracking parameters, was confirmed. Interestingly, subjects' scan paths when sight translating from Polish into Russian revealed that the test subjects frequently averted their gaze from the text. The scans show this as lines pointing sideways and extending beyond the text area (See Figure 7.4).

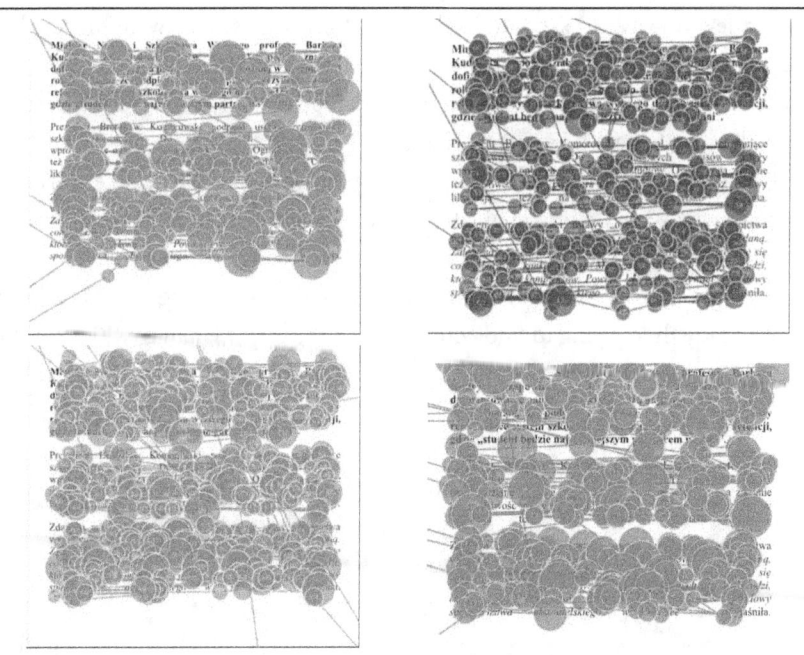

Figure 7.4 Selected scan paths illustrating spatial saccadic movements during sight translation from L1 (Polish) to L2 (Russian)

Such saccadic movements were also noted in my experiment on the SMI 500 eye tracker (Płużyczka 2015) that I presented earlier when discussing cognitive load results.[9] Later in the text I have provided selected scan paths of test subjects during sight translating. Saccades were directed mainly to the left, though the SMI eye tracker collected them all in the upper left corner, as can be seen in Figure 7.5. However, saccades pointing downward were also noted.

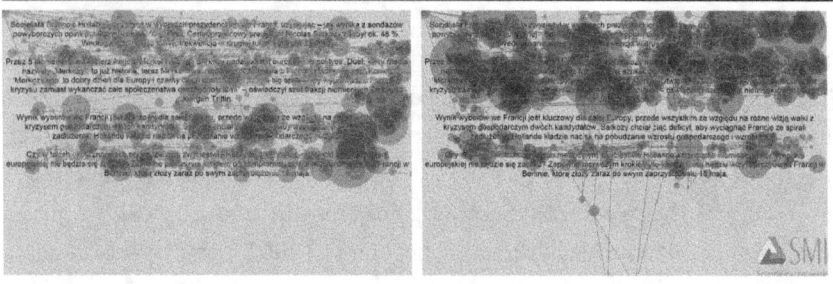

Figure 7.5 Selected scan paths illustrating spatial saccadic movements during sight translation

Interestingly, such saccadic movements did not occur during reading for comprehension (to be precise, only in one of the seventeen scan paths were there a few downward saccades). The video recordings (that were made while the subjects were sight translating) showed that averting the gaze from the stimulus (text) was performed when the test subjects were deliberating over the equivalent in the target language.

Spatial saccadic movements were also registered during the team experiment we conducted (see Grucza et al. 2019). We tested how pretranslational reading facilitates sight translation. Spatial saccadic movements were registered not only during sight translation but also during pretranslational reading because subjects were already then trying to find equivalents in the target language (Figure 7.6).

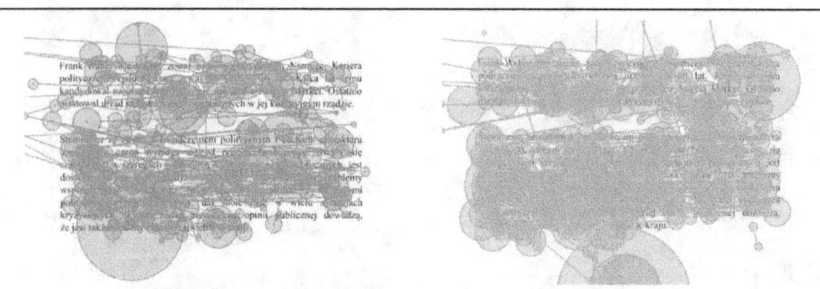

Figure 7.6 Selected scan paths illustrating spatial saccadic movements during sight translation (column 1) and pretranslational reading (column 2)

I have found no mention or analysis of such eye movements in the literature. Therefore, I attempted to explain them myself. I have linked them to psychological research conducted mainly with observational methods on the movement of the eyes when answering a question. It has been noted that people who were asked to answer a question in a survey tended to move their gaze beyond the questionnaire immediately after reading it, that is, when they were deliberating over an answer. There were various hypotheses as to why this occurred. One was that subjects wanted to avoid distractions in order to better focus. Another was that it might be related to NLP[10] theory. According to this theory, if subjects look to the left, they are making the answer up (lying), and if they look to the right, they are attempting to recall the information. I checked this theory during my experiments and found no correlation between gaze direction and subjects' making up or recalling information (in this case equivalent in target language). Then, it was thought that moving the eyes sideways while answering questions was linked to different types of memory (questions requiring imagination vs. questions relating to verbal issues) (see Płużyczka 2015, 2016, 2020, for more). However, it was only relatively recently that we came closer to what might be an explanation. Ehrlichman et al. (2007) and Micic, Ehrlichman, Chen (2010) in their studies showed that questions that exact a "search" for an answer in the long-term memory, that is, require strong memory involvement, generate high saccadic movement. Ehrlichman and Micic (2012) claimed that it reduces cognitive load by activating additional cognitive resources. The experiments of Christman et al. (2003) demonstrated that saccades activate sequences and alternately the left and right cerebral hemispheres. It appears that increased interaction between hemispheres facilitates the recollection of information, that is, scanning long-term memory. Assuming that the saccadic movements I had detected were the equivalent of what psychologists call "moving the eyes when responding," I decided to explore whether they were actually related to engaging long-term memory.

During sight translation, spatial saccadic movements, pointing in various directions and beyond the translated text, were reported for nearly all test subjects. The recordings of translations showed that subjects averted their gaze from the text when attempting to recall expressions in the target (in this case, the foreign) language that would correspond to the expressions in the source language (in this case, the native language for participants). This confirmed that spatial saccadic movements are tied to the activation of additional cognitive resources, which facilitates scanning the long-term memory to find the right equivalent. On the other hand, during reading for comprehension, spatial saccadic movements were rarely registered (only for one test subject were minor downward saccadic movements reported). This stems from the fact that the task did not require searching for information in the long-term memory and merely required retaining information for a short period (in the working memory). This translates to lower eye movement activity.

Thus, my experiments show that moving the gaze away from the stimulus (performing spatial saccadic movements) occurs in order to activate additional cognitive resources (irrespective of the direction to which they point) to scan the long-term memory. Therefore, I identified such saccadic movements as an indicator of cognitive load as well as an indicator of long-term memory. This has not been identified before.

11 Interpretation of the Results

Due to the analysis of the differences between the analyzed process and the reference process, it was possible to assess the scale of cognitive load during sight translation. It was found that the analyzed type of translation activity requires a several times greater cognitive load than does reading for comprehension. In this regard, the frequent practice of using sight translation as an exercise to prepare students for interpreting, especially in introductory interpreting classes, should be validated.

The significant differences detected in the perception and reception of text during reading for comprehension and reading for translation question the thesis (e.g., Gile 2009) that one of the components of sight translation is "reading for comprehension." The results suggest that we should instead talk about "reading for translation."

The fact that the experiment involved two processes that differed significantly in terms of cognitive load and that the selected eye-tracking parameters reflected this difference confirm the reliability of these parameters in studies comparing the two tasks. However, within one task on smaller units of analysis (e.g., paragraphs or sentences), the parameter of pupil dilation turned out to be unreliable (more: Płużyczka 2015, 2020). I have illustrated this using the example of paragraphs where the pupil dilation parameter did not indicate the most difficult paragraph for the participants, that is, the one causing the greatest cognitive load. Thus, in studies comparing text units in a single task, this parameter will be unreliable.

The detection of spatial saccadic movements has provided empirical evidence for the involvement of long-term memory in sight translation. Spatial saccadic movements, pointing in various directions and even beyond the translated text, were reported for nearly all test subjects during sight translation. These eye movements are tied to the activation of additional cognitive resources and scanning the long-term memory. This type of memory was not included in Gile's sight translation model. It was not until 2009 that Gile included any memory effort in the sight translation effort model (in his earlier work he did not include memory effort at all). Moreover, he noted that the memory effort in sight translation is a short-term memory effort. However, my experiments clearly proved that long-term memory is involved when searching for the equivalent in the target language. Min'âr-Beloručev also seemed to overlook this, identifying among the mechanisms "memorizing" but forgetting about the extraction of information from long-term memory. In 2004, Agrifoglio noted from her research that memory effort is present in sight translation, but she did not specify which kind of memory (short-term or long-term) is present.

Results of my experiments also verify the thesis of Just and Carpenter (1980), which has dominated eye-tracking studies for over forty years and which assumed that a word is being processed for as long as the fixation upon it lasts. However, it would be more plausible to say that a word is received perceptually during fixation on it, but it can also still be processed when fixation on it ceases.

12 Conclusions

The motivation for conducting eye-tracking experiments on sight translation was to determine to what extent such studies could help us expand our knowledge of the translation process. More precisely, it is to learn how they can help us understand the mental operations involved in translation as well as verify previous hypotheses about the mental modelling of the translation process. Additionally, the studies described fill the gap in the literature when it comes to sight translation. This type of translation is often neglected even in classifications.

I started conducting eye-tracking research in translation studies in 2011 when it was still not very common in the discipline. Moreover, there was no methodological framework on eye-tracking parameters and their exact application on various units of analysis and in between one task. I wanted to verify how reliable these parameters are and whether they could be used to indicate specific mental processes. Having discovered spatial saccadic movements in the pilot study, that is, saccades that go beyond the text, I turned my attention to them in each subsequent experiment to explain their occurrence. To my knowledge, this had not been done in translation studies (or even in text reception studies) or any eye-tracking experiments previously. Moreover, psychological studies on explaining moving the eyes while a subject is responding to a question were conducted using mainly the observational method.

The research questions I addressed in my experiments were (see also Section 4):

(a) What is the (level of) cognitive load during sight translation?
(b) Can it be assessed with the help of eye tracking parameters?
(c) Are selected eye-tracking parameters reliable in evaluating cognitive load on every unit of analysis?
(d) What mental processes can be distinguished by using eye tracking (and is it at all possible)?
(e) What is the visual perception during sight translation and how does it differ from reading for comprehension?

I answered the first question (a) by comparing visual activity during sight translation with that in the baseline process, reading for comprehension. The tested eye-tracking parameters reached values twice (fixation count), two and a half (dwell time), and even three times (revisits) higher than during the control process. The parameter of the average fixation was forty-eight milliseconds higher and the pupil was on average 0.73 millimeters wider during sight translation. The results are empirical confirmation of **a very high cognitive load in this type of translation**. Previously, researchers have been divided about this, with some not considering this type of translation highly difficult due to the source text being in front of the subject at the time.

To question (b) we can answer that **it is possible to assess cognitive load using eye-tracking parameters by comparing two different processes**. This is demonstrated in the answer to question (a). All eye-tracking parameters tested had values several times higher, indicating a much higher cognitive load. However, this is more of an estimation of cognitive load as high, medium, or low, as we do not yet have the tools and methodological framework to measure it accurately.

Regarding the validity of the selected parameters in measuring cognitive load (answer to question (c)), I found that they **all are credible in assessing the level of cognitive load when comparing two processes/tasks**. They all indicated a huge difference between the two analyzed tasks in terms of the mental load required to perform them. However, the research findings presented here showed that **not all parameters are reliable on smaller units of analysis (paragraphs, sentences, and words) when comparing them within one task**. Dwell time, fixation count, and revisits were found to be the most universal, neither dependent on the unit of analysis nor on whether it was a comparison between tasks or within a single task. The parameter of **pupil dilation was found to be unreliable on smaller text units** when they are compared with each other in a single task. That is, it did not indicate which paragraph (sentence, word) in the text that was sight translated was the most difficult. The reason for this might be the specificity of the biological response of our autonomic nervous system. The sympathetic nervous system works very quickly (the pupil dilates rapidly), but the parasympathetic nervous system is much slower (the pupil does not contract as quickly from one paragraph to another, even if that paragraph is much easier). As far as I know, there has not been such a study like this before.

The answer to question (d) seems to be one of the most revealing of the presented experiments. Research to date has not focused on which exact processes can be distinguished based on eye-tracking studies. Cognitive load is a very generalized concept that encompasses many mental processes. Therefore, the discovery that **we can identify a particular mental process and confirm its involvement** in translation is remarkable. We can identify the process of scanning long-term memory due to spatial saccadic movements that were registered in all presented experiments with sight translation. These eye movements are also tied to the activation of additional cognitive resources, so they could be an additional indicator of mental effort and cognitive load.

The demonstrated results also showed **the specificity of information perception during sight translation** (answer to question (e)). This perception is characterized by a very high number of fixations, a long fixation time, as well as irregular saccadic movement. As time is limited, peripheral vision also occurs. As perception during sight translation differs significantly from that during reading for comprehension (short fixations, fewer fixations, regular saccadic movement), **we should talk about "reading for translation"** rather than "reading for comprehension" or even better **"text reception for translation"** in regard to sight translation.

Regarding the mental models of translation discussed at the beginning of the article, we can note on the basis of the presented results that **some of their assumptions can be confirmed, while some should be rejected**. For example, the Effort Model of sight translation presented by Gile is not confirmed by the presented eye-tracking studies. Firstly, Gile does not include long-term memory effort in sight translation. The **involvement of scanning the long-term memory was proven** in my experiments. Secondly, although he singles out reading effort as an element of translation, we can see based on eye-tracking results that the reception of text during reading for comprehension differs significantly from that during sight translation. We should, therefore, rather speak of "reading for translation" or preferably "text reception for translation." Gile's model is generalized, and while his concept of processing capacity and the dependence of translation performance on this is relevant, we will not discuss it here. As for Min'âr-Beloručev's model, it also does not include long-term memory in sight translating but only memorizing. That is, the basic mental process is missing. Moreover, he avoids specifying mental operations, presenting instead the conditions for translation rather than the cognitive processes themselves. Nonetheless, it has to be noted that both Gile and Min'âr-Beloručev considered sight translation to be one of the most difficult types of translation, that is, requiring a high level of cognitive load. This assumption was empirically confirmed in the research presented in this article.

To summarize, the eye-tracking studies presented in this chapter have primarily demonstrated the possibility of identifying, via eye movement, specific mental processes involved in sight translation. To my knowledge, the involvement of long-term memory in sight translation has not previously been investigated or confirmed in empirical studies, especially not by using the eye-tracking method. Furthermore, I identified in my experiments **a new parameter of cognitive load and indicator of long-term memory, namely spatial saccadic movements**, or saccades that go beyond the text. I assume a higher number of spatial saccadic movements indicates a greater cognitive load. Such movements occur in order to reduce the cognitive load and scan the long-term memory. No such studies have been conducted in translation studies or linguistics before to the best of my knowledge. I have only come across such studies in the field of psychology, and these have mainly been studies conducted using the observation method. If eye tracking was used, it took into account often the frequency of saccades (Ehrlichman and Micic 2012) and not spatial saccadic movements as such. This was also the reason why I proposed a new term for such movements registered during translation.

In addition, an analysis was carried out to check **the reliability of selected eye-tracking parameters on different units of analysis**, which I also had not found in previous works. I have cited extensive literature that lists the eye-tracking parameters as indicators of cognitive load but does not check to what extent they actually indicate cognitive load. Because of the analysis of various eye-tracking parameters, and the fact that it was done on various units of analysis (Płużyczka 2015), the limitations of the pupil dilation parameter were discovered. It was also novel to compare sight translation to reading for comprehension to verify the reliability of the parameters and to empirically prove that in translation we are dealing with a specific kind of "reading for translation,"—one that cannot be called "reading" or "reading for comprehension."

In conclusion, eye-tracking research definitely expands the exploratory possibilities, and its results expand the cognitive boundaries in translation studies. It is now time to move from general results about, for example, the distribution of attention to the identification of specific mental processes. Additionally, I believe that further validation of eye-tracking parameters is needed because as we can see, each shows a different scale of magnitude, while some have limitations and are sometimes unreliable. We should also note that we are registering some indicators of mental processes without having direct access to the brain, so we can only make assumptions (of greater probability) as to what exact processes may be going on. There are great prospects for interdisciplinary research in this field, as without the support of neuroscientists and biologists it will be difficult for linguists or translation studies scholars to understand the foundation of translation processes or their biological determinants.

Notes

1 The experiments were supposed to continue in 2020–1, but the pandemic put those plans on hold.
2 I use the term "translation" in its general sense, that is, as an umbrella term covering the written transferring of the meaning expressed in a written source text (the narrow sense of the term "translation," which I will refer to as "written translation"), the oral transferring of the meaning expressed in an oral source text, which is referred to by the term "interpreting," and the oral transferring of the meaning expressed in a written source text, namely "sight translation," which is the focus of the research presented in my chapter.

3 I am aware of the "offset correction" option in the BeGaze eye-tracking data analysis software—but I have consciously not used it because it is manually moving the fixations, which I believe is a manipulation in the results.
4 Experiments were conducted at the same time of day, in the same place in the room, so that the light fell in the same way. Additionally, light amount was measured with a light meter so that there were no big differences.
5 Where t is the value of Student's t-test for specific samples, p—significance, Cohen's d—effect size measure, M—mean, SD—standard deviation.
6 Fixations mean "stopping the gaze" at a particular location in the text or image. It is a relatively stable (there are tiny movements and trembles) position of the eyeball. Fixations usually last for 200—300 ms (D. Richardson, M.J./ Spivey 2009; K. Rayner 1998). It is assumed that fixations are strongly correlated to the cognitive process, that is, during fixations stimuli reach the brain and are consciously processed.
7 Saccades are fast darts of the eye in between items. It is stipulated that during saccadic movements we do not really perceive information, meaning no cognitive process is occurring and the stimuli reaching the brain are not analyzed consciously. The duration of a saccade ranges between 10 and 20 ms. It is a voluntary movement, so saccades are the chief instrument of selective visual attention. The range of movement of the eyes during a saccade spans 1–20 symbols, and on average it is 7–9 symbols.
8 I proposed to create a name to describe saccades going beyond the text (and monitor) because I could not find research on them in the literature. I decided to call them "spatial" because they lead to fixations outside the area recorded by the eye tracker, so we do not know exactly where they point, but "spatial" does not mean a specific space.
9 This confirms that the registration of saccadic movements directed beyond the text is not dependent on the equipment (eye tracker) on which the study is conducted.
10 NLP (*Neuro-Linguistic Programming*). The concept was set up in the 1970s by a mathematician and therapist R. Bandler and a linguist J. Grinder as a form of psychotherapy and a method for self-development (R. Bandler/ J. Grinder 1975). It is, generally speaking, a set of communication techniques that is supposed to change perception and thinking patterns. The assumptions of NLP, which gained a lot of attention, in particular in business circles, have found no confirmation whatsoever in scientific research; in fact, they have been scientifically challenged and undermined (i.a., C. F. Sharpley 1987). At present NLP techniques are considered unscientific methods of persuasion or simply manipulation.

References

Agrifoglio, M. (2004), "Sight Translation and Interpreting: A Comparative Analysis of Constraints and Failures," *Interpreting*, 6(1): 43–67.

Ahern, S. K. and B. Jackson (1979), "Psychological Signs of Information Processing Vary with Intelligence," *Science*, 205: 1289–92.

Barhudarov, L. S. = Бархударов, Л.С. (1975), *Язык и перевод. Вопросы общей и частной теории перевода*, Москва: Международные отношения.

Barik, H. C. (1969), "A Study of Simultaneous Interpretation," Unpublished doctoral diss., University of North Carolina (On file with University Microfilms, Ann Arbor, Michigan; order no. 70-3192).

Bell, R. T. (1991), *Translation and Translating: Theory and Practice*, London and New York: Longman.

Christman, S. D., K. J. Garvey, R. E. Propper, and K. A. Phaneuf (2003), "Bilateral Eye Movements Enhance the Retrieval of Episodic Memories," *Neuropsychology*, 17: 221–9.

Dejean Le Féal, K. (1981), "L'enseignement des méthodes d'interprétation," in J. Delisle (ed.), *L'enseignement de l'interprétation et de la traduction: De la théorie à la pédagogie, (seria, Cahiers de traductologie,"* 4), 75–98, Ottawa: Editions de l'Université d'Ottawa.

Duchowski, A. T., (2007 [2003]), *Eye Tracking Methodology: Theory and Practice*, New York: Springer Verlag.

Ehrlichman, H. and D. Micic (2012), "Why People Move Their Eyes When They Think?," *Current Directions in Psychological Science*, 21(2): 96–100.

Ehrlichman, H., D. Micic, A. Sousa, and J. Zhu (2007), "Looking for Answers: Eye Movements in Non-visual Cognitive Tasks," *Brain and Cognition*, 64: 7–20.

Feldweg, E. (1996), *Der Konferenzdolmetscher im internationalen Kommunikationsprozess*, Heidelberg: Groos.

Gerloff, P. (1988), "From French to English: A Look at the Translation Process in Students, Bilinguals, and Professional Translators," UM Dissertation Services, University Microfilms International, Ann Arbor.

Gerver, D. (1971), "Aspects of Simultaneous Interpretation and Human Information Processing," Unpublished D.Phil. thesis, Oxford University.

Gile, D. (1983), "Des difficultés de langue en interprétation simultanée," *Traduire*, 117: 2–8.

Gile, D. (1995), *Basic Concepts and Models for Interpreter and Translator Training*, Amsterdam: John Benjamins Publishing.

Gile, D. (2009), *Basic Concepts and Models for Interpreter and Translator Training*, Rev. ed., Amsterdam: John Benjamins Publishing.

Grucza, S., A. Bonek, D. Kudła, M. Castelas, M. Płużyczka, and M. Patera (2019), *Czytanie pretranslacyjne a jakość tłumaczenia a vista. Wyniki longitudinalnego badania okulograficznego* [Pre-translation Reading vs. the Quality of Sight Translation. Results of a Longitudinal Eyetracking Study], Warszawa: Wydawnictwo Naukowe Instytutu Komunikacji Specjalistycznej I Interkulturowej.

Gutt, E.-A. (1991/2000), *Translation and Relevance: Cognition and Context*, Manchester and New York: St. Jerome.

Herbert, J. (1952), *Manuel de l'interprète. Comment on devient interprète de conférence*, Geneva: Georg.

Hoeks, B. and W. J. M. Levelt (1993), "Pupillary Dilation as a Measure of Attention: A Quantitative System Analysis," *Behavior Research Methods, Instruments & Computers*, 25: 16–26.

Hyönä, J., J. Tommola, and A.-M. Alaj (1995), "Pupil Dilation as a Measure of Processing Load in Simultaneous Interpretation and Other Language Tasks," *The Quarterly Journal of Experimental Psychology*, 48A: 598–612.

Just, M. A. and P. A. Carpenter (1980), "A Theory of Reading: From Eye Fixations to Comprehension." *Psychological Review*, 87(4): 329–54.

Just, M. A. and P. A. Carpenter (1993), "The Intensity Dimension of Thought: Pupillometric Indices of Sentence Processing," *Canadian Journal of Experimental Psychology*, 47(2): 310–39. https://doi.org/10.1037/h0078820

Kahneman, D. (1973), *Attention and Effort*, Engelwood Cliffs: Prentice Hall.

Kahneman, D. and J. Beatty (1966), "Pupil Diameter and Load on Memory," *Science*, 154: 1583–5.

Kahneman, D., L. Onuska, and R. E. Wolman (1968), "Effects of Grouping of the Pupillary Response in a Short-term Memory Task," *Quarterly Journal of Experimental Psychology*, 20: 309–11.

Kalina, S. (2003), "Stegreifübersetzen—Eine translatorische Übungsform," in B. Nord and P. A. Schmitt (eds.), *Traducta Navis. Festschrift zum 60. Geburtstag von Christiane Nord*, 103–17, Tübingen: Stauffenburg.

Kiraly, D. (1995), *Pathways to Translation. Pedagogy and Process*, Kent: The Kent State University.

Krings, H. P. (1986), *Was in den Köpfen von Übersetzern vorgeht. Eine empirische Untersuchung zur Struktur des Übersetzungsprozesses an fortgeschrittenen Französischlernern*, Tübingen: Narr.

Kussmaul, P. (1991), "Creativity in the Translation Process: Empirical Approaches," in K. M. van Leuven-Zwart and T. Naaijkens (eds.), *Translation Studies: The State of the Art. Proceedings of the First James S. Holmes Symposium on Translation Studies*, 91–101, Amsterdam and Atlanta: Rodopi.

Kussmaul, P. (1995), *Training the Translator*, Amsterdam: John Benjamins Publishing.

Kutz, W. (2002), "Dolmetschkompetenz und ihre Vermittlung," in J. Best and S. Kalina (red.), *Übersetzen und Dolmetschen. Eine Orientierungshilfe*, 184–95, Tübingen: UTB.

Lambert, S. (1988), "A Human Information Processing and Cognitive Approach to the Training of Simultaneous Interpreters," in D. L. Hammond (ed.), *Languages at Crossroads. Proceedings of the 29th Annual Conference of the American Translators Association*, 379–87, Medford and New York: Learned Information Inc.

Lambert, S. (1991), "Aptitude Testing for Simultaneous Interpretation at the University of Ottawa," *Meta: journal des traducteurs/ Meta: Translators' Journal*, 36(4): 586–94.

Lederer, M. (1981), *La traduction simultanée. Expérience et théorie*, Minard: Lettres Modernes.

Lederer, M. (1994), *La traduction aujourd'hui*, Paris: Hachette.

Lörscher, W. (1987), *Übersetzungsperformanz, Übersetzungsprozeß und Übersetzungsstrategien. Eine psycholinguistische Untersuchung*, Universität Essen: Mimeo.

Lörscher, W. (1991), *Translation Performance, Translation Process, and Translation Strategies. A Psycholinguistic Investigation*, Tübingen: Narr.

Matthews, G., W. Middleton, B. Gilmartin, and M. A. Bullimore (1991), "Pupillary Diameter and Cognitive Load," *Journal of Psychophysiology*, 5: 265–71.

Micic, D., H. Ehrlichman, and R. Chen (2010), "Why Do We Move Our Eyes while Trying to Remember? The Relationship between Non-visual Gaze Patterns and Memory," *Brain and Cognition*, 74: 210–24.

Min'âr-Beloručev, R. K. = Миньяр-Белоручев, Р. К. (1980), *Общая теория перевода и устный перевод*, Москва: Воениздат.

Moser-Mercer, B. (1997/2002), "Process Models in Simultaneous Interpretation," in F. Pöchhacker and M. Shlesinger (eds), *The Interpreting Studies Reader*, 149–61, London and New York: Routledge.

Muñoz Martín, R. and C. Martín de León (2020), "Translation and Cognitive Science," in F. Alves and A. Jakobsen (eds.), *The Routledge Handbook of Translation and Cognition*, 52–68, London: Routledge.

Olalla-Soler, Ch., J. F. Aixelá, and S. Rovira-Esteva (2020), "Mapping Cognitive Translation and Interpreting Studies: A Bibliometric Approach," *Linguistica Antverpiensia. New Series – Themes in Translation Studies*, 19. https://doi.org/10.52034/lanstts.v19i0.542

Oléron, P. and H. Nanpon (1965), "Recherches sur la traduction simultanée," *Journal de Psychologie Normale et Pathologique*, 62(1): 73–94.

Osgood C. E. and T. A. Sebeok, eds. (1954), "Psycholinguistics: A Survey of Theory and Research Problems," *The Journal of Abnormal and Social Psychology*, 49(4, Pt.2): i–203. https://doi.org/10.1037/h0063655

Paneth, E. (1957), "An Investigation into Conference Interpreting (With Special Reference to the Training of Interpreters)," Thesis for the Degree of M.A. in Education, London University.

Percival, Ch. (1983), "Techniques and Presentation," in C. Picken (eds.), *The Translator's Handbook*, 89–97, London: Aslib.

Płużyczka, M. (2013), "Eyetracking Supported Research Into Sight Translation. Lapsological Conclusions," in S. Grucza, M. Płużyczka, and J. Zając (eds), *Translation Studies and Eye-Tracking Analysis*, 105–38, Frankfurt am Main: Peter Lang Verlag.

Płużyczka, M. (2015), *Tłumaczenie a vista. Rozważania teoretyczne i badania eyetrackingowe [Sight translation. Theoretical Considerations and Eyetracking Research]*, Warsaw: Wydawnictwo Naukowe Instytutu Komunikacji Specjalistycznej I Interkulturowej.

Płużyczka, M. (2016), "Przestrzenne ruchy sakadowe a pamięć długotrwała [Spatial Saccadic Movements and Long-term Memory]," *Lingwistyka Stosowana/ Applied Linguistics*, 20(5): 101–18. https://doi.org/10.32612/uw.20804814.2016.5

Płużyczka, M. (2020), "Tracking Mental Processes in Sight Translation. Neurobiological Determinants of Selected Eye Tracking Parameters," *Translation, Cognition & Behavior*, 3(2): 209–23.

Pöchhacker, F. (2004), *Introducing Interpreting Studies*, London and New York: Routledge.

Rayner, K. (1998), "Eye Movements in Reading and Information Processing: 20 Years of Research," *Psychological Bulletin*, 124(3): 372–422.

Rayner, K. and A. Pollatsek (1989), *The Psychology of Reading*, Englewood Cliffs: Prentice Hall.

Renshaw, J. A., J. E. Finlay, R. D. Ward, and D. Tyfa (2004a), "Regressions Re-visited: A New Definition for the Visual Display Paradigm," in *CHI '04 Extended Abstracts on Human Factors in Computing Systems*, 1437–40, New York: ACM.

Renshaw, J. A., J. E. Finlay, R. D. Ward, and D. Tyfa (2004b), "Understanding Visual Influence in Graph Design through Temporal and Spatial Eye Movement Characteristics," *Interacting with Computers*, 16: 557–78.

Seleskovitch, D. (1968), *L'interprète dans les conférences internationales, problèmes de langage et de communication*, Washington, DC: Pen ad Booth.

Seleskovitch, D. (1975), *Langage, langues et mémoire: Étude de la prise de notes en interprétation consecutive*, Paris: Lettres modernes.

Seleskovitch, D. (1983), "Enseignement de la traduction à vue," *Revue de Phonetique Appliquée*, 66: 165–8.

Seleskovitch D. and M. Lederer (1984), *Interpréter pour traduire*, Paris: Didier.

Siegle, G.J., S. R. Steinhauer, C. S. Carter, W. Ramel, and M. E. Thase (2003), "Do the Seconds Turn into Hours? Relationships between Sustained Pupil Dilation in Response to Emotional Information and Self-Reported Rumination," *Cognitive Therapy and Research*, 27: 365–82.

van Hoof, H. (1962), *Théorie et Pratique de l'interprétation (avec application particuliere à l'anglais et français)*, München: Max Hueber Verlag.

von Wartensleben, G. (1910), "Beiträge zur Psychologie der Übersetzung," *Zeitschrift für Psychologie*, 57: 90–115.

Wilss, W. (1996), *Knowledge and Skills in Translator Behavior*, Amsterdam and Philadelphia: John Benjamins Publishing.

Wright, P. and D. Kahneman (1971), "Evidence for Alternative Strategies of Sentence Retention," *Quarterly Journal of Experimental Psychology*, 23: 197–213.

Yarbus, A. L. (also: Ârbus, A. L. = Ярбус А.Л., 1965), (1967), *Eye Movements and Vision*, New York: Plenum Press.

Żmudzki, J. (2015), *Blattdolmetschen in paradigmatischer Perspektive der anthropozentrischen Translatorik*, Lubliner Beiträge zur Germanistik und angewandten Linguistik, Frankfurt/M.: Peter Lang.

Conceptual Variations in Legal Translation between "Right" and "權利"

Junfeng Zhao and Jie Xue

1 Introduction

Legal transplant has long been an international practice of both legislature and judicature to import new concepts and rules of law that are available in foreign legal systems. Though the "transplant" metaphor, borrowed from botany and horticulture, has been criticized by many (Seidman 1975; Kahn-Freund 1975; Friedman 1979; Legrand 1997; Friedman 2001) for its oversimplification of the direct or indirect contact and mutual influence between different legal systems (or cultures), it is undeniable that the common grounds between the legal institutions in different countries at present can mostly be traced back to lessons drawn from one by another some years or centuries ago. However, Watson's assertion that the transplantation of a legal concept or rule could be quickly done without any knowledge of the "political, social or economic context of the foreign law" (Watson 1976: 79) still seems to carry things to the extreme. It would be unwise to deny such a possibility, but an extremely simple, mechanistic case of legal transplant is not likely to arouse the interest of researchers (Stein 1977: 209). In other words, scholars would be more intrigued with discovering the variations embedded in the process of legal borrowing and thus exploring potential causes. Now that legal transplant has become a "standard approach to comparative law" (Cairns 2013: 695), scholars in related fields probe into not only the macroscopic environment but also relatively microscopic factors. Geller (1994) and Miller (2003) investigate the environment where the legal concept or rule is fostered and where it is to be cultivated. Language issues involved in the process of legal transplant have also been examined (e.g., Clarke 2006; Wang 2010), as the circulation of legal ideas mostly happens interlingually. Langer

(2004) even suggests that the metaphoric expression of legal transplant should be replaced by legal translation, of course as a metaphor as well, to indicate the transformations that might take place when legal ideas are transferred from the source system to the target.

Traditionally, translation studies presuppose conceptual equivalence (Pym 2007), based on which researchers debate about topics like fidelity, faithfulness, or loyalty. It was once believed that there must be a concept and an expression of the concept in the target language that equals the original in the source language, and that translators are "equivalence-seeker" (Mossop 1983: 246). It also served as the fundamental motive for linguists to compile bilingual or multilingual dictionaries that grew thicker and thicker, as Borges (1984: 51) argues that "the dictionary is based on the hypothesis—obviously an unproven one—that languages are made up of equivalent synonyms." This prescriptive presumption could be valid under many circumstances when words are representations of the physical world because the universality of natural objects forms the basis for a linguistic equation. However, such equations could be broken even when signifying the natural world due to discrepancies in reality such as the cliché of Eskimo words for snow, let alone intellectual concepts in the mental world like law. A scientific, or even mathematical, understanding of equivalence, therefore, is unacceptable and misleading (Halverson 1997: 211). Though many other scholars (e.g., Snell-Hornby 1988: 22) also criticize or radically propose to discard the notion of equivalence in translation studies, Pym argues that equivalence is "a necessary and functional illusion" for demarcating what translation is and enabling translators to make a living (1995: 167). At least two crucial implications can be grasped based on these insightful opinions. For one thing, equivalence has never been reducible to formal correspondence in language alone due to the social nature of translation; for another, translation studies are actually more concerned with why translation is not equivalent than why it is. It would be no surprise therefore to encounter the "cultural turn" of translation studies in the late 1980s and 1990s (Bassnett and Lefevere 1990: 1). Since then, extensive research has been conducted to describe and explain translation in a cultural context through the theoretical lens of sociology, politics, history, and so on.

A sociological perspective of translation studies centers on the proposition that translation is a social practice that is shaped by social surroundings and induces social consequences (Buzelin 2013: 187). In other words, translation is regarded as an influential event in the real world instead of a code-switching activity simply at the linguistic level. Consequently, translators are no longer socially detached wordsmiths who devote all their effort to finding conceptual equivalents with which they cloak themselves in the process of translation. Instead, they become visible social agents who develop multifarious strategies to conform to or deviate from the fixed structure of the society (Wolf 2007: 19). This new perspective shifts focus onto the skopos, power, ideology, social measure, and any other cultural factors related to the role of translators but at the same time incurs risks of ignoring the blurred pixels of words and phrases through which the role of translators are staged (Lü 2004: 56; Singh 2007: 80). This gap between the traditional and new perspectives of translation studies, stressing, respectively, text and context, highlights the importance of an interface of cognition and sociology, that is, the study of how meaning is constructed and perceived under given social conditions.

2 A Cognitive-Sociological Approach to Legal Translation

Progress in cognitive linguistics in the twentieth century significantly propelled the development of sociological investigations into how language plays a part in the process of social interaction. One of the first scholars to name such a strand of sociology as "cognitive sociology" is Aaron Cicourel (1974), who pays special attention in his book to how social interaction is organized and represented through language and meaning, including nonverbal language. While Cicourel adopts a generative grammar or semantics approach to sociological issues, new achievements in embodied-cognitive linguistics enable cognitive sociologists to explore the ways in which humans form their conception of social structure.

Fauconnier and Turner (1998: 143, 2002: 46) propose a network model of conceptual integration or blending, in which conceptual elements in two or more input spaces are projected to the blend space(s) with some original elements missing and some new elements emerging. Between the input spaces exists a generic space in which each element can find a counterpart in both or all input spaces, thus constituting the lowest possibility for projection. Projected elements may undergo three kinds of operation: composition, completion, and elaboration. The composition of elements could be a fusion of counterparts or bringing in the counterparts separately. A composition can be completed unconsciously by background knowledge from the input spaces and further elaborated by recruiting new principles and logic in the blend space. These three processes construct an emergent structure of elements in the blend space. Fauconnier and Turner's network model is highly capable of explaining the meaning-making of new concepts not only in a monolingual context but also in the cognitive analysis of translation (Wang 2001). When a concept is translated into another language, translators have to represent the original conceptual structure with existing elements in the target language, which are generically partial counterparts but scarcely equivalent in all aspects, as previously discussed. It is thus inevitable that the original concept will be projected selectively and that new conceptual elements will be generated.

Adapting the original model, Wang (2019: 752) holds that, in the translation process, the author can be regarded as input space 1, that is, the author space, containing the source text and schemata; and the translator as input space 2, that is, the translator space, containing language proficiency and background knowledge. A blended text of translation is produced in the translation space on the basis of the counterpart connections in the generic space. Furthermore, Wang argues that the weight of the two input spaces varies in the blending, hence an inclination toward domestication or foreignization reflected in the style of a translation product (2019: 753–4). It is this unbalanced state in weight that gives rise to the sociological aspect of translation. The translator, situated in a particular sociocultural context, makes circumstantial decisions in the process of conceptual mapping and integration, and such decisions will stimulate the social settings or cultural context to change in an explicit or implicit manner.

Though cognitive scientists endeavor to discover the underlying mechanism for human cognition and have reached some convincing conclusions in laboratory settings, a complete understanding of cognition cannot be achieved without situating conceptual constructs in real social and cultural environment. Cognitive sociologists adopt a structuralist (e.g., Goffman 1986) or constructionist (e.g., Loseke 2003) view to analyze the representation, classification, and integration of social meaning. Their principal proposition is that human cognition deals with new information by classifying it according to the existing structure and integrating it with established constructs. Some other cognitive sociologists (e.g., Zerubavel 1999) probe into the phenomenon that members of a particular community tend to focus on certain people, places, objects, and events while ignoring others. For example, an employment culture that values social esteem over actual payment encourages the young to enter prestigious professions such as teachers, nurses, and firefighters, compared to less respected positions such as stockbrokers, business executives, and actors. Researchers believe that the attention scheme of the members of a particular community is socially molded to a large degree, though individual idiosyncrasy also exerts some effect (Cerulo 2005: 108). However, these attentional settings could be altered by influential historical events, for instance, by legal transplant, which is the transposition of law from one society to another.

Hart (1954: 41–7) maintains that the precise meaning of legal concepts derives from a given legal context where a particular legal system and many rules of law have been established. Legal concepts are closely bound up with social institutions (Cao 2002: 229). Therefore, in a cognitive-sociological account of legal transplant, conceptual variations in the process of translation can be analyzed by firstly comparing the asymmetry of attentional schemes (Brekhus 2015: 26) of the source and target cultures and then identifying and explicating the shift of focus resulting from interlingual and intercultural variations.

That China has been conducting legal transplants as an endeavor to establish its new system of law since as early as the mid-nineteenth century makes a perfect case for a cognitive-sociological analysis of legal translation. In the late Qing dynasty, many Chinese scholars were awakened by humiliating defeats in the wars with foreign powers and called desperately for learning from the West. Many academic works, including jurisprudential publications, were translated into Chinese. William A. P. Martin's Chinese translation of *Elements of International Law* written by Henry Wheaton is regarded as the "first full practice of legal translation in modern China" (He 2014: 200). This influential book coined numerous basic legal terms that are used extensively today. In 1892, the Qing government was compelled to formulate new legislation in conformity with its Western counterpart. Though these newly drafted laws did not come into effect eventually due to strong opposition from the conservatives (Liang 2013: 355), the tentative transplantation of the Western legal system aroused deep contemplation among Chinese legal scholars and provided chief cornerstones for the legal reform later undertaken by China.

3 The Translation of the Western Legal Concept Right into Chinese Law

As a rudimentary concept in law, the English word "right" would be translated by translators nowadays into 權利 without any hesitation. The concept is pervasive in legislation and judicial documents as well as in jurisprudential publications in academia and communications among laypeople. It appears that the fantasy of equivalence has been realized between these two words in different languages. However, such a conclusion comes under question when the transplantation of the Western legal concept right is observed via a cognitive-sociological lens.

Browsing through a dictionary of ancient Chinese language, we cannot find a clearly defined concept equivalent to the Western idea of right. Does that mean legal rights were utterly neglected in ancient China for thousands of years before the concept of right was transplanted? The answer to this question is hardly satisfactory with a simple yes or no. A credible explanation for this social reality needs to be sought by thoroughly investigating the traditional Confucian approach to law.

3.1 Reciprocal Obligation in Ancient Chinese Law

From the perspective of embodied cognition, it can be reasonably inferred that the relationship between rights and obligations must have been pondered by early philosophers in both China and the West ever since they had realized the social distinction between self and other(s). According to Confucius and his followers, social relations are divided into five different types: the relations between ruler and subjects, parents and children, husband and wife, elder and younger brothers, and between friends (Pan 2010). Nevertheless, the fundamental principle that governs ancient Chinese society is the Confucian philosophy of 和 (hé, harmony). By upholding peaceful engagement with others, ancient Chinese gave much more accentuation to personal obligations than private rights, which sharply contrasts with the West. Within a different philosophical framework, the social relations between self and other(s), cognized by Westerners as rights and obligations, are perceived by Chinese literati via 義 (yì, righteousness) and 利 (lì, benefit).

The traditional Chinese character 義 is vertically composed of two components: 羊 (yáng, sheep, the animal traditionally used as sacrifice) and 我 (wǒ, a particular weapon used to sacrifice, later evolved into a singular first-person pronoun). It denotes righteousness, justice, and good-natured interpersonal relationship. As for 利 in both traditional and simplified Chinese, it comprises the left part 禾 (hé, cereal crops), which signifies a mature agricultural plant, and the right part 刂 (dāo, a knife), which represents the sickle used to harvest. The adjective 利 is used to describe the sharpness of a blade, the nimbleness of a horse, and the smoothness of a process. Its nominal usage refers to benefits, advantages, interests, and profits.

As early as in the spring and autumn period, a great Chinese thinker had argued that "凡有血氣，皆有爭心，故利不可強，思義為愈。義，利之本也，蘊利生孽。" (All that have blood and breath have the disposition to contend, so benefits should not be obtained by force. It would be better to think of righteousness. Righteousness is the root of benefits. To accumulate benefits gives rise to evildoing. Our translation) (Guo, Cheng and Li 2012: 1727). However, the long-lasting debate between righteousness and benefit among Chinese scholars is generally believed to have started with Confucius's famous saying: "君子喻於義，小人喻於利。" (A gentleman understands things in terms of righteousness, while a lesser man understands things in terms of benefits. Our translation) (Yang 2017: 54). Confucius and his keen followers believe that human beings, born to become social members, should consider what is righteous in the society before what is beneficial to themselves and that personal gain can be realized through virtuous deeds of other social actors. The seemingly overwhelming stress put on righteousness, nonetheless, does not mean that benefits are unrecognized in the Confucian conception of social order. The implication of emphasizing righteousness over benefit consists in the condemnation of being actuated merely by mercenary views, and benefits obtained by reasonable and upright means are justly accepted.

Some researchers (e.g., Peerenboom 1995: 377) question the notion of mutual obligation among social beings by arguing that the Confucian version of benefits can be gained only when all members of the society constantly abide by ethical rules as expected, which is probably an illusion. After all, certain irreconcilable conflicts exist between righteous and beneficial social practices. What happens then if someone's misconducts cause harm to others' benefit? The ultimate solution of Confucians to this knotty issue is not to punish but to exhort people not to misbehave in the first place. Of course, punishment is also prescribed in the law apart from moral preaching. However, for a society that put 禮 (lǐ, rites) before 法 (fǎ, law), punishments are applied to restore balance when social beings break the harmonious state of nature. That also explains why ancient Chinese statutes are primarily penal codes.

It has to be admitted that the Confucian approach to law is not immune to innate deficiencies. Taking an obligation-oriented option of social relations obscures the concept of right in the background of legal philosophy. One of the consequences is that though "rights in fact" (Peng 2004: 343) relating to property and contract are indirectly established in ancient China, the concept of "civil rights" promoting equality and liberty did not grow autogenously in the soil of ancient Chinese philosophical and cultural traditions. The ancient Chinese legal system without the concept of civil rights had been operating in its way domestically and exerting far-reaching effects on the legal theories and practices in other Asian countries until an ancient China was forced to integrate with a modern world.

3.2 Conceptual Integration between Right and 權利

The English word "right," according to *Online Etymology Dictionary* (Harper 2021), owes its origin ultimately to the Proto-Indo-European root *-reg*, meaning move in a straight line, which produces Old English *riht*, Old Saxon *reht*, Middle Dutch *recht*, and Latin *rectus*. As is believed by embodied-cognitive linguists, humans base their cognition on what they see, hear, touch, smell, and taste in the physical world. Therefore, the rule for differentiating between a straight and bent line in geometry is metaphorically convenient for measuring whether social beings' conduct is acceptable. Social behavior is conceived as morally right when it is in agreement with generally acknowledged rules. Moral rights are universal and inherent in natural law theories. The transition from recognizing a moral right to claiming a legal right is a major step toward a positive law conception of right, which means that legal rights are those moral rights confirmed through legislative enactments or judicial decisions. The law sets only the minimum requirement for social actors. However, it is not always morally right to exercise a legal right. An example would be that a wealthy man wastes a large amount of food he bought with the money he earned by lawful means, which can be morally condemned but not legally punished.

It is believed that the key legal term "right" was first translated into Chinese as 權 or 權利 by William A. P. Martin, together with Chinese colleagues according to the preface, in the translation of Wheaton's *Elements of International Law* published in 1864. Before that, scholars referred to right by employing explanatory expressions such as 例 (rule), 道理 (principle), and 應當的 (obliged) in other translated works (He 2014: 194). The characters 權 and 利 and the compound word of the two used by Martin have their original meaning in traditional Chinese. The character 權 (*quán*) literally means a kind of tree and is often used to refer to the sliding weight of a steelyard, from which its figurative meanings as a verb such as to weigh, to balance, and to compare are derived, as well as its nominal signification of reins of power. The word 權利 can be found, for instance, in a classical Chinese literature *Xunzi*. In the first article of this collection of philosophical writings, Xun Kuang (荀匡) wrote: "是故權利不能傾也，群眾不能移也，天下不能蕩也。" (For this reason, power and benefit cannot tempt him; the multitude cannot influence him; and the entire world cannot sway him. Our translation) (Fang and Li 2011: 11). The translated term shares few, if not none, connotations and denotations with its original meaning in Chinese. Martin excuses himself for having no better alternative but to use 權 and sometimes with 利 to translate right (Wang 2001: 166). Nevertheless, for what reason Martin chose 權(利) as the Chinese counterpart for right in English, rather than simply offer a transliteration as it was the translation technique widely adopted at the time, still deserves to be investigated. After all, the decision-making of translators more or less reflects rationality despite the undeniable existence of contingency.

An analysis of the conceptual integration network can help dig into the profound schema that underlies lexical choices in translation. To answer the earlier question requires searching for the conceptual elements in the generic space, that is, counterpart connections between right and 權(利) (see Figure 8.1). According to Martin and his Chinese fellow translators in the Chinese version of *Introduction to the Study of International Law* written by Theodore Dwight Woolsey, the term 權 refers not only to "有司所操之權" (the power held by the authority, our translation) but also to "凡人理所應得之分" (the due every ordinary person deserves, our translation). The character 利 is added sometimes, such as in "庶人本有之權利" (the inherent right of the common people, our translation) (Li 1998: 120). As previously discussed, the Chinese character 權 has a figurative meaning of reins of power. It refers to the authority to make decisions in view of the relative weight (value or importance) of possible options. And 利 means the benefits, interests, or profits brought by certain actions. Therefore, the lexical choice in Martin's translation indicates an

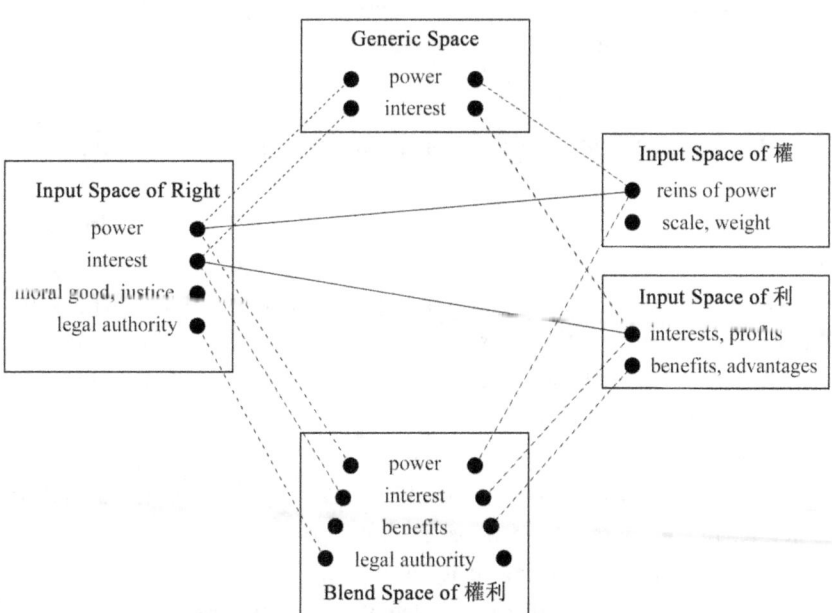

Figure 8.1 Conceptual integration between right and 權利.

understanding of right politically as power and economically as interest. Put in another way, the new term is invented by illustrating the concept by means of describing its epistemological properties, instead of directly defining right in its ontological nature of morality.

After identifying which conceptual elements of the input spaces are projected, it is subsequently crucial to inspect which elements are sifted out and which elements are emergent. The etymological meaning of straight and just fundamentally embedded in the concept of right is exceptionally elusive in its Chinese translation. Furthermore, by compounding two characters that have already been used together as a word suggesting a derogatory meaning in traditional Chinese literature, Martin may have purposelessly rendered a morally ideal and favorable concept into a somewhat realistic and negative one. What is emergent in the Chinese term can be exposed by an instance of back translation in the appendix to a later published work, the Chinese version of William Edward Hall's *International Law*, where Martin back translated 權利 into right and privilege (Liu 1999: 150). It seems that Martin's translation of right as 權利 is, to some degree, contingent due to the conceptual lacuna. However, the acceptance and prevalence of this translated term in the Chinese language and culture cannot be easily taken for granted. How the connotation and denotation of 權利 are constructed and perceived by the Chinese society at the turn of the century falls into the scope of a cognitive-sociological quest.

4 A Cognitive-sociological Analysis of Conceptual Variations

A cognitive-sociological view on translation explores how the cultures and societies interact via the bridge of the translator's linguistic operations. Regarding the translation of a concept as both a cognitive activity and a social practice, this view acknowledges the translator's role as social agent and recognizes the existence of a well-established structure of social constructs. The purpose is to figure out the social and cognitive mechanism for conceptual variations: what subjective and objective factors motivate translators to make linguistic choices and what effect is produced intentionally or unintentionally on the established structure. In the following sections, the rendition of right into 權利 will be examined by analyzing the social identity of the translator, the classification of the transplanted concept, and its integration and the preference of cultural attention in the Chinese society.

4.1 Right as Power and Interest

Though the concept of right, according to Hohfeld's analysis (Hislop 1967: 57), consists of the following elements: privilege, claim, power, and immunity, and the earliest modern use of right, referring to power and privilege, dates back to debates in the Middle Ages (Wenar 2020), special attention to power and interest in Chinese conception of right is still unneglectable.

As Wang (2005: 31) argues, an investigation into the Chinese translation of this key term cannot be persuasive enough without taking into account the historical circumstances under which Martin translated the book. Amid frequent diplomatic disputes between the Qing government and Western powers, Martin's translation of *Elements of International Law* was seen both by Western diplomats as a source of legal justification for invasion and by Chinese officials as a source of legal reasoning to defend sovereignty (Liu 1999). Personally, what Martin was trying to achieve as a translator, a missionary, and a diplomat may be to establish a common ground between Christian values and traditional Chinese philosophy, based on which the Qing court was expected to accept foreign claims to political and commercial rights such as consular jurisdiction and free trade. However, the establishment of such a ground and the justification of those rights are significantly frustrated by the historical fact that they were all obtained by military force. The conception of right as power is thus not surprising.

Power-oriented comprehension of right in China can also be attributed to the fact that the Western concept was first introduced to China through a book of international law. Though a considerable portion of the book touches on personal rights, the subject of rights mentioned therein mainly refers to states, not individual persons. Accordingly, the translated concept of right was a compound comprising both rights and powers for a very long period of time (Tong 2021: 1254). In a society placing insurmountable emphasis on the sense of belonging to the society, the earliest reference of 權利 in the law of nations, rather than the law of persons, further contributes to the rough division between the powers or authority of political entities and the rights of individuals.

A sociological consideration can also account for the close association of right with interest. As previously mentioned, although there may not be a specific legal term, the right to property was undoubtedly admitted in ancient China because the legal principle that a piece of property should be returned to its rightful owner has long been established. Numerous judgments on disputes over private property can be found to have applied this principle. Similarly, an injurer shall be liable for monetary damages to compensate for the harm caused to the injured, which means that ancient Chinese law protects both property rights to tangible objects and fundamental rights to the human body. However, such rights are all somehow related to economic interests. Early modern Chinese conception of rights is highly distracted by the focus on corporeal things as the object of rights. This proposition may be illustrated by the conservatives' strong objection to new family law during the legal reform initiated by the late Qing government. With a few disagreements about protecting real rights, they fiercely condemned the provisions prescribing children's rights against their parents (Liang 2013: 354). More specifically, they accommodated "right" to a legal concept to deal merely with economic relations among social members. However, family relations are not subject to the matter of rights because negotiating rights between parents and children dramatically undermines the family values of Confucianism (Tiwald 2011: 244).

Peerenhoom (1995: 361) maintains that the distinction between right and interest lies in the moral nature of right and the consequentialist and utilitarian implication of interest, but "the *li* of *quanli* gives a utilitarian cast to the term 'rights' by evoking negative connotations of self-interest" (365). The inherent and inalienable components of right resting heavily on the theoretical basis of natural law and individualism originated in the West did not enter into the Chinese conception of right within the feudal system and social hierarchy of ancient China, thus failing to raise full consciousness of civil rights among ordinary Chinese in the early nineteenth century.

4.2 Right Within the Framework of 義

It must be pointed out that not all Chinese scholars failed to escape the hidden pitfall in Martin's translation of right, at least not those who were able to read right-related Western literature in the original language. Though the utterly new semantic entry of 權利 was eventually listed in Chinese dictionaries, the Chinese translation of the concept of right was not always indisputable for many Chinese scholars.

A prominent figure in the Chinese history of translation, Yan Fu (嚴復), who translated many Western academic works such as Montesquieu's *The Spirit of Law*, Huxley's *Evolution and Ethics*, Spencer's *The Study of Sociology*, and Smith's *The Wealth of Nations*, puts up his opposition to Martin's translation of right. Yan holds that translating right into 權利 is like 以霸譯王 (recognizing a despotic warlord as the legitimate king, our translation), which brings about a highly adverse effect on the idealized account of right (Wang 1986: 519).

Rights are inherent to humans, not vied for with others by means of force or power. Therefore, he proposes to invent a pair of new terms 民直 (literally civil straight) or 天直 (literally heavenly straight) for right and 民義 (literally civil righteousness) for obligation because the meaning of right goes ultimately back to straight in English. However, after thirty years of dissemination within China and to and from Japan (Li 1998), 權利 had already become an established popular term in China. In spite of his proposal of another coinage for the academia, Yan himself had to use the ill-defined but widely used term in his publications in the early twentieth century.

It is fairly natural for Chinese scholars to realize that the traditional Chinese notion of 義 bears the meaning of moral righteousness that shares a highly similar connotation with the Western concept right. For over 2,000 years, the Chinese people built and managed their relations with others under the Confucian principle that 義 precedes 利, with the former constantly occupying the very center of morality and law. In a cultural environment with great confidence in the Chinese civilization, many eminent figures in modern Chinese history elaborate on the seeming coincidence between 義 and right and try to interpret right with this deep-rooted and rich-connotated traditional Chinese concept.

Liang Qichao is a significant intellectual who composed a pile of works to introduce the idea of right. He argues in an essay on rights that: "大抵中國善言仁，而泰西善言義。仁者，人也。我利人，人亦利我，是所重者常在人也。義者，我也。我不害人，而亦不許人之害我，是所重者常在我也。" (It can be generally concluded that Chinese focus on benevolence whereas Westerners on righteousness. Benevolence is concerned with others. A person who benefits others will benefit from others, hence the constant emphasis on others. Righteousness, on the other hand, is concerned with oneself. A person who does not harm others will not be harmed by others, hence a constant focus on oneself. Our translation) (Liang 2016: 92). It can be seen that the difference between Chinese and Western traditions in terms of right is interpreted simply as a matter of attention. By invoking another vital Confucian concept 仁 (*rén*, benevolence), Liang expressly incorporates the connotation of right into the notion of 義. Echoing Liang's conception is Cai Yuanpei's discussion on 公義 (literally public righteousness) and 公德 (literally public virtue) (Chen 2021: 62–6). Their discourses placing particular stress on the justness core of right all proceed from the traditional Chinese philosophical basis of righteousness. To sharply distinguish what is righteous from what is beneficial, they unanimously banished the appearance of the character 利 in their Chinese renditions of right. However, their conception of right within the framework of 義 is not immune to the traditional inclination to overemphasize obligations and ignore rights. Hu Shi's coinage of 義權 (literally righteous power) and 義分 (literally righteous duty) for translating right and obligation, respectively, handles the relationship between right and obligation not analogically to that between 義 and 利 but under the superordinate notion of 義. The dichotomy between 義 and 利 is dissolved, which means both rights and obligations can be righteous, and righteous benefit can derive from individual rights. In this view, the differentiation between rights and obligations in the West crosscuts the Chinese distinction between 義 and 利.

These reflections of Chinese scholars on the translation of right indicate a gradual change of attention scheme. The implicit connotation of moral good and the focus on individual rights that used to be neglected have been noticed and introduced into the Chinese understanding of 權利. While the closer attention on individual rights could be partly due to the spread of social Darwinism among Chinese scholars (Lin 2020: 411), the reason that they put an increasing emphasis on moral integrity in understanding rights is more likely the everlasting philosophical tradition of 義.

5 Conclusion

The present study adopts a cognitive-sociological approach to conceptual variations in legal translation. As believed by cognitive sociologists, social factors shape and guide human cognition. Thought cannot be examined as "merely a subjective or personal phenomenon" or "solely a universal or species-wide phenomenon" (Cerulo 2005: 108). Therefore, cultural differences are of centrality in the translation of legal concepts. On the sociolinguistic front, the translator's choice of existing concepts that have similar connotations with the original or the coinage of new terms combining separate words in the target language is undoubtedly subject to their fore-structure of interpretation. In terms of socio-legal reality, the translingual practice of a translated legal concept or a transplanted legal model cannot evade profound impacts of legal scholars' and practitioners' long-standing cognition of law. Meanwhile, an investigation into conceptual variations needs also to throw light on the historical contexts under which the translation took place.

Since Martin's translation of right into 權利, the Chinese conception of right has undergone several historical periods during which power, interest, righteousness, or obligation took a predominant position, respectively (Jin and Liu 2005: 99).

These historical orientations bequeath much conceptual and cultural legacy to contemporary understanding of rights and obligations in China. By analyzing different orientations of the varied conception of a legal concept translated from a foreign legal culture, we have no intention to confirm or create a more appropriate term or a so-called equivalent in Chinese. What is of true worth is to figure out how the meaning of a transplanted concept is cognitively and socially constructed and molded by linguistic agents and different groups of recipients.

Acknowledgments

This study is funded by the Centre for Translation Studies at Guangdong University of Foreign Studies (Project No. CTSZB202002).

References

Bassnett, S. and A. Lefevere (1990), "Introduction: Proust's Grandmother and the Thousand and One Nights: The 'Cultural Turn' in Translation Studies," in S. Bassnett and L. André (eds.), *Translation, History and Culture*, 1–13, New York: Pinter Publishers.

Borges, J. L. (1984), *Twenty-Four Conversations with Borges, Including a Selection of Poems: Interviews by Roberto Alifano, 1981–1983*, trans. N. S. Arauz, W. Barnstone, and N. Escandell, Housatonic: Lascaux Publishers.

Brekhus, W. H. (2015), *Culture and Cognition: Patterns in the Social Construction of Reality*, Cambridge: John Wiley & Sons.

Buzelin, H. (2013), "Sociology and Translation Studies," in C. Millán and F. Bartrina (eds.), *The Routledge Handbook of Translation Studies*, 186–200, New York: Routledge.

Cairns, J. W. (2013), "Watson, Walton, and the History of Legal Transplants," *Georgia Journal of International and Comparative Law*, 41(3): 637–96.

Cao, D. (2002), "Finding the Elusive Equivalents in Chinese/English Legal Translation," *Babel*, 48(4): 330–41.

Cerulo, K. A. (2005), "Cognitive Sociology," in G. Ritzer (ed.), *Encyclopedia of Social Theory*, vol. 1, 108–11, London: Sage.

Chen, Q. J. (2021), "From Righteousness to Rights: A Study from History of Idea and Philosophical Interpretation on Transformation of Moral Sense in Late Qing Dynasty and early Republic of China," *Philosophical Research*, 2: 57–68.

Cicourel, A. V. (1974), *Cognitive Sociology: Language and Meaning in Social Interaction*, New York: The Free Press.

Clarke, D. C. (2006), "Lost in Translation? Corporate Legal Transplants in China," *SSRN*, July 10. https://dx.doi.org/10.2139/ssrn.913784 (accessed July 20, 2021).

Fang, Y. and B. Li (2011), *Translation and Annotation to the Xunzi*, Beijing: Zhonghua Book Company.

Fauconnier, G. and M. Turner (1998), "Conceptual Integration Networks," *Cognitive Science*, 22(2): 133–87.

Fauconnier, G. and M. Turner (2002), *The Way We Think: Conceptual Blending and the Mind's Hidden Complexities*, New York: Basic Books.

Friedman, L. M. (1979), "Book Review," *British Journal of Law and Society*, 6(1): 127–9.

Friedman, L. M. (2001), "Some Comments on Cotterrell and Legal Transplants," in D. Nelken and J. Feest (eds.), *Adapting Legal Cultures*, 93–8, Portland: Hart Publishing.

Geller, P. E. (1994), "Legal Transplants in International Copyright: Some Problems of Method," *UCLA Pacific Basin Law Journal*, 13(1): 199–230.

Goffman, E. (1986), *Frame Analysis: An Essay on the Organization of Experience*, Boston: Northeastern University Press.

Guo, D., X. Q. Cheng, and B. Y. Li (2012), *Translation and Annotation to The Commentary of Zuo*, Beijing: Zhonghua Book Company.

Halverson, S. L. (1997), "The Concept of Equivalence in Translation Studies: Much Ado about Something," *Target. International Journal of Translation Studies*, 9(2): 207–33.

Harper, D., ed. (2021), "Right," *Online Etymology Dictionary*. https://www.etymonline.com/word/right#etymonline_v_15068 (accessed July 20, 2021).

Hart, H. L. A. (1954), "Definition and Theory in Jurisprudence," *Law Quarterly Review*, 70(1): 37–60.

He, Q. H. (2014), "The First Full Practice of Legal Translation in Modern China: A Study Based on the Chinese Translation (1864) of Wheaton's *Elements of International Law*," *Journal of Comparative Law*, 2: 190–200.

Hislop, D. J. (1967), "The Hohfeldian System of Fundamental Legal Conceptions," *Archives for Philosophy of Law and Social Philosophy*, 53(1): 53–89.

Jin, G. T. and Q. F. Liu (2005), "Studies of the Origin of Modern Chinese Thought and Database Methodology," *Journal of Historical Science*, 5: 89–101.

Kahn-Freund, O. (1975), "Book Review," *Law Quarterly Review*, 91(3): 292.

Langer, M. (2004), "From Legal Transplants to Legal Translations: The Globalization of Plea Bargaining and the Americanization Thesis in Criminal Procedure," *Harvard International Law Journal*, 45(1): 1–64.

Legrand, P. (1997), "The Impossibility of 'Legal Transplants,'" *Maastricht Journal of European and Comparative Law*, 4(2): 111–24.

Li, G. L. (1998), "On *quanli*," *Peking University Law Review*, 1: 115–29.

Liang, Q. C. (2016), *Discourse on the New Citizen*, Beijing: The Commercial Press.

Liang, Z. P. (2013), *Searching for Harmony in the Natural Order – A Study of Legal Tradition from a Cultural Perspective*, Beijing: The Commercial Press.

Lin, L. F. (2020), "A History of the Transplantation and Exchange of Right," *Peking University Law Journal*, 32(2): 402–17.

Liu, L. H. (1999), "Legislating the Universal: The Circulation of International Law in the Nineteenth Century," in L. H. Liu, S. Fish, and F. Jameson (eds.), *Tokens of Exchange – The Problem of Translation in Global Circulations*, 127–64, London: Duke University Press.

Loseke, D. R. (2003), *Thinking About Social Problems: An Introduction to Constructionist Perspectives*, New York: Routledge.

Lü, J. (2004), "The Ontological Return of Translation Studies – A Reflection of The Cultural Turn in Translation Studies," *Journal of Foreign Languages*, 4: 53–9.

Miller, J. M. (2003), "A Typology of Legal Transplants: Using Sociology, Legal History and Argentine Examples to Explain the Transplant Process," *The American Journal of Comparative Law*, 51(4): 839–86.

Mossop, B. (1983), "The Translator as Rapporteur: A Concept for Training and Self-improvement," *Meta*, 28(3): 244–78.

Pan, G. D. (2010), *Sociological Thoughts of Confucianism*, Beijing: Peking University Press.

Peerenboom, R. P. (1995), "Rights, Interests, and the Interest in Rights in China," *Stanford Journal of International Law*, 31(2): 359–86.

Peng, C. X. (2004), "The Absence of Civil Rights Concept in Ancient China – On the Cultural Roots of Private Rights from a Comparative Perspective," *Global Law Review*, 3: 331–43.

Pym, A. (1995), "European Translation Studies, Une Science qui Dérange, and Why Equivalence Needn't Be a Dirty Word," *TTR: Traduction, Terminologie, Rédaction*, 8(1): 153–76.

Pym, A. (2007), "Natural and Directional Equivalence in Theories of Translation," *Target. International Journal of Translation Studies*, 19(2): 271–94.

Seidman, R. B. (1975), "Book Review," *Boston University Law Review*, 55(3): 682–7.

Singh, R. (2007), "Unsafe at Any Speed? Some Unfinished Reflections on the 'Cultural Turn' in Translation Studies," in P. St-Pierre and P. C. Kar (eds.), *In Translation – Reflections, Refractions, Transformations*, 73–84, Amsterdam: John Benjamins Publishing.

Snell-Hornby, M. (1988), *Translation Studies: An Integrated Approach*, Amsterdam: John Benjamins Publishing.

Stein, F. (1977), "Uses, Misuses—And Nonuses of Comparative Law," *Northwestern University Law Review*, 72(2): 198–216.

Tiwald, J. (2011), "Confucianism and Human Rights," in T. Cushman (ed.), *Handbook of Human Rights*, 268–78, New York: Routledge.

Tong, Z. W. (2021), "The Origin, Spread and the Scope of 'Right' in Jurisprudence Written in Chinese," *Peking University Law Journal*, 33(5): 1246–64.

Wang, B. (2001), "Conceptual Integration and Translation," *Chinese Translators Journal*, 22(3): 17–20.

Wang, J. (2001), *Connecting the Legal Sense of Two Worlds: The Import of Western Law and Legal Terms in the Late Qing Dynasty*, Beijing: China University of Political Science and Law Press.

Wang, L. (2010), "Legal Transplant and Cultural Transfer: The Legal Translation in Hong Kong," *Across Languages and Cultures*, 11(1): 83–91.

Wang, L. J. (2005), *Intellectual Inquiry into Power and Right*, Beijing: China Legal Publishing House.

Wang, S., ed. (1986), *Yan Fu Collection*, Beijing: Zhonghua Book Company.

Wang, Y. (2019), "Revised Conceptual Blending Theory and Embodied-Cognitive Translation Process," *Foreign Language Teaching and Research*, 52(5): 749–60.

Watson, A. (1976), "Legal Transplants and Law Reform," *Law Quarterly Review*, 92(1): 79–84.

Wenar, L. (2020), "Rights," *The Stanford Encyclopedia of Philosophy* (Spring 2021 Edition), February 24. https://plato.stanford.edu/archives/spr2021/entries/rights/ (accessed October 8, 2021).

Wolf, M. (2007), "Introduction: The Emergence of a Sociology of Translation," in M. Wolf (ed.), *Constructing a Sociology of Translation*, 1–36, Amsterdam: John Benjamins Publishing.

Yang, B. J. (2017), *Translation and Annotation to the Analects of Confucius*, Beijing: Zhonghua Book Company.

Zerubavel, E. (1999), *Social Mindscapes: An Invitation to Cognitive Sociology*, Cambridge, MA: Harvard University Press.

9

Cognitive, Linguistic, and Discursive Elements in Metaphor Translation

Sui He

1 Introduction

The story of metaphor and translation is well documented in the recorded past. As Hermans (2004: 118) notes, the Latin translation of the Greek word *metaphorá* is *translatio*, which means the symbolic or physical movement of ideas and persons, covering the senses of "metaphor" and "translation" at the same time. This shared value of "movement" has an enduring legacy in contemporary scholarship: in translation studies, the production of metaphor can be seen as an intralingual translation activity that describes something in terms of something else; in metaphor studies, translation can be viewed as an interlingual phenomenon that involves the substitution of an item across languages and cultures. In this sense, translation studies and metaphor studies share a close relationship, and a proper collaboration between the two disciplines is bound to be a mutually beneficial one.

Since the 1980s, the perception of "metaphor" has witnessed a fundamental change from being a rhetorical device to a cognitive phenomenon, which has set the landscape for contemporary metaphor studies. In *Metaphors We Live By*, Lakoff and Johnson (1980: 1) introduce the idea of "conceptual metaphor," which denotes the manifestation of our conceptual system that defines "our everyday realities." Influenced by this idea, contemporary metaphor studies emphasize the cognitive function of metaphor, viewing metaphor as "the phenomenon whereby we talk and, potentially, think about something in terms of something else" (Semino 2008: 1). To clarify the conundrum of defining "metaphor," Kövecses (2010: 4–7) draws a line between conceptual metaphors (i.e., the way of thinking) and linguistic metaphors (i.e., the way of talking): conceptual metaphors resemble the understanding of one conceptual domain in terms of another conceptual domain, while linguistic metaphors (aka metaphorical expressions) are the linguistic manifestations of conceptual metaphors. In metaphor studies, research on conceptual metaphors holds a dominant position and the discussion on linguistic metaphors has served as a resource to elaborate relevant issues about conceptual metaphors.

As detailed in Section 2, the development of this cognitive view of metaphor sheds light on metaphor translation research. However, the application of cognitive metaphor theories to translation studies requires careful consideration. This is because metaphor studies following the cognitive pathway focus more on conceptual metaphors (Charteris-Black 2004: 11; Semino 2008: 9), whereas for translation research, the examination of linguistic metaphors in specific contexts plays a crucial role. Therefore, it is essential to incorporate the cognitive perspective of metaphor into the ongoing linguistic and discursive analysis of translation products and strengthen the connection between the cognitive, linguistic, and discursive facets of metaphor translation.

Building on a case study, this chapter explores metaphor translation following a descriptivist approach. As Johnstone (2018: 22–3) states, the primary goal of scholarly research following the descriptive pathway, in contrast to the critical pathway, is to "describe the world" and "only later, if at all, to apply scholarly findings in the solution of practical problems." Therefore, the current chapter aims to describe the cognitive, linguistic, and discursive underpinnings of metaphor translation, serving as the raw data for further generalization and comparison.

2 Metaphor Translation

2.1 Cognitive Metaphor Theories in Translation Studies

The development of cognitive metaphor research has fueled the advancement of metaphor translation research. In this trend, two prominent theories emerge: conceptual metaphor theory (CMT, Lakoff and Johnson [1980] 2003) and conceptual blending theory (CBT, Fauconnier and Turner 2002). In light of the two theories, the available research on metaphor translation typically falls into three categories: the application of CMT, CBT, and a combination of both.

CMT plays a vital role in establishing the collaboration between translation studies and metaphor studies, which remains dominant in the field.

Theoretically, it has been applied by translation scholars to discuss the issue of "cognitive translation" as featured in Mandelblit (1995), which brought into the horizon the idea that translation involves both linguistic and conceptual shifts. Recent research (e.g., Massey and Ehrensberger-Dow 2017; Massey 2021; Zhou 2021) has shown a growing trend in viewing translation products as clues for understanding the cognitive efforts of translators, which fills in the gap between product-oriented and process-oriented research. Similarly, enlightened by the cognitive function of metaphor, St. André (2010), Chesterman (2014), and Guldin (2016) approached the conceptualization of translation from the perspective of metaphor and showcased the potential impact that metaphor can have on the manifestation of translation theory and practice.

Methodologically, CMT has been proven helpful in describing translation shifts and distilling translation strategies. Producing lists of translation strategies is a classical topic in metaphor translation research. At the earlier stages, Newmark (1980: 95–7; 1988: 106–13) held the idea that different types of metaphors should be translated differently and prescribed two lists of translation procedures. The idea was later developed by Toury (1995: 82–3, 2012: 107–10). This categorization method for identifying translation procedures has inspired researchers to examine a specific type of metaphor with regard to CMT and describe how they were translated in practice (e.g., Merakchi and Rogers 2013; Tebbit and Kinder 2016).

The most significant advancement in recent years, however, is the methodological breakthrough introduced by Shuttleworth (2011, 2017). Drawing on CMT, Shuttleworth's method features a parametric analysis that deconstructs the complex compound of metaphor, offering the possibility to examine how different parts and types of metaphor are translated in practice. Metaphor parameters introduced in this line of research provide feasible perspectives to analyze metaphor translation, covering both quantitative and qualitative aspects of this complex activity. Drawing on a multilingual parallel corpus containing six target languages (French, German, Italian, Russian, Polish, and Chinese), this research provides higher credibility for generalizing patterns of metaphor translation across different languages with the help of metaphor parameters.

While much has been said about CMT in metaphor translation research, the literature related to CBT is comparatively scarce to find. Among the available resources, Rydning (2005) discusses the translation of metonymy (which is regarded as a type of metaphor by some scholars) in light of CBT; McElhanon (2006) offers a thorough demonstration of how CBT (and CMT, but independently) works and gives a list of translation strategies for translating conceptual blends; Wang (2009) utilizes CBT (and figure and ground theory) to illustrate how translators translate their personal interpretations where metaphors are involved. The existing studies prove the usefulness of CBT in metaphor translation research, yet when compared to CMT, the extent to which CBT can help with metaphor translation analysis remains a question.

Moving to the combined usage of CMT and CBT in translation analysis, Liang (2017) carries out a detailed discussion on Mo Yan's novel and the English version translated by Howard Goldblatt. Analyzing translation products in light of CMT and CBT is one of the highlights of this article, which showcases the complementary angle that these two models can offer. To align these two models and unleash the potential they have in translation analysis, He (2021) proposes a dual-model parametric approach inspired by the parametric method introduced by Shuttleworth (2017) as detailed in Section 3. With the help of CMT and CBT, it is possible to show the suitability of metaphor parameters for analyzing the cognitive and linguistic elements in metaphor translation.

2.2 Discursive Elements

The literature listed earlier touches upon certain aspects of metaphor translation informed by the recent development of cognitive metaphor theories. However, it is essential to provide a more comprehensive picture of the discursive elements alongside the cognitive and linguistic underpinnings because all these aspects hold particular relevance to translation research, especially for descriptive translation studies. Against this backdrop, the current study takes a step forward by adding a discursive facet to the dual-model parametric approach proposed earlier by He (2021), in the hope of displaying a more robust description with higher credibility against the logical fallacies that might influence the analysis of translation products. In the following paragraphs, I will briefly explain what "discourse" means in this article, before moving to the next section where the method being used to address the cognitive, linguistic, and discursive elements of this case study is unwrapped.

As Johnstone (2018: 36) summarizes, discourse, as a mass uncountable noun, means "any actual talk, writing, or signing." As a countable noun usually used in the plural form, it denotes "[the] conventional ways of talking that create and perpetuate systems of ideology, sets of beliefs about how the world works and what is natural" (2018: 36). Discourse analysis denotes the method that researchers can use to answer a wide range of questions related to the topic of discourse.

Based on the features of discourse listed in van Dijk (2011: 3–5), this study speaks to discourse analysis in three nonmutually exclusive ways: discourse as communication, discourse as contextually situated, and discourse as genres. First, for the communication facet of discourse, interaction by text and talk enables us to understand "the knowledge, intentions, goals, opinions and emotions of others" and "how we acquire and update socially shared and distributed knowledge and thus the very conditions of coordinated interaction" (p. 3). As a fundamental component of human communication, translation, either in its prototypical sense as interlingual translation (including sign languages and multimodal elements) or in its general sense as interpretation, is entwined with specific discourses. Second, for contextual situatedness, discourse is "part of a social situation in people's everyday lives, and as an experience among others" (p. 4). Elements involved in this situated experience, such as setting, participant identities, goals, and so on, all contribute to the definition of the context, which allows people to "engage in text or talk that is appropriate to the current communicative situation" (p. 4). Informed by this relatedness, this study includes paratextual parameters such as interviews and speculation on the medium (i.e., the two journals where the Chinese translations were published) to reshape the jigsaw of the discursive underpinnings of the specific translation activity. Third, for the genres facet, the case study looks into popular cosmological texts that are characterized by the typical structures falling into this genre.

3 Methodology

The source text (ST) discussed in this study was published in *Scientific American* and the target texts (TTs) were published in 《环球科学》 *Huanqiukexue* ("Global Science," published in Beijing in Simplified Chinese) and 《科学人》 *Kexueren* ("Science Person," published in Taipei in Traditional Chinese). The ST tells the story of the oldest supermassive black holes and discusses how they grew so massive and so quickly after the big bang. The information about the ST and TTs is presented in Table 9.1.

Following the metaphor identification procedure for scientific texts demonstrated in He (2021: 36–7), twenty-seven metaphorical expressions were identified in the ST. In the TTs, there is only one added example in *Huanqiukexue*. These examples were reviewed by two metaphor translation scholars to ensure the validity of this research. To unveil the cognitive and linguistic elements in this translation activity, the examples were analyzed with the dual-model parametric approach with two sets of metaphor parameters—projection and provenance.

Table 9.1 Information about the ST and the TTs

	Source Text	Target Text 1	Target Text 2
Publication Date	February 2018	March 2018	April 2018
Title	The First Monster Black Holes	宇宙巨婴：最初的超级黑洞 [Giant babies of the universe: the first black holes]	巨獸黑洞養成記 [The growing diary of giant monster black holes]
Word Count	2,259 words	3,724 characters	3,625 characters
Author/Translator	Priyamvada Natarajan	Yan-ting Dong Ye Feng Li-jun Gou (copyeditor) 董燕婷：中科院国家天文台博士；冯叶：北京工业大学（审校：苟利军中科院团队负责人） [Yanting Dong: PhD candidate, National Astronomical Observatories, Chinese Academy of Science; Ye Feng Beijing University of Technology (copyeditor: Li-jun Gou, lab leader, Chinese Academy of Science)]	Wo-lung Lee 李沃龍：臺灣師範大學物理系副教授 [Wo-lung Lee: Associate Professor, Department of Physics, Taiwan Normal University]
Bio-notes	Priyamvada Natarajan is a theoretical astrophysicist at Yale University whose research focuses on cosmology, gravitational leasing, and black hole physics.		

The projection parameter represents the conceptual content of metaphors in CMT (e.g., BLACK HOLES ARE ANIMALS) and the contextual information of linguistic metaphors in CBT (e.g., black holes would have had to *eat* faster than the Eddington rate). Conceptual metaphor is expressed in capital letters in the form of A IS B (Lakoff and Johnson 1980: 7), as shown in the BLACK HOLES ARE ANIMALS example. In this formula, A, known as the *target domain*, denotes the topic that a metaphorical expression is recruited to describe. B, known as the *source domain*, denotes the source that people refer to when describing the topical item. This formula is known as a *mapping*, which represents the systematic correspondences between A and B (Kövecses 2010: 7). While CMT provides a powerful lens to observe metaphor translation at a cognitive level, CBT offers a feasible framework to examine the translation of linguistic metaphors at a contextual level.

The provenance parameter denotes the knowledge source for metaphor cognition in CMT and cognitive mechanisms in CBT. For CMT provenance, this concept was initially brought up by Lakoff (1987: 194–5), who proposes four categories of metaphor based on knowledge source: (1) image schematic metaphor, which involves basic cognitive structures derived from repeated bodily experience (e.g., "the *growing* black hole"); (2) propositional knowledge-based metaphor, which refers to the mapping of knowledge from one domain to another with an emphasis on the idea of social knowledge on top of the basic bodily experience (e.g., "*freak* quasars"); (3) image metaphor, which denotes one-time physical resemblance (e.g., "stars . . . *dotting* the sky"); (4) Aristotle's metaphor, which stands for a very simple and general type of metaphor following the syntactic format of "SOMETHING IS WHAT IT HAS SALIENT PROPERTIES OF."

For CBT provenance, this parameter features four cognitive mechanisms: simplex network, mirror network, single-scope network, and double-scope network. These cognitive networks were introduced by Fauconnier and Turner (2002: 119–35) in the seminal book *The Way We Think*. The scope of CBT is more general than CMT: CBT focuses on human cognition but CMT only works with metaphor. The categorization criterion of these networks rests in the key concept of "frame," which refers to long-term schematic knowledge that connects mental spaces such as the frame of walking along a path (Fauconnier and Turner 2002: 40). According to the authors, a simplex network has one frame and one value in each input space (e.g., "dark matter *candidate*"); a mirror network has one frame with one out of several values chosen for blending (e.g., "stars . . . *dotting* the sky"); a single-scope network usually has two frames in two input spaces but only one of them is chosen for blending (e.g., "*freak* quasars"); and a double-scope network often has more than one frame in the blend, which is either sourced from a mixture of original frames or an extension of a dominating frame (e.g., "not even light can *escape*").

To discuss the correlation between metaphor parameters and translation solutions, a list of grand translation solutions was adopted: (1) retention, where the original mapping is retained; (2) modification, where the original mapping is replaced by a different mapping; (3) removal, where the metaphoricity of the ST is removed but the literal meaning is carried through; (4) omission, where both the metaphoricity and the literal meaning are omitted; and (5) addition, where translators add a metaphorical expression in the TT when there is none in the ST.

To fulfil the need for providing discursive information for consolidating the description of this translation activity alongside the textual analysis, this study draws on different resources that are accessible at the moment, including biographical information, interviews with two of the translators (Ms. Ye Feng and Professor Wo-lung Lee), speculation on the editorial policies, and the usage of identified metaphorical expressions in English and Chinese popular scientific writings.

To demonstrate how the three intertwined layers help to describe this specific discourse of metaphor translation, the next section is divided into three parts, featuring the cognitive, linguistic, and discursive elements of the case study, respectively.

4 A Case Study—First Monster Black Holes

Before moving on to the details, Table 9.2 shows the overall distribution of the grand translation solutions adopted by the translators in the TTs.

For the ST, most of the metaphorical expressions were retained in the TTs, followed by removal, modification, and omission examples. Even though the

Table 9.2 Translation Solutions Overview

	Huanqiukexue	*Kexueren*
Retention	19	18
Modification	2	1
Removal	5	7
Omission	1	1
Total (ST)	27	27
Addition	1	0
Total (ST + TT)	**28**	**27**

current dataset is small in size, this list of frequency is in line with the findings of large corpus-based research such as Schmidt (2015: 259) and Shuttleworth (2017: 147). One added metaphorical expression was found in *Huanqiukexue*. Detailed information on how these metaphors were translated is presented in the following sections.

4.1 Cognitive Elements

Guided by the method described in Section 3, the cognitive elements of this case study are revealed by CMT provenance, CBT provenance, and CMT projection.

In the dataset, five of the metaphorical expressions were identified as image schematic metaphors. The majority of metaphors fall into the propositional knowledge-based category (twenty-one examples) with only one identified as image metaphor. No Aristotle's metaphor was identified in the ST or the TTs. Figure 9.1 shows the movement of metaphorical expressions before and after translation in light of the CMT provenance parameter. In Figure 9.1, the distribution of CMT provenance categories is presented in the central bar, with the *Kexueren* and *Huanqiukexue* presented to the left and right sides, respectively. Each category is highlighted in different colors: image schematic metaphors in indigo blue; propositional knowledge-based metaphors in light blue; image metaphors in aqua blue; Aristotle's metaphors in orange; and null cases are represented in grey. Gradient-colored ribbons showcase movement from one category to another.

As Figure 9.1 shows, for image schematic and propositional knowledge-based metaphors, translators chose to either keep the original knowledge source or to take away the metaphoricity conveyed in the ST. For propositional knowledge-

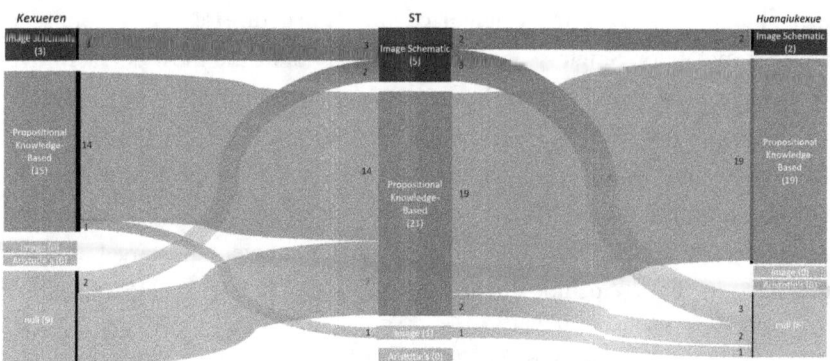

Figure 9.1 Movement of CMT provenance categories in translation.

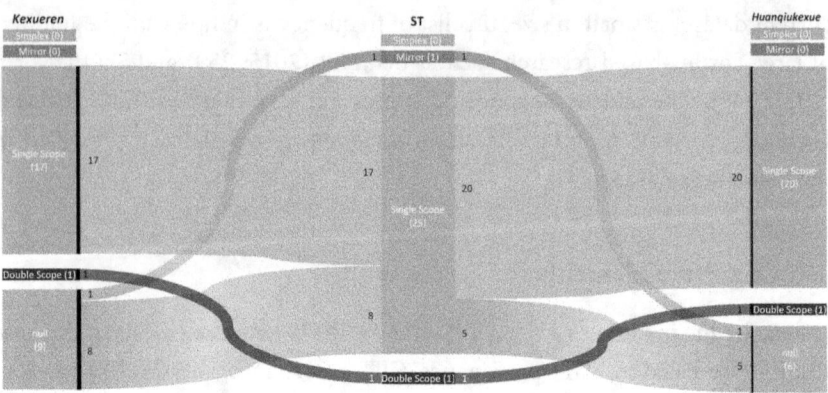

Figure 9.2 Movement of CBT provenance categories in translation.

based metaphors, the translators of *Huanqiukexue* prefer to preserve the original knowledge structure than taking away the metaphoricity. Interestingly, for the only image metaphor example, while it was removed in *Huanqiukexue*, the translation in *Kexueren* utilizes a metaphorical expression of a propositional knowledge-based nature to render this image metaphor. Detailed information about this example is discussed in Section 4.2.

In the ST, twenty-five examples were identified as single-scope network metaphors, alongside one mirror network metaphor and one double-scope network metaphor. No simplex network metaphor was identified. Figure 9.2 shows the movement of metaphorical expressions with regard to the CBT provenance parameter. Similarly, different categories of metaphors under the CBT framework are represented in different colors.

For the mirror and double-scope network examples, the movement is identical among the TTs: removing the metaphoricity of the mirror network metaphor and keeping the original cognitive structure of the double-scope network metaphor. Single-scope network metaphors—the most pervasive type of metaphor—were either kept in the single-scope network or taken away. In comparison, *Huanqiukexue* translators chose to preserve more of the single-scope network metaphors than the *Kexueren* translator, which echoes the previous findings under the CMT provenance parameter.

Finally, in terms of the CMT projection parameter, the target domains identified in the ST include GALAXIES (2), BLACK HOLES (15), COSMOS (1), UNIVERSES (2), LIGHT (1), QUASARS (2), STARS (3), STARS AND GALAXIES (1), with their frequencies indicated in the brackets. The source domains include ANIMALS (11), LIVING CREATURES (9), HUMANS (4),

CORPSES (1), DOTS (1), and MONSTER (1). While the target domains are subject to the topic of this specific article, the source domains embedded in the metaphorical expressions show a strong emphasis on the humanization[1] and personification[2] elements, perhaps except for the DOTS example where the appearance of stars and galaxies is described as "dotting in the sky." As the TTs show, this portfolio is connected with the source domains chosen by the translators, especially for the added example in *Huanqiukexue*, where the mapping for this special case resonates with the personification tendency of the ST. Compared to Shuttleworth (2017: 75), cosmological articles rely more on humanization and personification tropes. For example, black holes can "feed" to "grow," with the potential danger of "choking"; stars have "birth" and "death," and even galaxies can become "obese." Under the cognitive mappings presented by the CMT projection, these concrete linguistic realizations listed in the quotation marks are depicted in light of the CBT projection parameter in Section 4.2.

4.2 Linguistic Elements

Building on the cognitive architecture of the CMT projection, CBT projection provides concrete insights into metaphor translation at a linguistic level. As the examples show, there is no guarantee that a metaphorical expression, such as "grow," would be translated consistently even in the same article. Therefore, instead of going through each mapping, the interdependent linguistic facet of the case study is structured with the five grand translation solutions listed in Section 3. Given that the discourse of this case study is dynamic, the following content only attempts to present the highlighted translation features following the descriptivist approach.

Starting with the most popular translation solution, retention is associated with two extreme cases: (1) conventionalized metaphorical expressions in English and Chinese popular scientific discourses; and (2) explicit metaphorical expressions.

For example, when describing the phenomenon of quasars or black holes absorbing surrounding cosmic entities by gravitational force, the author used "eat," "feast," and "gobble"—wordings that can be frequently found in cosmological articles. These expressions are metaphorical by nature. Take "eat" as an illustration, the context of this example is "they [quasars] would have had to eat faster than the Eddington rate." In CBT, the projection of this example can be explained as follows: input space 1 contains the factual information that quasars can absorb the stars, gases, and other cosmic entities that fall close enough to the field of its gravitational force; input space 2 contains the literal meaning of "eat" as "to put food in your mouth and swallow it" (*Macmillan Dictionary Online*). These input spaces facilitate further blending, where the meaning of this metaphorical expression is obtained. In the TTs, the Chinese translations—进食 jìn shí (*Huanqiukexue* in Simplified Chinese) and 進食 jìn shí (*Kexueren* in Traditional Chinese)—share the same blending network as the English original.

For explicit metaphorical expressions, the translators of both TTs chose to retain the expression "choking," together with the double quotation marks in the ST. The usage of double quotation marks indicates the metaphorical nature of this expression, which functions in the same way as using metaphor indicators such as "is," "are," and "as," and so on. When the mind decodes the meaning of this segment, the appearance of the double quotation marks evokes an additional mental space that contains the knowledge structure of rhetorical devices. Together with the meaning-bearing input spaces, the contextual meaning is obtained in the blend. In this retention example, the complete network with three activated input spaces is then transferred into Chinese. Even though there is only one such example, this type of metaphorical signposting can often lead to the direct retention of the source segment, as suggested by the larger corpus in the umbrella project detailed in He (2022).

Interestingly, although retention is the most popular choice, removing the metaphoricity of the source segments turns out to be the second. There are two main features among the removal examples: (1) the emphasis on meaning over metaphoricity and (2) linguistic variations showcased by different word choices.

For example, in *Huanqiukexue*, the translation of "the oldest supermassive black holes" is a typical one where the delivery of meaning outweighs the preservation of metaphoricity. This example was found in the lede that summarizes the main content of this article. While the translation in *Kexueren* retains the original expression, the translation in *Huanqiukexue* presented here opts for the literal meaning as 那些非常遥远的超大质量黑洞 *nà xiē fēi cháng yáo yuǎn de chāo dà zhì liàng hēi dòng* (those supermassive black holes that are very far away). This translation draws on the connection between "distance" and "age" given that the light seen by us on Earth has travelled for a long time before reaching our retinae. By delivering the meaning through "very far away," the metaphoricity conveyed by the "oldest" in the ST is removed in this example.

Considering the variation in word choices, the translations of "birth" and "death" are exemplary. The linguistic instantiations of meaning are dynamic—they can be metaphorical or literal. This can lead to different translation solutions. For example, "the birth and death of stars" were translated as 恒星的诞生与死亡

héng xīng de dàn shēng yǔ sǐ wáng in *Huanqiukexue* and 恒星生滅 *héng xīng sheng miè* in *Kexueren*. Both TTs contain the literal meaning conveyed in the ST. Considering the word choice, however, the expression recruited in *Kexueren* is literal in nature, which leads to the removal of metaphoricity in this example. In comparison, the usages of 誕生 *dàn shēng* and 死亡 *sǐ wáng* in other segments in *Kexueren* retain the original metaphorical expressions. The potential reasons for the word choice are discussed in Section 4.3 in light of the discursive information.

Moving on to modification, this type of translation solution is closely related to conceptual consistency concerning the translation of headings and subheadings. "The First Monster Black Holes" is the main heading of the article, and "Feeding a Black Hole" is one of its subheadings. Both expressions belong to the general mapping BLACK HOLES ARE MONSTERS. In *Huanqiukexue*, this mapping was replaced by BLACK HOLES ARE GIANT BABIES, with the title translated as 宇宙巨婴：最初的超级黑洞 *yǔ zhòu jù yīng: zuì chū de chāo jí hēi dòng* (the giant babies in the universe: the first super black holes) and the subheading rendered as 怎样把黑洞养大 *zěn yàng bǎ hēi dòng yǎng dà* (how to raise a black hole).

To understand this conceptual shift, I referred to the British National Corpus and the Peking University Chinese Corpus.[3] As the result shows, describing supermassive black holes as monsters is rare to find in both languages. To understand how this MONSTER-infused metaphor was translated into other languages, I looked up the French and the Japanese versions as references. In the French version *Pour la Science* (For Science), the title was rewritten as "Le Paradoxe des Quasars Jeunes" (the paradox of the young quasars). Similarly, in the Japanese version 《日経サイエンス》 (Nikkei Science), the title goes directly as "巨大ブラックホール爆誕の謎" (the riddle of the sudden formation of gigantic black holes). Apparently, these rewritings, together with the modified title in *Huanqiukexue*, indicate that the original metaphorical expression imposed a certain level of difficulty for the translators.

Employing the MONSTER source domain could be the author's idiosyncratic perception or writing style,[4] but in the English scientific community, metaphorical expressions that convey a hostile or colonial attitude toward the universe are not rare to find. For example, the expression "taming the multiverse" found on the *New Scientists* website[5] and the Research News[6] of the University of Cambridge in memory of Professor Stephen Hawking, as well as other typical expressions. To understand this case study, the interview data presented in Section 4.3 provides a clue.

For omission, the only example identified in the dataset is presented below, where the metaphoricity and the meaning conveyed by "growing" were omitted.

ST	the mass of the growing black hole will briefly exceed that of the stars
Huanqiukexue	黑洞的质量将会短暂地超过恒星的总质量
Back Translation	The mass of the black hole will briefly exceed the total mass of the stars.
Kexueren	黑洞質量將短暫超越所有恆星
Back Translation	The mass of the black hole will briefly exceed all the stars.

This example shows that the omission solution is influenced by the importance of a segment in the context and the redundancy that retaining the original information might cause in the TTs. "Growing" evokes the mental space of a living creature getting bigger in size by consuming nutrition, which is in line with the main mapping BLACK HOLES ARE LIVING CREATURES in the ST. However, the context of this example includes sufficient information of "growing," which functions as a basic knowledge point for the readers to grasp the meaning. With the help of "briefly," the importance of including the "growing" element in translation is further weakened. This could be a reason why this segment was omitted in both TTs.

Finally, the only addition example was found in *Huanqiukexue*, where "early in cosmic history"—a literal expression—was rendered as 在宇宙诞生不久 *zài yǔ zhòu dàn shēng bù jiǔ* (shortly after the cosmos was born). This example is informed by the mapping THE COSMOS IS AN ANIMAL identified in the ST, where the mental space of birth is activated to describe the existence of the cosmos.

By examining the translations of these linguistic metaphors facilitated by CBT projection, it is shown that the translation of metaphorical expressions is dynamic—it is undoubtedly influenced by the conceptual metaphors that govern the linguistic realizations, but at the same time, contextual elements also play a part. To have a more rigorous insight into these specific decisions made by translators, Section 4.3 delves into the discursive elements with the aim to offer more descriptive information to understand this particular discourse.

4.3 Discursive Elements

As the cognitive and linguistic analyses show, quantitative findings and qualitative observations can be extracted from textual analysis. However, without discursive information, discussions on these texts-based observations remain solely speculative. For example, we can see that *Kexueren* seems to have a stronger tendency to retain the original metaphorical expressions compared to *Huanqiukexue* and that *Huanqiukexue* seems to pay more attention to the delivery of meaning than the preservation of metaphoricity (e.g., "dots" and "oldest" examples). These textual realizations are the tip of the iceberg in these decision-making processes. To better understand these phenomena, it is indispensable to know more about the decision-makers and the environment in which these decisions were made. Given that the editorial boards of the two Chinese versions are not accessible, the following contents describe paratextual observations and interview information obtained from the translators.

According to the official website of *Scientific American*, there are altogether fourteen language editions available in more than thirty countries. In the two Chinese versions, the aims are clearly stated on the individual websites. To preserve the original essence of *Scientific American*, *Huanqiukexue* inherits the seriousness of *Scientific American* and sticks to the editorial guidance of "scientists + translators + journalists" (*Huanqiukexue* 2020). On the other hand, *Kexueren* aims to deliver the most futuristic knowledge in an easily understandable manner for its target audience, comprising industrial elites, educated families, and teachers and students in high schools and higher education settings (*Kexueren* 2020). Additionally, it is shown that in both Chinese versions, accessibility and readability play an important part in translation commissions. For example, the deputy director of *Huanqiukexue* explains their view of a good translation as "even a reader with little background knowledge can understand and enjoy reading our translation; otherwise, it will not be a good one" (Liu 2014: 35–6). Similarly, Liao (2011: 364) observes that the editors and the translators of *Kexueren* regard themselves as "mediators between more advanced scientific developments and Taiwanese society" to "make scientific knowledge more accessible to their readers." These features may have certain influence on translation policies. However, without further evidence, this speculation is for information only.

In comparison, the interviews with the translators are more informative for understanding the translation examples discussed in the previous sections. The *Huanqiukexue* translation was conducted by two translators and one proof editor. The *Kexueren* translation was conducted by one translator. Two semi-conducted interviews were held in total for the current project: one with a translator of *Huanqiukexue* (Ms. Ye Feng) and another with the translator of *Kexueren* (Dr. Wo-lung Lee). The focus of these interviews is on the translators' general translation experience and their reflection on translating the ST. This provides an insight into the operational context and controls the potential biases that may be introduced with the presence of myself as an observer. The intention of the interview was made clear to the interviewees with the consent given.

Starting with the translation process, both translators mentioned that the editors played a part in reviewing and providing feedback to their translations, proving that the TTs are collaborative outputs. Concerning the attitude toward the unknown in the universe, Ms. Feng shared her viewpoint that our thinking and horizon could be rather confined because "we are living on a blue dot in the vastness of the universe." Reflecting on the translation of "monster" into "giant babies," she mentioned that there were multiple drafts but the final decision on "giant babies" was made by the editor. Talking about the perception of culture in science, Dr. Lee mentioned that because it is science, the cultural differences in science between Western and Chinese scientific communities are trivial. Drawing on his academic training background in the United States, Dr. Lee stated that having received relevant training for a long time, his attitude toward science and scientific questions is pretty much in line with the Western tradition. However, in popular science, the usage of myths can be very different, and this is one of the challenges that he encounters when translating.

Sharing their approach and attitude to translation, Ms. Feng noted that to translate a text, one must have a solid understanding of it: if one can understand the logic and the content of the text, s/he can translate in an accessible way; if the readers find it difficult to understand the translated article, then this could be an implication that the translators themselves might not understand the original text. A solid understanding of the ST requires the translator to grasp the logical structure of the article, to think in the same way as the author would think, and for most of the time, the translator does not need to add personal ideas to the translation. Additionally, when reflecting on her translation style, she expressed the idea that using expressions closer to the target audience's daily life can allow the readers to better understand the text. She carried on commenting that this is usually the case for nonterminological segments and a perfect word choice can come as a eureka moment—sometimes a better word choice is not strictly the corresponding term in Chinese, but it just appears, timely and perfectly.

Drawing on her extensive translation experience of popular scientific articles and books from English into Chinese, Ms. Feng commented that while understanding the content of hard science can impose difficulties, the differences in culture and narrative style can also lead to considerable challenges. For example, she explained, there was a book that includes a section on the installation of an instrument. The procedure of this installation was described differently from the way that Chinese engineers would do: it used cultural-specific elements and it did not come with an illustration. This caused great trouble for her translation. To solve this problem, she carried out research to build the essential knowledge infrastructure to understand the mechanism of this installation. In her translation, she decided to provide complementary information for Chinese readers who might not understand the mechanism without translator's notes. This echoes her motivation for translating popular scientific texts during her extracurricular time. As she mentioned, the popularization of scientific knowledge can bring science closer to people's lives; there should not have been a gap between science and human because science is everywhere. The function of popularizing science is to narrow the gap and tell people that everyone has the potential to chase the fascination of science.

The keyword accessibility was also highlighted by Dr. Lee. For him, the motivation for translating for *Kexueren* is twofold—for his research enthusiasm and for learning about science communication. Dr. Lee mentioned that although the topics of some translations are not within his research expertise, they are essentially relevant. Additionally, as a university professor, he also shared the idea that reading and translating popular scientific texts enable him to reflect on his teaching activity and to know how to better communicate with his students. Concerning the approach and perception of translation, Dr. Lee viewed it as a second creation. He commented that the function of translators is like a bridge, that is, to transfer something that they can access to wider society. The most interesting thing about translation, he commented, is to recreate the English texts in Chinese. This recreation should only be built on the condition that the meaning of the ST should not be distorted or changed. But at the same time, as he noted, there is room for him to make certain changes and play around with languages. Also, Dr. Lee mentioned that he was inclined to translate concisely and precisely without using redundant elements.

As the interview detail shows, there are similarities and differences among the translators, and most of the insights shared by the translators also resonate with the translation patterns that can be observed in the texts, for example, why "monster" was modified as "giant babies" in *Huanqiukexue* and was retained in *Kexueren*, why "dotting the sky" was removed in *Huanqiukexue*, why the "growing black hole" example was simultaneously omitted in both translations, and so on. However, it is also shown that idiosyncratic features can have a considerable influence on translation. Therefore, without obtaining specific insights, it can be dangerously misleading to draw conclusions solely based on textual information.

5 Concluding Remarks

This chapter presents a case study that makes an attempt to describe the cognitive, linguistic, and discursive aspects of metaphor translation. As the literature shows, the study of metaphor translation is no longer limited to identifying translation strategies based on linguistic clues. Instead, it involves fruitful discussions on the cognitive aspect of metaphor translation and requires further inclusion of discoursal elements that can complete the picture of metaphor translation alongside the linguistic and cognitive dimensions. To take a step forward into this direction, the description of the case study presented in this chapter is divided into three sections: cognitive facet in light of CMT, linguistic and contextual facet facilitated by CBT, and discursive facet, which comprises paratextual speculation of the publishing media and focused interviews with the translators. The case study reveals that metaphor translation, or translation activity in general, is a complex decision-making activity in a certain discourse mediated by human agents. The generalizable patterns of activity as such require scrutiny and sufficient information. To describe translation strategies or any other patterns identified in translation to a decent level of credibility, one must have a broader picture of the operational context to minimize the potential risk of falling into logical loopholes.

This case study, however, has certain limitations. In addition to the methodological defect listed in He (2021), a pertinent case in point is the organization of discourse elements. In the current study, more thoughts have been given to editorial policies at a general level instead of specific editorial decisions due to the lack of information. Although this general insight can contribute to the analysis of translation behavior at an organizational level, the extent to which it holds for this specific translation commission remains questionable. Relatedly, the failure to get in touch with the editor and the author unavoidably leaves a black space in the re-presentation of the discourse. Also, using interviews to provide discursive information has been critically assessed in the literature (e.g., Potter 2004: 618). This makes it necessary to dive deeper into the methodological framework of discourse analysis to support relevant analysis. Despite the defects, it is hoped that this case study can shed light on the future development of metaphor translation research and invite researchers to think about the potential application of discourse analysis and cognitive theories to translation studies.

Acknowledgments

I would like to thank Ms. Ye Feng and Dr. Wo-lung Lee for kindly agreeing to participate in the interview regardless of their busy agenda and for their willingness to help facilitate the research on metaphor translation in the popular scientific context. My gratitude also extends to Dr. Li-jun Gou for his help in putting me in touch with Ms. Ye Feng.

Notes

1 Humanization, aka anthropomorphism, means "mappings from a non-human entity (i.e., animals, objects or abstracts) to a human one" (Shuttleworth 2017: 73).
2 Personification means "mappings from abstract concepts or inanimate objects to sentient beings, whether or not these are specifically non-human" (Shuttleworth 2017: 74).
3 http://bncweb.lancs.ac.uk/ and http://ccl.pku.edu.cn:8080/ccl_corpus/.
4 In the "more to explore" section at the end of the ST, the author cited another journal article entitled "Seeds to Monsters: Tracing the Growth of Black Holes in the Universe" (Natarajan 2018: 29).
5 https://www.newscientist.com/article/mg17122994-400-taming-the-multiverse/.
6 https://www.cam.ac.uk/research/news/taming-the-multiverse-stephen-hawkings-final-theory-about-the-big-bang.

References

Charteris-Black, J. (2004), *Corpus Approaches to Critical Metaphor Analysis*, Houndmills, Basingstoke, Hampshire, and New York: Palgrave Macmillan.
Chesterman, A. (2014), "Translation Studies Forum: Universalism in Translation Studies," *Translation Studies*, 7(1): 82–90.
Fauconnier, G. and M. Turner (2002), *The Way We Think: Conceptual Blending and the Mind's Hidden Complexities*, New York: Basic Books.
Guldin, R. (2016), *Translation as Metaphor*, London: Routledge.
He, S. (2021), "Cognitive Metaphor Theories in Translation Studies: Toward a Dual-Model Parametric Approach," *Intercultural Pragmatics*, 18(1): 25–52.
He, S. (2022), "Translating Scientific Metaphors in Specialised Texts: Observations from Chinese Translations," PhD diss., University College London, London.
Hermans, T. (2004), "Metaphor and Image in the Discourse on Translation. A Historical Survey," in Harald Kittel , Armin Paul Frank , Norbert Greiner , Theo Hermans , Werner Koller , José Lambert and Fritz Paul (eds.), *An International Encyclopedia of Translation Studies*, 118–28, Berlin: Walter de Gruyter.

Huanqiukexue (2020), "About Us." https://huanqiukexue.com/plus/list.php?tid=46 (accessed December 12, 2020).

Johnstone, B. (2018), *Discourse Analysis*, London: John Wiley & Sons.

Kexueren (2020), "About *Kexueren*." https://sa.ylib.com/about.aspx (accessed December 12, 2020).

Kövecses, Z. (2010), *Metaphor: A Practical Introduction*, Oxford: Oxford University Press.

Lakoff, G. (1987), "Position Paper on Metaphor," in *Theoretical Issues in Natural Language*, 194–7, New Mexico State University: Association for Computational Linguistics. https://dl.acm.org/doi/10.3115/980304.980348.

Lakoff, G. and M. Johnson (1980), *Metaphors We Live By*, 1st ed., Chicago: University of Chicago Press.

Lakoff, G. and M. Johnson (2003), *Metaphors We Live By*, 2nd ed., Chicago: University of Chicago Press.

Liang, X. (2017), "Different Conceptual Blending with Different Cultural Frames: Goldblatt's (Mis-)Construal of Mo Yan's Metaphor in Big Breasts and Wide Hips," *Comparative Literature Studies*, 54(4): 771–94.

Liao, M. H. (2011), "Interaction in the Genre of Popular Science: Writer, Translator and Reader," *The Translator*, 17(2): 349–68.

Liu, F. (2014), "《环球科学》的坚持与改变 [Persistence and modification of Huanqiukexue]," *Chinese Journalist*, 5: 35–6.

Mandelblit, N. (1995), "The Cognitive View of Metaphor and its Implications for Translation Theory," in M. Thelen and B. Lewandowska-Tomaszczyk (eds.), *Translation and Meaning PART 3*, 483–95, Maastricht: Hogeschool.

Massey, G. (2021), "Re-framing Conceptual Metaphor Translation Research in the Age of Neural Machine Translation: Investigating Translators' Added Value with Products and Processes," *Training, Language and Culture*, 5(1): 37–56.

Massey, G. and M. Ehrensberger-Dow (2017), "Translating Conceptual Metaphor: The Process of Managing Interlingual Asymmetry," *Research in Language*, 15(2): 173–89.

McElhanon, K. A. (2006), "From Simple Metaphors to Conceptual Blending: The Mapping of Analogical Concepts and the Praxis of Translation," *Journal of Translation*, 2(1): 31–81.

Merakchi, K. and M. Rogers (2013), "The Translation of Culturally Bound Metaphors in the Genre of Popular Science Articles: A Corpus-based Case Study from Scientific American Translated into Arabic," *Intercultural Pragmatics*, 10(2): 341–72.

Natarajan, P. (2018), "The First Monster Black Holes," *Scientific American*, 318: 24–9.

Newmark, P. (1980), "The Translation of Metaphor," *Babel: International Journal of Translation*, 26: 93–100.

Newmark, P. (1988), *A Textbook of Translation*, Hemel Hempstead: Prentice-Hall International.

Potter, J. (2004), "Discourse Analysis," in M. Hardy and A. Bryman (eds.), *Handbook of Data Analysis*, 607–42, New York: Sage.

Rydning, A. F. (2005), "The Return of Sense on the Scene of Translation Studies in the Light of the Cognitive Blending Theory," *Meta: Journal des traducteurs*, 50(2): 392–404.

Schmidt, G. (2015), "Applying Conceptual Metaphor Theory in Cross-Linguistic and Translation Research," in B. Belaj (ed.), *Dimenzije značenja*, Zagreb: Filozofski fakultet sveučilišta u Zagrebu.

Semino, E. (2008), *Metaphor in Discourse*, Cambridge: Cambridge University Press.

Shuttleworth, M. (2011), "Translational Behaviour at the Frontiers of Scientific Knowledge: A Multilingual Investigation into Popular Science Metaphor in Translation," *The Translator*, 17(1): 301–23.

Shuttleworth, M. (2017), *Studying Scientific Metaphor in Translation: An Inquiry into Cross-lingual Translation Practices*, London: Routledge.

St. André, J. (2010), *Thinking through Translation with Metaphors*, Manchester: St. Jerome.

Tebbit, S. and J. J. Kinder (2016), "Translating Developed Metaphors," *Babel*, 62(3): 402–22.

Toury, G. (1995), *Descriptive Translation Studies and Beyond*, 1st ed., Amsterdam: John Benjamins Publishing.

Toury, G. (2012), *Descriptive Translation Studies and Beyond*, 2nd ed., Amsterdam: John Benjamins Publishing.

van Dijk, T. A. (2011), *Discourse Studies: A Multidisciplinary Introduction*, New York: SAGE Publications.

Wang, B. (2009), "Translating Figure Through Blending," *Perspectives: Studies in Translatology*, 16(3): 155–67.

Zhou, L. M. (2021), "The Translator as Cartographer: Cognitive Maps and World-Making in Translation," *Target*, 33(1): 1–25.

10

Human-Machine Symbiosis to Enhance Overall Understanding

Ming Qian

1 Introduction

The prerequisite of translation[1] is understanding and interpretation. All translations begin with subjective understanding of the source text. The source text is then interpreted by the translator who then transfers the interpreted meanings into another language. During this process, the translator has to choose the most appropriate versions of the interpretation. In other words, the translator is essentially a decision-maker and problem solver. In this chapter, we focus on how enhancing understanding between human and machine can be achieved through human-machine symbiosis (Stephanidis 2019: 1229–69). The enhancements are bidirectional: machine can augment human understanding using pretrained language models as knowledge bases while human understanding can be conveyed to machines through "teaching" (Figure 10.1).

The vision of human-machine symbiosis is that a human will work closely and harmoniously with the machine and the machine is designed to have physical (e.g., exoskeleton to help humans carry more weight or augmented senses to enhance human perception) or cognitive capabilities (e.g., superior memorization and processing power) that enhance and augment natural human capabilities (Grigsby 2018: 255–66; see also Stephanidis 2019: 1229–69). In order to achieve this vision, systems need to be "intelligent" and capable of understanding humans but do not necessarily need to recreate how humans think. In the context of translation for human-machine collaboration, a vision of human-machine symbiosis is to build a teaming mechanism between human translators and machine translators.

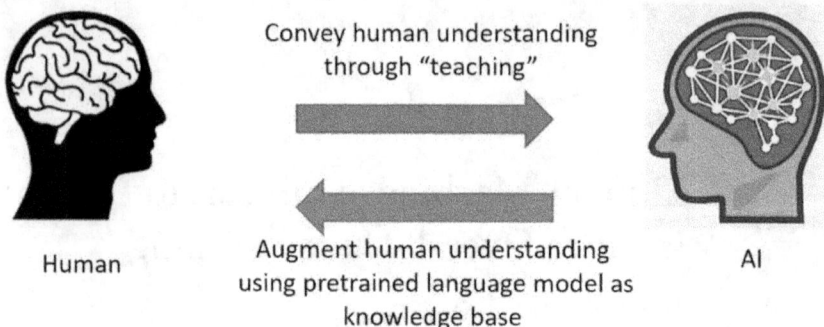

Figure 10.1 Enhanced understanding through human-machine symbiosis

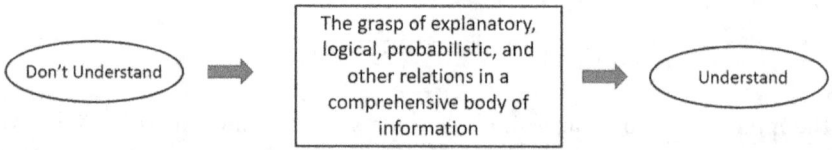

Figure 10.2 Understanding as a cognitive achievement through the grasp of explanatory, logical, probabilistic, and other relations in a comprehensive body of information

On the outset of this wider context, examples related to issues of collaboration between human translators and AI-powered MT may be enhanced in different ways. They will be discussed in detail from the following perspectives:

- How do human translators gain understanding from each other?
- How can machines, powered by AI tools, help humans understand better?
- How can human input inform machine understanding?

2 Human-to-Human Understanding and Explanation

Understanding requires "seeing the way things fit together" (Riggs 2003: 218) or "grasping of explanatory and other coherence-making relationships in a large and comprehensive body of information" (Kvanvig 2003: 192). Riggs (Riggs 2003: 219) argued that understanding can be evaluated based on three criteria: accuracy, explanatory power, and coherence (see Figure 10.2).

In the field of computer science and artificial intelligence, a traditional machine-oriented definition views understanding as the processing of information, which is numerical and/or symbolic. At an early stage of development of AI systems, if a machine generates correct output, it is assumed that the machine "understands" the input content it processes (Wilkowska 2013: 88). Therefore, understanding is regarded as an outcome or a state. Consequently, a single test is sufficient for demonstrating that one AI agent understands correctly or not. But, later on, Blaha (2022: 2) argued that understanding is a process that depends on learning, interpreting, generalizing, and acting upon information. Therefore, no single test is sufficient for demonstrating that one AI agent understands another. Therefore, to evaluate understanding requires executing a series of probing to check the manner and extent to which information has been learned, interpreted, generalized, and acted upon. To probe and demonstrate degree of understanding requires natural language.

In translation studies, understanding (subjective comprehension and interpretation) can be considered to be a "process" that can shift around during the course of translation: even when the same translator is translating the same sentence in the same context, potentially different decisions may be made, as translators' affect/emotion is always present in their decision and in their cognition. That is probably why a piece of translation normally requires a (separate) reviser, other than the translator him/herself, to revise the translation in the professional translation industry (ISO 17100 https://www.iso.org/standard/59149.html).

Explanation (models) can take on many different forms to achieve various degrees of understanding (Baumberger 2017: 8) in terms of breadth and depth. In the context of translation, an experienced translator can teach a less experienced translator to translate by utilizing knowledge drawing from rule-based inferences and statistics-based induction.

Table 10.1 shows some Chinese-to-English and English-to-Chinese examples (column 1) in terms of the reasoning behind how target words are chosen by translators. Column 2 shows possible human-to-human (teacher-to-student) explanations on why the target words are selected (or cannot be determined). The first example illustrates the deductive-nomological model of explanation or reasoning (Eidlin 2010: 285) where the phenomenon is explained as a particular case of a known general law—the rules of the verbs in third-person singular. The second example illustrates the inductive-statistical model (Hájek 2011: 99–135) where an explanation was rendered probable in accordance with statistical law (e.g., a conditional probability of past occurrences).

To understand something is not simply to know but to know of its relation to other knowledge in the context and to being aware of these relations (Baumberger 2017: 1–29). For example, for the last example in Table 10.1, the word "Psybrid"

Table 10.1 Different types of explanations: Deductive-Nomological, Inductive-Statistical, and Failure to Explain

Sample Source and Target Texts (bold font highlights the words/phrases in focus)	Human-to-Human (Teacher-to-Student) Explanations	Explanation Models
Chinese: 他在沃尔玛工作. English: He **works** in Walmart.	Third-person singular verb ending with suffix -s or -es is an English grammar rule (that does not apply in Chinese).	**Deductive-nomological model**: infer particular instances from general law (i.e., grammatical rules).
Chinese: 权利要求书 English: **claims**	I have translated 100+ patent documents before. Every time we translate the Chinese word "权利要求书" into "claims."	**Inductive-statistical model**: make decisions based on statistical observations.
English: Qualitative **Psybrid** Question (on a patient survey form for MRI scan)	No explanation. The word does not exist in the dictionary (linguistic knowledge repository); and it is not a term for MRI operation (domain knowledge base).	Fail to find any knowledge related to the word. Fail to connect this word to contextual knowledge (e.g., MRI).

Source: From Wu, H. (2022), "How to Semi-Automate Google Search to Aid Translation," ATA-CLD Blog Post, June, http://www.ata-divisions.org/CLD/how-to-semi-automate-google-search-to-aid-translation (accessed October 2, 2022).

is not a word in the dictionary, and translators have a hard time linking this word to any domain knowledge in the context—the context seems to be related to an MRI scan and patient survey—which leads to the failure of understanding and explaining.

As AI technology develops, AI has better or equivalent capabilities than humans in terms of deductive, inductive, and selective abductive reasoning while humans are unchallenged in the domain of creative abductive reasoning (Littlefield 2019). One example of selective abductive reasoning is that a translator needs to determine whether to translate a Chinese phrase "驱动单元" into "drive unit" or "driving unit" (Wu 2022). To arbitrate between two hypotheses, the translator does Google searches on both phrases plus the original Chinese phrases: the search based on "驱动单元 driving unit" returns nine results while the search based on "驱动单元 drive unit" returns 191 results. Even though it is possible that the abductive reasoning, providing the best answer available, may be wrong, it has a very good chance of leading to correct solutions. This kind of selective abductive reasoning, in contrast to creative abductive, can be categorized as a special type of inductive reasoning. Creative abduction, on the other hand, relies on creative features, such as the expert use of background knowledge and ontology—forming new concepts while searching heuristically among the old concepts in unconventional ways (Magnini 2004).

3 Human Understanding Enhanced by AI Tools— Localization and Culturalization Applications

In this section, we will explore and analyze how machines, powered by AI tools, may help humans (e.g., translators) understand better. The focus is on how AI tools, in particular, BERT and GPT-3, can provide knowledge and/or connections of knowledge to enhance human understanding.

3.1 Self-Supervised Learning Models Using BERT and GPT-N Language Models

The emergence of Transformer-based deep learning architectures (Vaswani 2017; see also Wang 2019) provides new approaches of natural language understanding. The Transformer architecture is similar to the sequence-to-sequence model with an encoder-decoder pair (illustrated in Figure 10.3) where the encoder encodes an input sequence and the decoder generates the output sequence. In addition, the Transformer architecture adds the attention mechanisms within the encoder and decoder where attention can be modeled as a weighted sum mapping between a set of input source words and an output target word.

Transformers enable the language pretrained models, which are trained on massive text datasets and then adapt to specific downstream tasks. Two powerful categories of the pretrained language models are encoders (e.g., Google Bidirectional Encoder Representations from Transformers—BERT) that provide contextualized representations for NLU and decoders (e.g., Generative Pretrained Transformer-based language model—GPT-3) that are good at text generation tasks. We show how we can enhance human understanding using these two self-supervised learning approaches.

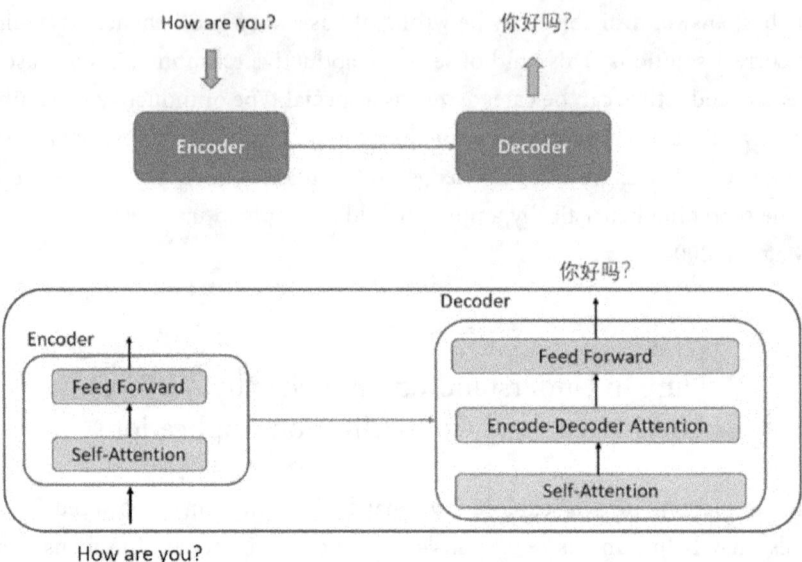

Figure 10.3 Simplified illustrations of sequence-to-sequence model and Transformer architecture with attention mechanism where attention weights indicate the impacts of input words on an output word (e.g., the input source-language words "you" and "are" carry larger weights to determine the target-language word "你")

BERT (Devlin 2018), developed by Google, makes use of the Transformer architecture that learns contextual relations between words in a text: the encoder reads the text input and the decoder produces a prediction for the fill-in-blank task. GPT-3 is also a Transformer-based language model (Brown 2020) that takes input and generates text from it. GPT-3 takes any text prompt, such as several phrases or sentences, and returns a text completion in natural language (Figure 10.4). Users can also program GPT-3 by showing just a few examples (few shots).

3.2 Localization and Culturalization Examples

Localization refers to the adaptation of a document's content to meet the linguistic, cultural, and other requirements of a specific target market (https://www.w3.org/International/questions/qa-i18n). Culturalization is how one can adapt content for other cultures and other geographies beyond just normal localization (https://www.dell.com/es-es/perspectives/is-culturalization-the-key-to-achieving-global-success/). During our research, we explored the approaches of using BERT and GPT-3 for localization and culturalization tasks (Qian and Liu 2021; see also Qian Newton, and Qian 2021). Table 10.2 lists some

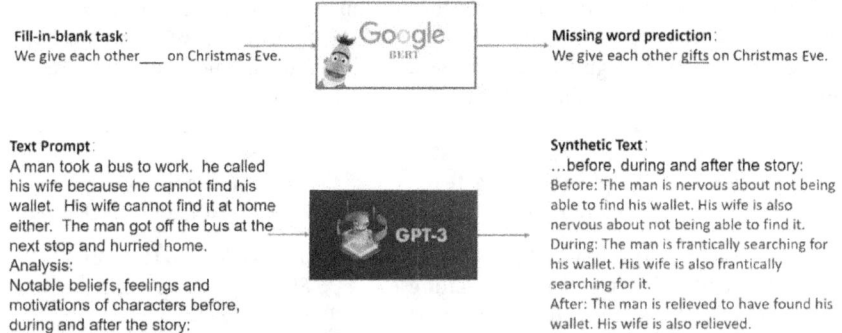

Figure 10.4 Self-supervised language models: BERT (Devlin 2018) and GPT-3 (Brown 2020). The input for BERT can be a fill-in-blank task, and the output of BERT can be a missing word prediction. The input for GPT-3 is prompted text provided by a human user, and the output is synthetic text that can make reasonable predictions and infer/reason about things not written in the prompting text

examples: column 1 describes the knowledge types; column 2 shows the set-up of the self-supervised task—BERT provides the rest of the sentence as context while GPT3 provide prompt text; column 3 shows the results generated by the self-supervised language models—BERT generates predictions on the masked word, and GPT-3 generates synthetic texts.

Table 10.2 shows six examples in which AI provides localization and culturalization knowledge. Example 1 shows an example of a missing logical connective. The Chinese language often omits logical connectives that are considered essential in English (Pinkham 2000). While Chinese readers can understand a text without these connectives, native speakers of English are likely to expect more help from the connective words. In this example, the logical relation between two clauses is cause-effect. The top choice by BERT is the connective word "because." The result shows that the language model captures the cause-effect relation implied by the context.

Example 2 shows an example of cultural-related emotional schema. A Chinese emotional (sadness) schema can be described as: a person experiences sadness when he/she senses a gap or lacking of ability when he/she compares himself/herself to others. This Chinese cultural sadness schema indicates inferiority, self-pity, and helplessness (Xu 2017: 65–84). BERT helps to find the interpretation in the Western culture through a masked word task. The top emotions found are "awkward," "inferior," and "embarrassed" in Western culture.

Example 3 shows an example of geopolitical factoid knowledge across different cultures: sovereignty over the Falkland Islands (Spanish: Islas Malvinas)

Table 10.2 Localization and culturalization examples (Qian and Liu 2021; see also Qian, Newton, and Qian 2021): BERT and GPT-3 Can Identify Cross-cultural and Cross-language Linguistic Knowledge and Nonlinguistic Knowledge Such As Emotional Schema, Geopolitical Knowledge, and Social Norms

No.	Set Up the Task Using Context (for BERT) and Prompting Text (for GPT-3)	Outputs Generated by Self-Supervised Language Models
1	**Set up a masked task after a literal translation from Chinese (the leading connective is missing)** [MASK] most coal mines in Hunan are located in remote hilly areas, and the province encourages laid-off workers there to switch to agriculture to earn a living.	**Mask prediction (by BERT)** 36.8% Because (top choice) 19.9% Although 14.0% While 13.0% Since 9.3% As The top choice identifies the correct logical connective.
2	**Set up a masked task to find the corresponding emotion schema in the Western culture** My English vocabulary is too small, and I feel [MASK] every time I compare myself to a native English speaker.	**Mask prediction (by BERT)** 10.3% awkward (top choice) 5.6% sick 5.3% inferior 4.4% embarrassed 3.7% stupid The top choice identifies the proper emotion schema (awkward) in the Western culture.
3	**Set up a prompt-prediction task** *Prompt* The islands were called the Falkland Islands by the British, and in Argentina it was called . . .	**GPT-3 generated text** The islands were called the Falkland Islands by the British, and in Argentina it was called <u>Islas Malvinas</u>. The GPT-3 has the factoid knowledge.
4	**Set up a prompt-prediction task** *Prompt* The Greek equivalent of a middle finger in the United States is . . .	**GPT-3 generated text** The Greek equivalent of a middle finger in the United States is <u>the Moutza, where you fling your hand out, fingers pushed apart.</u> The GPT-3 has the factoid knowledge.
5	**Set up a masked task to find the social norm** *Prompt* This guy walked into the building right in front of me. He was very nice to [MASK] the door for me.	**Mask prediction (by BERT)** open 75.3% hold 9.3% The BERT knows the social norm (door etiquette).

Table 10.2 (Continued)

No.	Set Up the Task Using Context (for BERT) and Prompting Text (for GPT-3)	Outputs Generated by Self-Supervised Language Models
6	**Set up a masked task to find the social norm** *Prompt* 他家老人去世了，在地上[MASK]紙。 (English translation: The old man of his family passed away, they [MASK] paper on the ground.)	**Mask prediction (by BERT)** 撒 13% (throw) 写 6.8% (write) 烧 5.7% (burn) *The BERT knows the social norm followed by Chinese mourners.*

Source: Data from Qian, M. and J. Liu (2021), "Assisting Text Localization and Transcreation Tasks Using AI-Based Masked Language Modeling," in International Conference on Human-Computer Interaction, 427–38, New York: Springer. Qian, M., C. Newton, and D. Qian (2021), "Cultural Understanding Using In-context Learning and Masked Language Modeling," in International Conference on Human-Computer Interaction, 500–8, New York: Springer.

is disputed by Argentina and the UK. GPT-3-generated synthetic text provides the proper Spanish result.

Example 4 shows an example of cultural factoid knowledge across different cultures: gestures in different countries could carry different meanings. GPT-3-generated synthetic text provides the proper answer for the Greek equivalent of a gesture that is well known in the United States.

Example 5 shows an example of social norm knowledge—etiquette refers to the conventions and norms of social behavior. They are accepted codes of conduct in social life. The example shows that BERT-generated result reflects door etiquette: when entering and exiting with other people, it is a stereotypically polite behavior to hold and open a door for the person behind you.

Example 6 shows a Chinese example of social norm knowledge: The process of throwing and lighting paper "money" into fire symbolizes the practice of sending or mailing money that the dead ancestors could use while "living" in another world. Again, BERT-generated results recognizes this social tradition that is followed by Chinese mourners.

In these examples, as long as the correct outputs are generated based on the input content, we can claim that the machine "understands" the input content it processes. For all the examples here, the solutions provided by the AI tools agree with the solutions by human experts. Therefore, if a human user does not have that understanding, the AI-generated results can point them to the right direction. Consequently, AI can enhance human understanding by providing correct knowledge, explanations, and statistical information.

These examples show that self-supervised pretrained models can provide accurate machine-oriented understanding (or at least generating a list of possible outputs for translators) based on the provided context. Armed with the output and knowledge provided by the AI tools, human translators, who may not be familiar with a different cultural or linguistic phenomenon, can gain full or at least partial understanding that can be broadened and deepened through further investigation (e.g., collecting more evidence). Therefore, we can claim that human understanding can be enhanced by leveraging the knowledge, explanations, and statistical information provided by the self-supervised AI language models.

Some recent studies (Petroni 2019; see also Kassner 2021) found that BERT (without fine-tuning) had good performance as knowledge base. As larger and more powerful language models become available, these AI tools' capabilities to enhance human understanding across linguistic and cultural barriers will also grow more significantly.

4 Machine Understandings Based on Human Inputs—Customized Machine Translation Application

In this section, we will explore and analyze how human inputs can help AI tools to understand customized machine translation text patterns defined and specified via active few-shot learning. Few-shot learning refers to the practice of feeding a machine learning model with a very small amount of training data, contrary to the normal practice of using a large amount of data (Wang 2020: 1–34). GPT-3 represents a good few-shot learner (Brown 2020: 1877–901).

4.1 Few-Shot Learning

A human student can generally perform a new language task from only a few examples or from simple instructions from a human teacher. For example, an experienced translator can teach a less experienced translator how to translate one type of words or sentence structures by giving several examples. By giving these examples, human teachers transfer their understanding—including linguistic and cross-cultural knowledge and how various knowledge in the context is connected—to human students.

To illustrate this point, we focus on an application of generating augmented text data, customized for English-Chinese simultaneous interpreting (SI), to train a customized machine translation engine. Few-shot learning that is based on human inputs illustrates a case of mutual enhancement: a human teaches the machine first using a few examples, then the machine combines the learned knowledge with its strength of memorizational and computational power to augment human capability in terms of efficiency, efficacy, and effectiveness.

4.2 Examples of Customized Machine Translation for Simultaneous Interpreting

To rival the best in human SI, a simultaneous machine translation solution needs to deliver nonrevisable translation (once giving a word utterance, the interpreter cannot go back to utter a revised version of the same translation) with one-second latency. Nonrevisability is a minimum requirement as one cannot listen to what is being said and simultaneously listen to a revision of what has been said. The one-second latency is something that many in the interpreting profession consider it to be impossible to sustain for long. For instance, research has shown that English-to-Chinese interpreters typically lag three seconds or more behind the words they are hearing (Lin 2014).

Formulaic techniques, such as the KLSI method for English-to-Chinese simultaneous interpretation, have been developed (Lin 2021: 394–412). Several KLSI techniques are illustrated in Table 10.3: repeat, replace, and skip-add-insert (SAI).

Repeat is an effective and mechanical way of resolving English post-modifiers for ST. In Chinese, the same modifiers are usually pre-modifiers. For example, the Chinese counterpart of the post-modifier "quickly" in an original English sentence "They finished the work ***quickly***" is "很快地." In conventional translation, the post-modifier in English needs to be brought forward and translated into pre-modifiers in Chinese: 他们很快地结束工作 (Back translation: They ***quickly*** finished the work). But, in SI, when an English speaker utters the word "quickly," the interpreter already translates the first few words into Chinese. As a coping strategy, the interpreter would repeat the verb "finished" to reestablish the word "quickly" as a pre-modifier: 他们结束工作， 很快地结束 (Back translation: They finished the work, quickly finished).

Replace means to replace a preposition with a verb. This enables the interpreter to repeat the verb at the beginning of a preposition phrase/clause instead of at the end as is the case in the example of the repeat strategy. It improves the quality of output and saves time. For example, the Chinese counterpart of the

Table 10.3 Generating Training Samples for KLSI repair, replace, and SAI Techniques (The Italicized Text Are the Input Teaching Examples and the Bolded Sentence Is the GPT-3-Generated Synthetic Samples.)

Techniques	GPT-3 Prompts and Generated Synthetic Text
Repeat	*They finished the work quickly.* *They finished the work, quickly finished.* *Tom beats the POW violently.* *Tim beats the POW, violently beats.* *The teacher shows every step carefully.* *The teacher shows every step, carefully shows.* ... *The woman weeps silently.* **The woman weeps, silently weeps.**
Replace	Our business is growing at 20 percent per year. Our business is growing, reaching 20 percent per year. The high-speed train is travelling at 350 kilometers per hour. The high-speed train is travelling, reaching 350 kilometers per hour. ... The US unemployment rate fell to a post-recession low of 6 percent. **The US unemployment rate fell, reaching a post-recession low of 6 percent.**
SAI	The children we saw earlier are now here. Whom we saw earlier, the children are here now. The policeman we met yesterday will inspect this facility again today. Whom we met yesterday, the policemen will inspect the facility again today. ... The customer you had argument before come to the food court again this week. **Whom you had argument before, the customer came to the food court again this week.**

Source: Lin, K. and M. Qian (2021), "KLSI Methods for Human Simultaneous Interpretation and Towards Building a Simultaneous Machine Translation System Reflecting the KLSI Methods," in International Conference on Human-Computer Interaction, 394–412, New York: Springer.

prepositional phrase "at 20% per year" in an original English sentence "Our business is growing at 20% per year" is "以每年 20% 的速度." In conventional translation, the prepositional phrase in English needs to be brought forward in Chinese: 我们的业务以每年 20% 的速度增长 (Back translation: Our business, at 20% per year, is growing). But, in SI, when an English speaker utters the prepositional phrase "at 20% per year," the interpreter already translates most words before the phrase into Chinese. As a coping strategy, the interpreter would replace the preposition word "at" to a verb "reaching" to resolve the post-modifier/pre-modifier mapping problem between English and Chinese: 我们的业务在增长. 每年达到20% (Back translation: Our business is growing, reaching 20% per year).

SAI (Skip, Add, and Insert) resolves the issue of modifying clause, rather than using Repeat strategy, to achieve better-quality output. For example, in an original English sentence "The children that we saw earlier are now here." There is a prepositional phrase "that we saw earlier," which can be literally translated into "我们之前看到的." In conventional translation, the modifying clause in English needs to be brought forward in Chinese: 我们之前看到的孩子们现在这里 (Back translation: The children that we saw earlier are now here). But, in SI, when interpreters hear the word "that" after the word "children," they know that a modifying clause would follow. As a coping strategy, interpreters can choose to skip the translation of the phrase "The children," wait to translate the modifying phrase ("that we saw earlier") first, then insert the phrase "the children" afterward. Therefore, the simultaneous interpretation becomes: 我们稍早看到的孩子现在在这里 (Back translation: Whom we saw earlier, the children are here).

One of the challenges of building a customized simultaneous machine translation system to reflect human experts' techniques is the lack of training samples provided by human experts. Commercial NMT machine translation requires millions of pairs of sentences in two languages, that is, parallel corpora (Geitgey 2020). Unlike traditional MT, which can be trained using web text, Wikipedia, and a corpus of books, it is unrealistic to obtain enough (verbal) parallel texts in English and Chinese reflecting unique techniques for training a NMT simultaneous translation system. An alternative approach is to pretrain the NMT model on a large corpus of text followed by fine-tuning on specific sentence types. The fine-tuning approach would require fine-tuning datasets with thousands or tens of thousands of examples. Moreover, even meeting this requirement is difficult, given it is difficult to obtain recorded interpretation sessions in which formulaic techniques were practiced Armed with only a small training set, a NMT system cannot generate translation results reflecting specific techniques.

Humans can perform a new language task from only a few examples (few-shot learning). It has been shown that scaling up language models (e.g., GPT-3) can achieve few-shot performance on many language tasks (Brown 2020).

Few-shot learning is ideal to the application of the abovementioned scenario: first a human expert can provide a couple of examples. Then, the AI system can quickly learn the patterns (e.g., repeat, replace, and SAI) from those examples and automatically make the relevant changes toward all similar sentences in the training corpus, which can be parallel corpora based on web text, Wikipedia, and corpora of books. Using the modified training corpora, a NMT system can produce output reflecting specific school of techniques. For few-shot learning, only a couple of examples are fed to the GPT-3 language model, then similar sentences in the training corpora can be identified using natural language processing tools (Farouk 2019) or keyword matching (Lin 2021). Accordingly, the GPT-3 can modify those sentences to reflect the unique techniques. Since the whole workflow has been automated, a human user's task is simply to enter a couple of examples. This requires human intelligence, but it is not time-consuming.

Table 10.3 shows several examples of using GPT-3 to generate training samples for KLSI's repeat, replace, and SAI techniques. The italicized texts are the input sentences, and the bolded sentences are the generated samples.

For the repeat technique, three examples are given as few-shot examples to train GPT-3. The English post-modifiers "quickly," "violently," and "carefully" are used with repeated verbs: "quickly finished," "violently beats," and "carefully shows." The fourth (testing) example shows that once the GPT-3 learns the pattern, it can revise an input sentence using the same pattern ("silently weeps").

For the replace technique, two examples are given as few-shot examples to train GPT-3. The propositional clause "at 20% per year" can be revised into "reaching 20% per year" and "at 350 kilometers per hour" into "reaching 350 kilometers per hour." The third (testing) example shows that once the GPT-3 learns the pattern, it can revise an input sentence using the same pattern ("to a post-recession low of 6 percent" is converted to "reaching a post-recession low of 6 percent").

For the SAI technique, two examples are given as few-shot examples to train GPT-3. "Whom we saw earlier" and "Whom we met yesterday" are inserted into at the beginning of the sentence while the subject words 'children' and "policemen" are adjusted accordingly. The third (testing) example shows that once the GPT-3 learns the pattern, it can revise an input sentence using the same pattern ("Whom you had argument before" and the subject word "customer" switches their positions).

Consequently, we can revise any number of sentences with the different patterns (reflecting various techniques) to generate a large quantity of augmented (synthetic) training samples: into English with the new pattern first, then the English sentences associated with the new patterns can be translated into Chinese to build parallel corpora with thousands or tens of thousands bilingual sentences.

5 Machine Understanding Based on Human Inputs—Stylometry Application for GPT-3

In this section, we will explore and analyze how human inputs can help AI tools on stylometry applications through active few-shot learning.

5.1 Examples of Stylometry Application—Understanding and Detecting Linguistic Phenomena

Stylometry (Neal 2017) studies linguistic styles of authors. It focuses on the analysis of variations in literary style between one writer and another writer. It is often used to attribute authorship to written documents with unknown authors. In Schick's study (2020), it is shown that human users can combine task description and few-shot examples to obtain good performance results on multiple natural language processing tasks. In the present study, we experimented to use human-input few-shot teaching samples to help GPT-3-based system understand linguistic concepts, including word contraction, oxford comma, and adverbs pre-modifying or post-modifying verbs (see details in Table 10.4). For the word contraction pattern, three pairs of few-shot teaching examples ("contraction" versus "no contraction") were given by humans. For the oxford comma pattern, multiple few-shot teaching examples (with or without oxford comma or invalid condition to apply oxford comma) were given by humans. For the post-/pre-modifier pattern, multiple few-shot teaching examples were given by humans. The testing results using new sentences show that the GPT-3-based model learns to recognize the patterns after only a few given teaching examples.

Once GPT-3 grasps the understanding, it can go through a large text corpus and label a large number of sentences with corresponding linguistic phenomena in a very short period of time. This is the value of stylometry applications: quickly generating statistics on authors' preferences on linguistic styles.

Table 10.4 Few-shot learning using GPT-3: Humans Can Use Several Examples to Teach GPT-3 Tool on Linguistic Concepts Such As Word Contraction, Oxford Comma, and Pre-modifier Versus Post-modifier for Verbs (Left Column). After the GPT-3 Tool Learned the Pattern, It Has the Ability to Detect These Linguistic Phenomena as Illustrated in the Right Column

GPT-3 Prompting Text (Few-Shot Training Examples)	Testing (Detect the Feature on New Sentences)
Word Contraction Example	
(format: sample sentence + description and classification label + highlighted text in the sentence related to the classification)	
"I haven't walked on this path before."	"Once summoned, the police should've quickly showed up to the house!"
In this sentence, the contraction form is "contraction": "haven't."	The contraction form is "contraction": **"should've."**
"I have not walked on this path before."	
In this sentence, the contraction form is "no contraction": "have not."	
"It would've made a better shot."	
In this sentence, the contraction form is "contraction": "would've."	
"It would have made a better shot."	
In this sentence, the contraction form is "no contraction": "would have."	
"She could not go to any college she wanted to."	
In this sentence, the contraction form is "no contraction": "could not."	
"She couldn't go to any college she wanted to."	
In this sentence, the contraction form is "contraction": "couldn't."	
Oxford Comma Example	
(format: sample sentence + description and classification label + highlighted text in the sentence related to the classification)	

"The panda eats, shoots, and leaves."
In this sentence, the Oxford comma form is "Oxford comma": "shoots, and leaves."

"After he walked all the way home, he shut the door."
In this sentence, the oxford comma form is "invalid condition": "home, he shut the door."

"Please bring me a pencil, eraser and notebook."
In this sentence, the Oxford comma form is "no Oxford comma": "eraser and notebook."

"I admire my parents, Gandhi, and Mother Teresa."
In this sentence, the Oxford comma form is "Oxford comma": "Gandhi, and Mother Teresa."

"Once upon a time, there is a snake living in the mountain."
In this sentence, the Oxford comma form is "invalid condition": "time, there is a snake."

"To my parents, Ayn Rand and God."
In this sentence, the Oxford comma form is "no Oxford comma": "Ayn Rand and God."

"Once summoned, the police should've quickly showed up to the house."
In this sentence, the Oxford comma form is "invalid condition": "police should've quickly showed up."

"My usual breakfast is coffee, bacon, and eggs."
In this sentence, the Oxford comma form is **"Oxford comma": "coffee, bacon, and eggs."**

"My usual breakfast is coffee, bacon and eggs."
In this sentence, the Oxford comma form is **"no Oxford comma": "coffee, bacon and eggs."**

Post-Modifier versus Pre-Modifier Example

(format: sample sentence + description and classification label + highlighted text in the sentence related to the classification)

"It ended abruptly."
In this sentence, the verb is post-modified: "ended abruptly."

"She calmly announced her retirement."
In this sentence, the verb is pre-modified: "calmly announced."

"She sings beautifully."
In this sentence, the verb is post-modified: "sings beautifully."

"She greedily ate the chocolate cake."
In this sentence, the verb is pre-modified: "greedily ate."

"The police quickly surrounded the house."
In this sentence, the verb is **pre-modified: "quickly surrounded."**

Table 10.5 GPT-3 tool extrapolating to unknown conditions: The Training Examples Cover Verb, Adverb, and Adjective. The Test Condition Is for Noun

GPT-3 Prompting Text (Few-Shot Training Examples)	Testing (Detect the Feature on New Sentences)
"I mised the train.": misspelled verb. "He walked sloly into the park.": misspelled adverb. "They look disapointed.": misspelled adjective.	"He is a profesor.": **misspelled noun.**

5.2 Examples of Extrapolating Linguistic Knowledge

In real life, new linguistic phenomena can emerge over time. Therefore, a human expert cannot be expected to give an exhaustive list of possible patterns and provide coverage for all patterns that could emerge in the future. In addition, it is not reasonable to ask human experts to update knowledge on handling emerging phenomena frequently. Therefore, it would be beneficial for an AI tool to extrapolate knowledge to cover emerging patterns that are similar to well-defined existing patterns. In Table 10.5, we show a simple example in which GPT-3 tool can extrapolate existing knowledge (e.g., how to detect misspelled verb, adjective, and adverb) to unknown situations (e.g., misspelled noun) through inductive inference without explicit example given on the new category. An author might have a habit of misspelling certain word so that it can serve as a stylometry.

6 Conclusion

The vision of human-machine symbiosis is that a human will work closely and harmoniously with the machine. Section 2 lists various definitions of human-to-human understanding/explanations and showed examples about how human translators gain understanding from or provide explanations to each other using relevant deductive, inductive, and abductive models. Section 3 shows how human understanding may be enhanced by AI tools for localization and culturization purposes. Sections 4 and 5 show how human inputs can be used to inform machine understanding for customized machine translation and stylometry applications.

As we illustrated in multiple examples in this study, humans and machines obviously have different strengths and weaknesses of understanding: humans have unique creative abductive reasoning capability that generates novel and creative solutions and share human experiences/traits while AI systems can advise by providing knowledge to enhance human understanding, by memorizing, processing, learning through a huge amount of data in a very short period of time, and by repeating or extrapolating a pattern.

In a wider context, we foresee a future in which each human expert can team up with their own AI assistant and provide customized results. Since different human experts can teach their AI assistants different traits and techniques, every human-AI team will provide their own unique expertise and values. The human-machine symbiosis approach will bring upon a further step in the direction of enhanced performance in terms of quality and efficiency for multilingual and translation tasks.

Note

1 In this chapter, the term "translation" is considered to be interlingual exchanges in a more general sense, irrespective of its mode of communication. In other words, interpreting is also considered to be a form of (verbal) translation, in this chapter.

References

Baumberger, C., C. Beisbart, and G. Brun (2017), "What Is Understanding? An Overview of Recent Debates in Epistemology and Philosophy of Science," in S. Grimm, C. Baumberger, and S. Ammon (eds.), *Explaining Understanding: New Perspectives from Epistemology and Philosophy of Science*, 1–34, New York and London: Routledge, Taylor and Francis Group.

Blaha, L. M., M. Abrams, S. A. Bibyk, C. Bonial, B. M. Hartzler, C. D. Hsu, S. Khemlani, J. King, R.S. Amant, J. G. Trafton, and R. Wong (2022), "Understanding Is a Process," *Frontiers in Systems Neuroscience*, 16: 800280.

Brown, T., B. Mann, N. Ryder, M. Subbiah, J. D. Kaplan, P. Dhariwal, A. Neelakantan, P. Shyam, G. Sastry, A. Askell, and S. Agarwal (2020), "Language Models Are Few-Shot Learners," in *Advances in Neural Information Processing Systems*, vol. 33, 1877–901, Cambridge, MA: MIT Press.

Devlin, J. and M. W. Chang (2018), "Open Sourcing BERT: State-of-the-Art Pre-training for Natural Language Processing," *Google AI Blog*, November 2. https://ai.googleblog.com/2018/11/open-sourcing-bert-state-of-art-pre.html (accessed October 2, 2022).

Eidlin, F. (2010), "The Deductive-Nomological Model of Explanation," in A. Mills, G. Durepos, and E. Wiebe (eds.), *Encyclopedia of Case Study Research*, 284–6, London: Sage.

Farouk, M. (2019), "Measuring Sentences Similarity: A Survey," arXiv preprint arXiv:1910.03940, October 6. https://arxiv.org/abs/1910.03940 (accessed October 2, 2022).

Geitgey, A. (2020), "Build Your Own Google Translate Quality Machine Translation System," medium.com, May 4. https://medium.com/@ageitgey/build-your-own-google-translate-quality-machine-translation-system-d7dc274bd476 (accessed October 2, 2022).

Grigsby, S. S. (2018), "Artificial Intelligence for Advanced Human-Machine Symbiosis," in *International Conference on Augmented Cognition*, 255–66, New York: Springer.

Hájek, A. (2011), "Conditional Probability," in P. Bandyopadhyay and M. Forster (eds.), *Philosophy of Statistics*, 99–135, Amsterdam: North-Holland.

Kassner, N., P. Dufter, and H. Schütze (2021), "Multilingual LAMA: Investigating Knowledge in Multilingual Pretrained Language Models," arXiv preprint arXiv:2102.00894, February 1. https://arxiv.org/abs/2102.00894 (accessed October 2, 2022).

Kvanvig, J. (2003), *The Value of Knowledge and the Pursuit of Understanding*, New York: Cambridge University Press.

Lin, K. (2014), *Field Simultaneous Interpreting*, Beijing: Foreign Language Teaching and Research Press.

Lin, K. and M. Qian (2021), "KLSI Methods for Human Simultaneous Interpretation and Towards Building a Simultaneous Machine Translation System Reflecting the KLSI Methods," in *International Conference on Human-Computer Interaction*, 394–412, New York: Springer.

Littlefield, W. J. (2019), "Abductive Humanism: Comparative Advantages of Artificial Intelligence and Human Cognition According to Logical Inference," Master Thesis, College of Arts and Sciences, Case Western Reserve University.

Magnani, L. (2004), "Creative Abduction as Active Shaping of Knowledge. Epistemic and Ethical Mediators," *Proceedings of the Annual Meeting of the Cognitive Science Society*, 26(26): 879–84.

Neal, T., K. Sundararajan, A. Fatima, Y. Yan, Y. Xiang, and D. Woodard (2017), "Surveying Stylometry Techniques and Applications," *ACM Computing Surveys (CSuR)*, 50(6): 1–36.

Petroni, F., T. Rocktäschel, P. Lewis, A. Bakhtin, Y. Wu, A. H. Miller, and S. Riedel (2019), "Language Models as Knowledge Bases?," arXiv preprint arXiv:1909.01066, September 3. https://arxiv.org/abs/1909.01066 (accessed October 2, 2022).

Pinkham, J. (2000), *The Translator's Guide to Chinglish*, Beijing: Foreign Language Teaching and Research Press.

Qian, M. and J. Liu (2021), "Assisting Text Localization and Transcreation Tasks Using AI-Based Masked Language Modeling," in *International Conference on Human-Computer Interaction*, 427–38, New York: Springer.

Qian, M., C. Newton, and D. Qian (2021), "Cultural Understanding Using In-context Learning and Masked Language Modeling," in *International Conference on Human-Computer Interaction*, 500–8, New York: Springer.

Riggs, W. D. (2003), "Understanding 'Virtue' and the Virtue of Understanding," in M. DePaul and L. Zagzebski (eds.), *Intellectual Virtue*, 203–26, Oxford: Clarendon Press.

Schick, T. and H. Schütze (2020), "Exploiting Cloze Questions for Few-Shot Text Classification and Natural Language Inference", arXiv preprint arXiv:2001.07676, January 21. https://arxiv.org/abs/2001.07676 (accessed October 2, 2022).

Stephanidis, C., G. Salvendy, M. Antona, J. Y. Chen, J. Dong, V. G. Duffy, X. Fang, C. Fidopiastis, G. Fragomeni, L. P. Fu, and Y. Guo (2019), "Seven HCI Grand Challenges," *International Journal of Human–Computer Interaction*, 35(14): 1229–69.

Vaswani, A., N. Shazeer, N. Parmar, J. Uszkoreit, L. Jones, A. N. Gomez, Ł. Kaiser, and I. Polosukhin (2017), "Attention Is All You Need," *Advances in Neural Information Processing Systems*, 30: 6000–10.

Wang, C., M. Li, and A. J. Smola (2019), "Language Models with Transformers," arXiv preprint arXiv:1904.09408, April 20. https://arxiv.org/abs/1904.09408 (accessed October 2, 2022).

Wang, Y., Q. Yao, J. T. Kwok, and L. M. Ni (2020), "Generalizing from a Few Examples: A Survey on Few-Shot Learning," *ACM Computing Surveys (csur)*, 53(3): 1–34.

Wilkowska, M. (2013), "A Philosophical Investigation in Machine Understanding. The Case of Implicit Meaning," *Semina Scientiarum*, 1(12): 83–96.

Wu, H. (2022), "How to Semi-Automate Google Search to Aid Translation," *ATA-CLD Blog Post*, June 9. http://www.ata-divisions.org/CLD/how-to-semi-automate-google-search-to-aid-translation/ (accessed October 2, 2022).

Xu, Z. and F. Sharifian (2017), "Unpacking Cultural Conceptualizations in Chinese English," *Journal of Asian Pacific Communication*, 27(1): 65–84.

Contributors

Sui He received her PhD degree in translation studies from University College London, UK in 2022. She works as a lecturer at the School of Culture and Communication at Swansea University, UK. Her research interest lies in metaphor translation in the contexts of popular science and health communication.

Zhiai Liu is Assistant Professor in Translation and Interpreting Studies at CUHK (Shenzhen, China). Dr. Liu's research focuses on interpreters' roles, accuracy and faithfulness, ethical and emotional challenges in legal interpreting. She is also an experienced interpreter/translator, a Chartered Linguist of CIOL, and a full-status member of the NRPSI in Britain.

Kirsten Malmkjær is Emeritus Professor of Translation Studies at the University of Leicester, UK. She is especially interested in translation theory and has developed the approach to translation-focused text analysis known as Translational Stylistics. Recent publications include *Translation and Creativity* (2020) and *The Cambridge Handbook of Translation* (2022).

Monika Płużyczka is Professor (dr hab. prof. ucz.) of Linguistics and Translation Studies at the University of Warsaw (Faculty of Applied Linguistics), Poland and Head of the Laboratory for Experimental Eye Tracking Linguistics (LELO Lab) and the Department of Translation Studies at the Institute of Specialised and Intercultural Communication.

Ming Qian is an experienced research scientist in the field of designing and developing cognitively and linguistically motivated computational paradigms. He has been a Chinese to/from English translator/interpreter for more than ten years. He holds sixty-three US/international patents. He has a PhD in electrical and computer engineering and is a certified PMP.

Claire Shih is Associate Professor in Translation and Interpreting Studies at University College London, UK. She publishes widely in the field of translation process research (TPR), eliciting data from think-aloud protocols (TAPs), retrospective interviews, screen recording, and eye tracking. Her recent publication focuses on translators' online information-seeking behaviors and translation pedagogy. She is currently coediting *The Routledge Handbook of East Asian Translation*. Her publications can be found here: https://orcid.org/my-orcid?orcid=0000-0002-7232-6275.

Anu Viljanmaa works as a university instructor at the Languages Unit in the Faculty of Information Technology and Communication Sciences at Tampere University, Finland. She has been teaching German and English interpreting since 2009 and is an active, certified interpreter (EMCI). Her research interests focus on interpreting as interaction and the professional listening competence of dialogue interpreters.

Binhua Wang is Chair/Professor of Interpreting and Translation Studies at University of Leeds, UK. His research interest lies mainly in interpreting and translation studies, in which he has published over fifty articles in refereed CSSCI journals and SSCI/A&HCI journals. He has authored the monographs *Theorising Interpreting Studies* (2019) and *A Descriptive Study of Norms in Interpreting* (2013) and edited with Jeremy Munday *Advances in Discourse Analysis of Translation and Interpreting* (2020).

Caiwen Wang is Senior Lecturer in Translation and Interpreting Studies at the University of Westminster, UK, and Associate Professor (Teaching) at University College London, having taught translation and interpreting at both the theoretical and the practical level. Her research interests are theoretical and empirical studies of translation and interpreting and the broad field of linguistics and applied linguistics. Her publications can be found here: https://orcid.org/0000-0002-6610-7244. Dr Wang is also a very experienced professional translator and interpreter.

Jie Xue is a PhD candidate in the School of Interpreting and Translation Studies at Guangdong University of Foreign Studies, China. His current research interest is legal translation and terminology translation. He has also been a translation practitioner and has contributed to the translation of several academic works in law.

Junfeng Zhao holds a PhD in forensic linguistics and is Professor and Director of the Centre for Translation Studies, Guangdong University of Foreign Studies, China. He is the vice chairman of the China National Committee for Translation and Interpreting Education and vice president of WITTA. He has published extensively in translation and interpreting studies, especially in legal translation and court interpreting.

Index

abductive reasoning   200–1, 215
affect   1–14, 19, 22–5, 27, 30–1, 37, 199
anxiety   57–9, 77
artificial intelligence   107, 121, 198
attention   5, 12–13, 19–21, 24, 38, 40–2, 45, 48–52, 59, 83–4, 88–9, 102, 108, 120, 129, 138, 148, 151–2, 159–60, 166–7, 169–70, 189, 201–2
augmented   197, 206, 211
awareness   9–10, 39, 51–2, 60–1, 85, 102

black box   5, 109, 129

cognition/cognitive   1, 3–10, 13, 15, 35, 37, 41, 51, 55–6, 58, 83, 86–7, 89–90, 93–4, 101, 103, 109, 117, 128, 147, 159–60, 162, 164, 170–1, 176, 179, 181–5, 188, 192, 198–9
cognitive behavior/cognitive behavioral   1, 6, 9–10
cognitive capacity   60, 94, 99, 108, 197
cognitive load/cognitive overload   83, 100–1
cognitive metaphor   100–1, 110, 125, 131–2, 134–41, 143–51
cognitive process/cognitive processing   1, 2, 4–5, 8, 11, 13, 19, 84, 89, 90, 107–8, 126
cognitive psychology/cognitive psychologist   1, 2, 4–6, 8, 11, 13, 176, 178
cognitive sociology/cognitive sociological   4, 84, 90, 107, 110–11, 113–15, 152, 159–61, 166, 170
comparative law   157
competence(s)   9, 36, 43, 50, 102, 113–14, 121
comprehension   4, 83, 97, 101, 107–9, 120, 132–8, 140–2, 144–6, 148–51, 167, 199
conceptual metaphor   175–6, 181, 188
covert self-talk   35–51
customized machine translation   206–7, 214

dialogue interpreters/dialogue interpreting   35–8, 40, 42–3, 46, 48–50, 111, 115–16

effective communication   84, 97
effort model   85, 87, 92, 102, 128, 147, 150
emotion/emotions   1–3, 5, 23–5, 30, 36–8, 42, 49–50, 56–9, 61, 71–2, 74–5, 78, 138, 179, 199, 203–4
emotional intelligence   7, 9–11, 14
empirical Studies/empirical experiments   12, 14, 20, 83, 86, 90, 92, 133, 150
experiment(s)   10, 12, 14, 41, 88, 107, 110, 112, 121, 125, 132–4, 138, 142–4, 146–52
eye tracking   3, 5, 13, 125, 127, 131–4, 136, 140, 143, 146–52

failure sequence   99–100
few-shot learning   206–7, 209–12, 214
first-person self-talk   41–2, 44–50
fixation(s)   132, 134–42, 147–9, 152

generic space   159–60, 165

Holocaust   23
human-machine symbiosis   197–8, 214–15

inner voice/inner speech   36, 39, 43–4
instructional self-talk   40–1, 45–51
internal listening filters   35–42, 45–51

legal interpreters/legal interpreting   55–9, 61–3, 65–8, 75–8
legal translation   157, 159, 161, 170
linguistic metaphor   176, 181, 188
listening filters   35–51
localization   201–5, 214
long-term memory   128–30, 142, 145–50

machine translation 206–9, 214
mediation of cross-cultural interaction 119
mental models/mental modelling 128–9, 131, 147, 150
mental processe(s)/processing 5, 100, 125–8, 130–2, 140, 142, 148–51
mental space 181, 186, 188
meta cognition/metacognitive 2, 36–7, 43
metaphor 175–9, 181–5, 188
motivational self-talk 40–1, 45–7, 51

non-first-person self-talk 41–2, 44–50

occupational stress 56, 60–1, 65, 76
omission(s) 83–103, 114–15, 117, 120, 182, 189
organizational support 60–1, 65

philosophical tradition 163, 170
popular science/popular scientific 182, 185, 190–1
professional listening competence 36, 50
pupil dilation 7–8, 132, 134–5, 138–41, 146, 149, 151

reading for comprehension 132–5, 137, 140–2, 144, 146, 148–51
reading for translation 132–3, 149–51
redundancy/redundancies 88, 95–7, 114, 117, 188

reflective self-talk 45–7, 50
retrospection(s) 89, 91, 94, 97
rights and obligations 170
risk analysis 87, 102

saccadic movements 134, 136, 141–50, 152
Scientific American 179, 189
self-directed self-talk 37–8
self-supervised language model 203–6
self-supervised learning 201
self-talk 35–51
sight translation 125, 128–38, 140–51
simultaneous interpreting 85–7, 90–2, 97, 99, 101–2, 108–10, 126, 128, 131, 206–9
simultaneous machine translation 207–9
social agent 159, 166
spelling errors 26–7, 29
stylometry 211, 214

think aloud 1–2, 20, 126
trigger 95, 97–100

unconscious omissions 91, 95

vicarious traumatization/trauma 58, 65, 71, 74, 76
visual attention 20, 152
visual perception 132, 148

wandering thoughts 36, 38

www.ingramcontent.com/pod-product-compliance
Lightning Source LLC
Chambersburg PA
CBHW071833300426
44116CB00009B/1533